The Future of Child Protection

The Future of Child Protection

∿ How to Break the Cycle
of Abuse and Neglect

JANE WALDFOGEL

HARVARD UNIVERSITY PRESS

Cambridge, Massachusetts, and London, England 1998

Library of Congress Cataloging-in-Publication Data

Waldfogel, Jane.
    The future of child protection : how to break the cycle of abuse
and neglect / Jane Waldfogel.
      p.   cm.
    Includes bibliographical references and index.
    ISBN 0-674-33811-1 (alk. paper)
    1. Child welfare. 2. Child welfare—United States. 3. Child
abuse—Prevention. 4. Child abuse—United States—Prevention.
I. Title.
HV713.W27   1998
362.76'8'0973—dc21   98-20429

Acknowledgments

In the fall of 1994 I was invited to join Frank Hartmann, Mark Moore, and Julie Wilson in leading an Executive Session on Child Protective Services at the Kennedy School of Government at Harvard University. The Executive Session convened an outstanding group of individuals—Marylee Allen, Ira Barbell, Richard Barnum, Michael Breslin, Karl Dennis, Frank Farrow, Sidney Gardner, Neil Gilbert, Beverly Jones, Susan Notkin, Frances Pitts, Bill Purcell, Linda Radigan, Susan Schechter, Patricia Schene, Lisbeth Schorr, Carlos Sosa, Gary Stangler, Joyce Thomas, Stewart Wakeling, Michael Wald, Michael Weber, and Carol Williams—who worked closely with us over the next three years to develop a deeper understanding of the current child protective services system, to articulate a vision for a new system, and to devise a strategy to get from here to there. The contribution of the Executive Session to this book is immense, and I am deeply grateful to all the members for their insights and support. I am also grateful to Stacey Rosenkrantz, who coauthored an earlier version of Chapter 4 and allowed me to include it here.

The Boston case-record data used in Chapters 1 and 2 were gathered as part of a study that Julie Wilson and I conducted of cases referred to child protective services. The study would not have been possible without the cooperation of the Massachusetts child protective services commissioner, Linda Carlisle. I would also like to thank the intake social workers, supervisors, and area director of the office that participated in the study. Their participation enriched both it and this book.

The Malcolm Wiener Center for Social Policy at the Kennedy School provided funding for the Boston case-record study and supported this book in many other ways. I would especially like to thank the director at the Wiener Center, Julie Wilson, and my former advisers at the Kennedy School, Mary Jo Bane and David Ellwood, for their continuing help and encouragement.

Two other institutions, and many other people, have contributed to this book. When I moved to Columbia University School of Social Work in 1995, I found a community of scholars working on child protective, child welfare, and other social policy issues. I am grateful to my colleagues in the Child Welfare Research Center and to my colleagues in the policy faculty for their help and support. I want especially to thank Sheila Kamerman, who encouraged me to write this book and read and commented on several chapters. I am also grateful to Kathryn Conroy and Ann O'Rielly for their help with Chapter 8.

The other institution that provided support and assistance is the Suntory-Toyota International Centre for Economics and Related Disciplines (STICERD) at the London School of Economics, where I have been a frequent visitor for several years now. STICERD proved to be a wonderful base to research and write the chapters that use British data and several others. I am grateful to my colleagues there for their continuing support. I would also like to thank Eileen Munro for her help with Chapter 7.

The Annie E. Casey Foundation and the Edna McConnell Clark Foundation provided funding for the Executive Session. This funding allowed me to spend some of my time working on child protection from 1994 to 1997. Starting in 1997, I also received support from Columbia University and from the W. T. Grant Foundation. Susan Grundberg, Wen-Jui Han, and Cheryl Krauth provided excellent research help. I am also grateful to Jeff Kehoe and Ann Hawthorne at Harvard University Press for valuable guidance on the manuscript. The opinions expressed in this book and any errors remain mine alone.

The largest thank-you goes to those who helped out on the home front—my husband, David Delison Hebb, and our daughter, Katie. This book is dedicated to them.

Contents

The Future of Child Protection

Chapter 1

Child Abuse and Neglect Today

Our image of child abuse and neglect, and of the role of child protective services, is often drawn from the case of one particular child who has been in the headlines or the television news. For many Americans, that child could be Lisa Steinberg. Illegally adopted by a lawyer who then battered her and her adoptive mother, Lisa was reported to child protective services in New York City on numerous occasions by concerned neighbors and others in the community. Tragically, despite these reports Lisa continued to be abused, and in 1987 she died at the hands of her adoptive father.

Eight years later, in 1995, the most visible case of child abuse in New York City, and the one providing the clearest proof that something was terribly wrong with the system, concerned Elisa Izquierdo, a six-year-old girl who died of abuse at the hands of her mother. Elisa's short life came to symbolize all that was wrong with the child protective services system. Elisa was well known to the public child protective services agency, having been reported several times as a suspected victim of abuse or neglect. Others in her community, including some 23 professionals from schools and community agencies, also knew she was being abused, yet, as *Time* magazine's cover story on her case concluded, "somehow nobody managed to stop it."[1] In the final months of her life, Elisa was so badly hurt from frequent beatings by her mother and stepfather that she was kept home from school; yet even with her history of abuse, no one followed up to check on her condition.

Elisa's case seemed all the more tragic when it came to light that her life might well have taken a different course. Elisa lived with her father until his death in 1994, when she was four and a half. At that time another relative stepped forward to take care of Elisa, while a patron, Prince Michael of Greece, offered to pay her tuition at the private school she had been attending. Instead, a judge placed her with her mother and stepfather despite evidence that the mother had abused Elisa in the past and that both the mother and stepfather were addicted to crack cocaine. Over the next year and a half the mother and stepfather systematically mistreated Elisa, and in November 1995 the mother beat her to death. Elisa's mother was convicted of second-degree murder and sentenced to 15 years in prison; her stepfather, who was in jail on a cocaine charge at the time of Elisa's death, pleaded guilty to assault charges and was sentenced to up to three years in prison. Elisa's death and the ensuing publicity placed a spotlight on the child protective services system. In the ensuing months reports of suspected abuse and neglect increased dramatically in New York and in other parts of the country. Elisa's death also prompted a series of reforms, including a reorganization of New York City's child protective services agency (discussed in Chapters 8 and 9).[2]

Across the nation similarly tragic instances of abuse have provoked public outrage. In the spring of 1995 Los Angeles residents were horrified at the death of Lance Helms, a two-year-old boy known to the child protective services system, who was returned home by court order over the objections of the child protective services workers. When the boy was beaten to death by his father's girlfriend, there was a perception that the system as a whole had failed this child. As in New York, the Los Angeles case refocused attention on the issue of child maltreatment, and reports of child abuse and neglect rose dramatically over the next few months.[3]

The cases of Lisa Steinberg, Elisa Izquierdo, and others like them around the country are tragedies in two respects. First, parents in these cases, instead of protecting and nurturing their children, beat, tortured, and murdered them. Second, the individuals whom we would expect to step in and protect children in such instances—teachers, doctors, judges, and particularly child protective services workers— knew the abuse was happening and yet failed to stop it. This latter failing makes these cases of physical abuse doubly horrible, and deserving of public attention, scrutiny, and remedy.

Another type of child maltreatment that has recently attracted increased public attention involves not physical abuse but rather neglect. Neglect cases usually come to public attention only when a child dies or if many children are involved, as in the notorious Chicago case in which police officers investigating a drugs complaint came upon a crack house where 19 children from several different families were living in horrendous conditions.[4]

In St. Louis, the case of Michelle Gray has come to epitomize the potential severity of chronic neglect, and the risks involved when a child protective services agency fails to respond appropriately. Michelle was a two-year-old who died of malnutrition and dehydration. At the time of her death her twin sister was also badly malnourished, and three older siblings showed signs of having been neglected for years. Michelle's parents did not deliberately set out to kill her or to harm her siblings, but neither parent was capable of providing adequate care. The mother was seriously depressed, the father was alcoholic and seldom employed, and there were allegations of domestic violence. The Gray family was first reported to child protective services in 1987, when the first child was an infant. Between 1987 and Michelle's death in 1995, the family was reported at least 15 times. Each time, the allegations were similar—the house was filthy, the children malnourished. On several occasions one or more of the children were diagnosed as "failure-to-thrive," and medical intervention was required. Each time the case was opened, the parents were cooperative (for example, they would bring the children to the doctor as requested), conditions in the home would improve marginally, and the case would be closed, only to reopen with the next report of neglect. Child welfare expert Patricia Schene, who reviewed the handling of the case at the request of the child protective services agency in St. Louis, concluded that the agency misread the parents' lack of resistance, interpreting it as a positive indicator when in fact it was merely symptomatic of their generally neglectful parenting style and in particular of the mother's depression.[5] The agency also failed to see the cumulative harm to the children as this neglect persisted.

At first glance the case of Nadine Lockwood, who died of neglect in New York City in 1996, seems eerily similar to that of Michelle Gray. Nadine, like Michelle, starved to death. In Nadine's case, however, the neglect in fact was intentional maltreatment. After Nadine died of malnutrition, investigators and the public learned that the mother had systematically denied food to this one child while providing adequate nutrition to the other, more favored siblings. When social workers were called and came to check on Nadine's condition, the mother lied to hide the maltreatment; on one occasion she alleged that this daughter was down south with relatives, and on another occasion she borrowed a neighbor's daughter to pass off as Nadine.

Nearly half of child fatalities involve neglect, not active physical abuse.[6] Neglect often serves as early warning of a situation that might escalate into more serious maltreatment; indeed, many of the children who are known to child protective services and subsequently die of maltreatment were originally reported to child protective services for neglect.[7] Chronic neglect cases can be particularly dangerous because of the risk that a system that focuses on investigating one incident at a time may fail to see the cumulative harm being done over time.

The third major type of child maltreatment is sexual abuse. Although the vast majority of child sexual abuse occurs in the child's home at the hands of a family member or a family friend, the best-known cases have involved allegations of abuse in day-care centers, churches, or other out-of-home settings. Many of the verdicts in these notorious cases have ultimately been overturned because of lack of proof. The public has been left with the impression that the children in these cases made false accusations, perhaps because they had been inadvertently coached to do so by well-meaning prosecutors and therapists so eager to protect children that they had seen maltreatment where it did not really exist. As a cover story in *Parade Magazine* pointed out in November 1996, the public is now skeptical about how much child sexual abuse really exists.[8] At the same time, when allegations are proved to be true, these cases prompt a strong public reaction.

Widely publicized individual cases rightly evoke anguish for the children involved and anger toward the people responsible for their well-being. We expect parents to treat their children with love and affection and not to harm them. As citizens and taxpayers, we also demand that the public systems we have established for child protection perform their role when parents fail to do so. But it would be a mistake to generalize from a few well-known cases to a typology of child maltreatment. The cases that arouse public outrage are not a random, representative sample of child abuse and neglect cases. Rather, they are special in some way, usually in that they involve either the death of a child or the maltreatment of several children and, more often than not, the failure of the child protective services system. These special cases may be useful for examining how well the system protects children under the most extreme circumstances, but they provide no insight into the overall population of children in need of protection and the general operations of the child protective services system. To move beyond the headlines, we must look at children in need of protection from several different vantage points, comparing those in the United States today both with those in earlier times and with populations of maltreated children in other, comparable countries.

The Role of Child Protective Services

The term *child protective services* (CPS) refers to a highly specialized set of laws, funding mechanisms, and agencies that together constitute the government's response to child abuse and neglect. Although definitions vary by jurisdiction, CPS is concerned principally with the abuse and neglect of children by their parents or guardians; in many areas CPS also investigates cases involving nonparental caretakers such as teachers or day-care providers.

All states and the District of Columbia have laws requiring certain categories of professionals and other individuals who have frequent contact with children (such as teachers and doctors) to report suspected child abuse and neglect to CPS. Reports from these mandated reporters constitute the majority of all referrals received by CPS, with teachers forming the single largest group of reporters.[9] Reports are also accepted from concerned citizens, family members, and children themselves; some states also allow reports to be made anonymously.

Child protective services intervention has several stages.[10] In the first stage, *reporting*, a mandated reporter or other person contacts the public CPS agency to allege that a child is being abused or neglected. In the second stage, *screening*, a decision is made whether the report should be investigated by child protective services. At this stage a report may be "screened out" if it clearly falls outside the mandate of the agency or if there is insufficient information to locate the family for an investigation; otherwise the report is "screened in" and assigned to a social worker for investigation.

In the third stage, *investigation,* a social worker sees the child and family and speaks with others who know them. One purpose of the investigation is to determine whether the child has been abused or neglected. If so, the report is "substantiated" (or "founded" or "supported"); if not, the report is "unsubstantiated" (or "unfounded" or "unsupported").[11] A second purpose of the investigation is to decide whether the child and family need ongoing services to prevent further maltreatment. If so, the case is opened for services; if not, the case is closed. In cases in which a child is at immediate risk of harm and cannot be protected at home, the CPS agency may take steps to obtain legal custody of the child and/or to place the child in "substitute care" (placement with a relative, foster care, group care, or some other form of out-of-home care). However, most children whose cases are opened for services remain in their own homes with some form of oversight by a social worker.

Typically, CPS agencies identify several stages of involvement with cases that remain open after the investigation. These stages include *assessment and service planning, ongoing service provision,* and periodic *case review.* The final stage of CPS intervention is *case closing.*

The Demographics of Children in Need of Protection

In 1996 CPS agencies in the United States received three million reports of alleged child maltreatment, representing a rate of 47 reports per 1,000 children.[12] As Table 1.1 shows, this rate is much higher than in past years. The American reporting rate is also much higher than in comparable countries. Neil Gilbert found that in 1992 the U.S. rate was 43 per 1,000 children under the age of 18, twice as high as that in the country with the next-highest rate, Canada (21 per 1,000 children under the age of 15).[13] The U.S. reporting rate is also much higher than England's (17.5 per 1,000 children under 16).[14]

These statistics raise several questions about the large number of children being reported to CPS agencies in the United States. Who are these children, why are they are being reported, and what happens to them after the report? Are there really more instances of abuse and neglect in the United States, or simply more reports? Data from national statistics, from recent and historical case-record samples in Boston, and from other countries (discussed in the next chapter) go a long way toward helping us answer these questions.

Table 1.1 Reports of child abuse and neglect, selected years, 1967–1996

Year	No. of reports	Reports per 1,000 children
1967	9,563	<1
1968	10,931	<1
1975	294,796	4
1976	669,000	10
1977	838,000	13
1978	836,000	13
1979	988,000	15
1980	1,154,000	18
1981	1,225,000	19
1982	1,262,000	20
1983	1,477,000	24
1984	1,727,000	27
1985	1,928,000	31
1986	2,086,000	33
1987	2,157,000	34
1988	2,265,000	35
1989	2,435,000	38
1990	2,559,000	40
1991	2,684,000	42
1992	2,909,000	45
1993	2,967,000	45
1994	3,074,000	46
1995	3,120,000	46
1996	3,126,000	47

Sources: 1967 and 1968: David Gil, *Violence against Children: Physical Child Abuse in the United States* (Cambridge: Harvard University Press, 1970); 1975–1986: American Association for the Protection of Children (AAPC), *Highlights of Official Child Abuse and Neglect Reporting—1986* (Denver: American Humane Association, 1987), and earlier reports; 1987–1996: Ching-Tung Wang and Deborah Daro, *Current Trends in Child Abuse Reporting and Fatalities: The Results of the 1996 Annual Fifty-State Survey* (Chicago: National Committee to Prevent Child Abuse, 1997) and earlier reports by the National Committee to Prevent Child Abuse (NCPCA).

Note: Data not available for 1969–1974. Figures from the *Child Maltreatment* reports by the U.S. Department of Health and Human Services, National Center for Child Abuse and Neglect (NCCAN) (Washington, D.C.: U.S. Government Printing Office, 1998 and earlier) for the period 1990–1996 are comparable to the NCPCA figures used here.

Table 1.2 Types of maltreatment in substantiated child abuse and neglect cases, 1986 and 1996 (%)

Type of maltreatment	1986	1996
Neglect	55	58
Physical abuse	28	22
Sexual abuse	16	12
Emotional maltreatment	8	6
Other	13	15
Total	100	113

Sources: 1986: AAPC, *Highlights—1986;* 1996: NCCAN, *Child Maltreatment 1996: Reports from the States to the National Child Abuse and Neglect Data System* (Washington, D.C.: U.S. Government Printing Office, 1998).

Note: The 1996 total exceeds 100% because more than one type of maltreatment may have been reported per case.

Data from 1986 and 1996, shown in Table 1.2, indicate that neglect cases make up over half of all reports in the United States. Physical abuse accounts for a quarter of all reports, about the same share as in 1986. Contrary to public perceptions, sexual abuse reports, the third most common type, have declined over the last decade, to 12 percent. Emotional maltreatment makes up 6 percent of all reports today. The remaining 15 percent consists of other types of maltreatment (the exact definition depends on the state).

Although the children reported to child protective services are a diverse group, those from racial and ethnic minorities are disproportionately represented, as are children from lone-mother families and poor families. In 1996 over 40 percent of children reported to CPS were from racial or ethnic minority groups: 27 percent were African-American, 11 percent were Latino, 2 percent were Native American, 1 percent were Asian, and 2 percent were from other minority groups.[15] However, the interpretation of these statistics is not straightforward.[16] Some researchers have found that with all other factors held equal, children from racial and ethnic minority groups are more likely to be reported to the system for physical abuse or neglect, though not for sexual abuse.[17] Other researchers, however, have found that controlling for income and family structure eliminates most or all of the effects of race and ethnicity on reporting, especially in reports of neglect.[18]

In fact low income, rather than race or ethnicity, seems to be the prime determinant of the higher rates at which minority children are reported to CPS. Several studies have found that with all other factors held equal, poor children are more likely than nonpoor ones to be reported to CPS.[19] Others have found that children living in poor communities are more likely to be reported.[20] Since children from racial or ethnic minority groups are three to four times more likely to be poor (and more likely to live in poor neighborhoods) than white non-Hispanic children and are likely to remain in poverty for longer, it may be poverty, rather than race or ethnicity per se, that largely explains their overrepresentation in the CPS system.

Why might poor children be more likely to be reported? One possibility is that poor families are under more stress, and that the heightened stress leads to more instances of child abuse or neglect; moreover, poor families, especially those living in poor neighborhoods, may have fewer family and community resources to draw upon in times of need.[21] There may also be a link between poverty and parenting styles that are harsh or punitive.[22] Although we lack good data on the true incidence of child maltreatment, there is some evidence that the incidence of abuse and neglect may be higher among poor children. For instance, the most recent national incidence study found that children in poor families (those with incomes below $15,000) were more than twice as likely as children from middle-income families (those with incomes from $15,000 to $29,000) to be identified as abused or neglected.[23] Another possibility is that the effects of poverty are mistaken for neglect; for instance, it may be hard for a reporter to determine whether a child lacks suitable winter clothing or is coming to school hungry because of parental neglect or because of inadequate family income. The largest gap between poor and middle-income children is in their risk for "physical neglect"—the lack of provision of adequate health care, supervision, food, clothing, and so on—with poor children more than four times as likely as middle-income children to be identified as victims of physical neglect, but only twice as likely to be identified as victims of physical abuse or sexual abuse.[24] Yet another possibility is that poor families are more likely to come into contact with individuals in the community, such as welfare workers or hospital emergency room personnel, who are accustomed to making reports of abuse or neglect. Indeed, individuals in the community may be more likely to refer families who are poor in the hope that a referral to CPS will help the families obtain forms of financial or other assistance that might otherwise not be available to them.[25]

The demographics of substance abuse, and the increasingly common practice of testing newborns for drug exposure, may also help explain the disproportionate representation of minority children in the CPS system. In a landmark study published in the *New England Journal of Medicine,* Ira Chasnoff and his associates found that African-American women, though no more likely than white women to use drugs or alcohol during their pregnancy, are ten times more likely to be reported to child protective services.[26] One reason for this discrepancy is that African-American women and their newborns are more likely to be tested for drug use at birth, as are poor women and women living in urban settings. A second reason is that, among those tested, black women are more likely to have used cocaine, whereas white women are more likely to have used other drugs such as marijuana. In most jurisdictions, a newborn who tests positive for exposure to cocaine is automatically reported to child protective services. Inevitably, then, a greater share of drug-affected newborns will be reported among black children than among white children.

Consequences of Reporting

On average, just over half of reports are screened in and assigned to a social worker for investigation, and 40 percent or fewer of all reports are "substantiated" or indicated.[27] The exact meaning of these terms varies somewhat across states, but generally a substantiated case is one in which the investigating social worker has found reasonable cause to believe that a child has been abused or neglected or is at elevated risk of abuse or neglect, while an indicated case is one in which there is some evidence that abuse or neglect has occurred but in which the evidence does not meet the threshold for substantiation.

What happens to a child and family after abuse or neglect is substantiated depends greatly on the jurisdiction in which the child resides. Some states provide services to only 40–44 percent of cases in which abuse or neglect is substantiated;[28] in other states the rate of service provision is much higher. In 1993, on average 74 percent of substantiated cases received some type of service in the 23 states that provided data on this question to the National Center on Child Abuse and Neglect.[29]

Surprisingly, only 5 percent of children reported to child protective services are removed from their homes; even among children in substantiated cases of child abuse and neglect, only 14 percent are removed.[30] Since about 74 percent of substantiated cases receive some type of services, this means that approximately 60 percent of children in cases of substantiated abuse or neglect remain in their own homes with their cases monitored by the CPS agency. Some of these children may subsequently be removed if their situation deteriorates or if new information comes to light, but the majority will remain at home throughout their involvement with child protective services. Typically, these children and their families will receive periodic visits by a social worker. They may also receive services such as counseling, day care, or other social services, depending on their needs and on what services are available in their area.

Racial and ethnic differences are more pronounced with regard to placement rates than they are with regard to reporting or substantiation rates. In 1980, 9.5 of every 1,000 African-American children were in placement, as opposed to 3.1 per 1,000 Caucasians.[31] Ten years later, data from the five states with the largest foster-care populations indicated that African-Americans continue to be disproportionately likely to be placed. Table 1.3 shows that African-American children are three times more likely than white children to be placed if they live in Texas, five to six times more likely in California and Michigan, eight times more likely in Illinois, and over thirteen times more

Table 1.3 Children in foster care per 1,000 children, by race and ethnicity, 1990

State	White	Hispanic	African-American	African-American/white placement rates
California	6.98	5.23	44.39	6.36
Illinois	2.85	2.73	23.70	8.36
Michigan	2.67	2.06	13.44	5.03
New York	3.11	12.86	42.10	13.54
Texas	1.41	1.45	4.15	2.94

Source: Robert Goerge, Fred Wulczyn, and Allen Harden, *Foster Care Dynamics, 1983–1992: A Report from the Multistate Foster Care Data Archive* (Chicago: Chapin Hall Center for Children at the University of Chicago, 1994), pp. 51, 54, 57, 60, 63.

likely in New York. Hispanic children had the same placement rate as non-Hispanic white children in 1980 but are now disproportionately represented in the foster-care caseload in some jurisdictions.[32] In New York, for example, Hispanic children have a placement rate over four times that of non-Hispanic white children. Though not shown in the table, Native Americans are also overrepresented in the foster-care system, with a placement rate of 8.8 per 1,000 in 1980 and a rate three to four times higher than other children in 1986.[33]

Data from New York City suggest that poverty plays an important role in these findings. Children in ghetto poverty neighborhoods— those with poverty rates 40 percent or higher—are five times more likely (14.5 per 1,000) to be placed than are children from neighborhoods where the poverty rate is under 20 percent (2.9 per 1,000). Moreover, controlling for income differences explains most or all of the racial and ethnic differences in placement rates.[34] Similarly, Duncan Lindsey finds that income differences explain the higher rate of placement of children from single-parent homes.[35]

National statistics tell us a little about which children are referred to CPS, why they are referred, and what happens afterward. But only case-record data can provide fuller answers about whether children are safer—better protected from abuse or neglect—as a result of having come to the attention of the child protective services system.

The Boston Case-Record Sample, 1994

The case-record sample used for analysis comes from reports made in 1994 to one of the Boston offices of the Massachusetts child protective services agency, the Department of Social Services (DSS).[36] Massachusetts DSS is state-run, with 26 local offices around the state, including 5 in the city of Boston, and has a better-than-average state-run management information system. In many respects DSS is a typical CPS agency, with screening and substantiation rates close to the national average. Statewide, DSS receives close to 5,000 reports of alleged child abuse or neglect each month. Just over half of these reports are screened in (54 percent, consistent with the national average of 53 percent), and over a quarter are ultimately substantiated (27 percent, a rate that at first glance is notably lower than the national average of 37 percent for 1994; but, as we shall see, different states calculate this statistic differently).[37] The screening and substantiation rates for the 5 offices covering Boston are somewhat higher. Altogether, the Boston offices receive some 750 reports per month. Two-thirds (67 percent) of these are screened in and investigated, and over half (55 percent) of all investigations result in a decision to substantiate abuse or neglect. Thus about 37 percent of all reports in Boston are substantiated, a rate in line with the national average.

There are several advantages to using Boston as a study site. Boston has a demographic mix close to the national average for big cities.[38] About a quarter (25.6 percent) of Boston's 574,000 residents are black; 20 percent are foreign-born.[39] Fifteen percent of Boston's families are poor; the poverty rate for families with children is about twice as high (28 percent). Just under half of children in Boston (35 percent of white children and 63 percent of black children) live in single-parent families.

The office selected for the case-record sample serves a diverse population of about 125,000. The study area differs from Boston as a whole in several ways. First, a larger share of the population is black and/or foreign-born; the area includes some predominantly African-American neighborhoods as well as a neighborhood that is the center of the city's Haitian community. Second, a larger share of children lives in two-parent families and in owner-occupied homes than in Boston overall; the area includes many working-class and middle-class families. This economic mix is reflected in the housing stock, which is predominantly multifamily houses built close together but also includes many single-family homes on suburban-sized lots as well as a few large housing projects.[40]

The local office selected for the case-record sample has a fairly high level of compliance with departmental regulations, policies, and procedures; practice is generally in line with departmental expectations. The office has a reputation of being well-managed, and the morale of staff appears good. Moreover, although staff turnover is fairly high, the intake unit, with responsibility for screening and investigating reports, has been relatively stable: in 1994 the supervisor had been with the department for more than 10 years, as had the social worker with primary responsibility for screening. Thus, casework practice in this office was likely to be representative of good practice in other Massachusetts offices and indeed in many other CPS offices nationwide.

The sample includes every family reported to the office for child abuse or neglect from June 20 to July 14, 1994.[41] The 188 children reported, from 122 families, were followed through the screening process, and those screened in were followed through the investigation phase. Massachusetts regulations require that screening be done within 24 hours and an investigation completed within 10 working days, and in fact the overwhelming majority of cases are handled within these timelines. Thus, initially the children were followed for up to two weeks after the report to CPS. The second stage of the study tracked outcomes for the children three years later.

The types of maltreatment reported to the Boston office, shown in Table 1.4, mirror the national pattern seen in Table 1.2: neglect is the most common type of referral, followed by physical abuse and then sexual abuse. This pattern persists in the subset of substantiated cases, as it does in the national data.

With regard to family structure, race, and ethnicity, Table 1.5 shows that the children reported to this CPS office are more likely to be black or Hispanic than the average for children in the city. At least part of this result reflects the fact that this area of the city has a large minority population.

Table 1.5 also shows that reported children are no more likely than the average child to be from single-parent families. This finding suggests that single-parent families may not be more likely to be reported to CPS than others in their neighborhoods. The Boston case records do not record family income, but the demographic profile of these cases suggests that many children reported to CPS are poor. Over 40 percent are living in one-parent families, and over half are members of racial or ethnic minority groups.

Table 1.4 Types of maltreatment in Boston case-record sample, 1994 (%)

Type of maltreatment	Reports	Substantiated cases
Neglect	60.2	70.8
Physical abuse	27.6	27.1
Sexual abuse	9.2	4.2
Emotional maltreatment	3.0	0.0
Total	100.0	102.1

Note: All tabulations for Boston are calculated from data in the Boston case-record sample.

Note: Total for substantiated cases exceeds 100% because more than one type of maltreatment may have been substantiated.

Table 1.5 Family structure, race, and ethnicity of children reported to Boston CPS (%)

Characteristic	Children reported	All children in Boston
Family structure		
Two parents	51.6	54.4
Lone mother	41.0	40.7
Other	7.4	4.9
Race and ethnicity		
White	19.1	74.4
Black	52.7	25.6
Biracial	8.5	—
Hispanic	9.0	—
Asian	1.1	—
Unknown	9.6	—

Source: All children in Boston: estimates from 1990 census by Julie Boatright Wilson, "Mattapan: A Community in Transition" (Paper prepared for Executive Session on Child Protective Services, Kennedy School of Government, 1994).

The Boston case records also reveal something about the coexistence of various risk factors such as substance abuse and domestic violence. DSS in recent years has emphasized the importance of risk factors such as substance abuse and domestic violence, and workers frequently note such factors in the case records. However, because these records reflect only what is learned and documented about families in the initial report and in the screening and investigation, they are likely to underestimate the prevalence of risk factors that may not be immediately apparent or that may not be divulged to CPS. The figures shown in Table 1.6 should be taken as lower-bound estimates of the prevalence of various risk factors in these cases. As such, they suggest that an important share of the reported cases, and an even larger share of the substantiated cases, involve families with risk factors such as substance abuse, domestic violence, criminal activity, or mental illness.

Perhaps the most surprising characteristic of the sample is the share of children already known to the agency before this report—53 percent. About two-thirds of these repeat cases had been opened but

Table 1.6 Risk factors present, Boston sample (%)

	All reported children	Substantiated cases
Substance abuse	20.5	29.9
Domestic violence	11.5	20.8
Parent has criminal record	5.7	10.4
Parent has mental illness	2.5	4.2

subsequently closed; the remaining third were open cases at the time of the new report. Clearly, many of the same children are cycling through the system more than once.[43]

The following brief descriptions of the first 15 reports in the sample provide a fuller portrait of the types of families reported to CPS. These case vignettes highlight many of the features already discussed: the dominance of neglect, as opposed to physical or sexual abuse; the high share of racial and ethnic minorities, single-mother families, and poor families; high rates of substance abuse, domestic violence, and other risk factors such as a parent's own childhood history of abuse or neglect; and repeat reportings to the system.

1. Sexual abuse. Single mother with two children, ages 6 and 3 (race and ethnicity not specified). Case closed 5 years ago. Mother alleges that ex-boyfriend sexually abused her son, age 6. Screened in. During investigation, ex-boyfriend says mother made false report because they had an argument. Mother confirms this. Case unsubstantiated and closed.
2. Neglect. Caucasian single mother with two children, ages 7 and 2. Open case. Family is homeless and staying in a motel. Neighbor at the motel alleges that mother provides inadequate care for the children. DSS social worker says she saw family recently and has no concerns. Family recently had an argument with the reporter. Screened out.
3. Neglect. African-American single mother with two children, ages 2 and 11. Case closed five months ago. Mother brought 11-year-old to hospital because he is suicidal and sets fires, but would not agree to hospitalization. Screened in. During investigation, maternal grandmother, who has custody of child, had child admitted to hospital. Case unsubstantiated and

closed, but is then reopened on a voluntary basis at the family's request. Older child remains in hospital (and is placed in group care at discharge); 2-year-old remains at home.

4. Physical abuse. Hispanic two-parent family with four children, ages 8 to 15. Prior case closed. Father drinks and is physically abusive with mother and children. Father punched oldest son last night. Mother is unable to protect children. Screened in for emergency response. Substantiated and case opened. Children remain at home.

5. Neglect. Caucasian single parent with two children, ages 13 and 17. Prior case closed. The 13-year-old girl is using drugs and running wild; the 17-year-old was arrested for car theft. Screened out because there were no protective issues. Case remains closed.

6. Neglect. African-American family with three children under age 6; parents are separated. Case closed a year and a half ago. Father alleges that mother drinks and smokes cocaine and leaves youngest son with anyone at hand (the two older children live with relatives). Screened in. Mother denies using drugs or alcohol and says father made false report; maternal grandmother concurs with this. Father did not return social worker's calls. Case unsubstantiated and closed.

7. Neglect and physical abuse. African-American two-parent family with one child, age 10. Open case. Child called police to say he didn't want to be in the home any longer. Both parents use drugs, and father hit child a few weeks ago. Screened out, no new protective issues.

8. Physical abuse. Caucasian single mother with one child, age 4. Open case. Child told day-care staff that mother burned her with a cigarette. Report screened out; child's injury is minor and no new protective issues.

9. Neglect and physical abuse. Hispanic single mother with two children, ages 4 and 2. Prior case closed. Mother was physically and sexually abused as a child and has history of substance abuse. Mother brought children to health clinic saying that she is unable to handle the 2-year-old. Screened in for emergency response. Mother says the 2-year-old is "wild" and "bad." She hits him sometimes, most recently this morning. The 4-year-old is well-behaved, currently staying at grandparent's because she

got upset when someone fired a gun into the apartment last week. Report substantiated and case opened. The 2-year-old remains home with mother at the conclusion of the investigation (but is placed in foster care a few days later).

10. Neglect and physical abuse. Biracial family with four children; parents are divorced and mother is remarried. No previous record. The 10-year-old came back from visiting father with a black eye. Father was abusive to mother in the past. Screened in. Father denies abuse, says 10-year-old walked into a tree. Father alleges mother drinks and uses drugs. Mother denies this. Child has a black eye but says he bumped into a tree. Case unsubstantiated and closed.

11. Neglect. African-American single mother with two children, ages 2 and 1 day. Prior case closed. Two-year-old lives with grandmother. Mother took the new baby out of state for illegal adoption and told father the baby died. The next day, mother changed her mind and asked police for help. Police got baby back and brought it to hospital. Father was abusive to mother during pregnancy and is threatening her now. Screened in for emergency response. Mother was in foster care as a child. Mother gave up new baby because she thought father didn't want child. Case substantiated and opened. DSS filed a care and protection petition and obtained temporary custody of both children.

12. Neglect. African-American two-parent family with six children, ages 1 to 13. Case closed four years ago. Children do not receive necessary medical and dental care. Screened in. Mother is overwhelmed. Father has kidney condition and does not help much. Children are clean but house is dirty and in disarray. Case substantiated and opened.

13. Neglect. African-American single mother with two children, ages 4 and 14. Prior case closed. Grandmother alleges that mother is using and selling drugs. Screened in. Mother says she stopped using drugs four years ago. Says grandmother is alcoholic and is asking for money but mother will not help her any more. School and doctor have no concerns. Older child denies there are drugs in the house. Case unsubstantiated and closed.

14. Neglect. African-American single mother with one child, age 2. No prior case. Father alleges that mother uses drugs and

leaves child with grandmother. Child recently grabbed a curling iron and got burned. Screened in. Mother denies using drugs except for marijuana. Burn was an accident. Health clinic (where mother and child attend a group) says child is well cared for. Mother says father made report to harass her. He has threatened her and she has a restraining order against him. Police confirm this. Case unsubstantiated and closed.

15. Neglect and physical abuse. Caucasian two-parent family with two children, ages 3 and 2 weeks. No prior case. Neighbor alleges that mother hits the 3-year-old and leaves him alone in the yard. Screened in. Mother denies leaving child alone. Child has behavior problems: he bangs his head and hits himself. Mother hits child sometimes on hands or buttocks but uses open hand. Child has no bruises or marks. Health center has no concerns about mother and will help refer her to appropriate services for the 3-year-old. Case unsubstantiated and closed.

These vignettes also indicate the extent to which the system seems to be used for family and other quarrels. Several of the cases involved disputes between ex-spouses or partners, between other family members, or between neighbors. Although former spouses and partners, family members, and neighbors often make truthful reports, it appears that they also sometimes make vindictive and false reports. Indeed, most of the conflictual reports in these first 15 cases turned out to be untrue.

The other noteworthy feature of these cases is their heterogeneity. No two are alike. Even in the entire sample of nearly 200 reported children, one is hard pressed to find situations that can easily be grouped together as similar types of cases. Rather, each case seems to present a different, complex, and evolving set of issues.

In the Boston sample, 77.9 percent of the reports were screened in, and half of these (50.5 percent) were substantiated. This means that 39.3 percent of all reports were substantiated; the remaining 60.7 percent were either screened out or were screened in and then not substantiated. But the relationship between substantiation and the provision of services is not a straightforward one. Table 1.7 shows the array of possible outcomes. Although cases that are not substantiated are typically closed, some percentage of unsubstantiated cases may be kept open if the CPS agency perceives a need for services and the family shows willingness to receive services, or if it was already an

Table 1.7 Case outcomes after investigation (%)

	Screened out or unsubstantiated	Substantiated
United States		
Closed	—	12
Open	—	28
Total	60	40
Boston		
Closed	50	3
Open	11	36
Total	61	39

Source: U.S.: projections from data in NCCAN, *Child Maltreatment 1993.*

open case with the agency before the latest report. Conversely, some substantiated cases will be closed after investigation because there is no need for services from CPS, or because a family refuses services and there are insufficient grounds to impose them involuntarily. There are no national figures on the share of cases falling into each of the four outcomes. However, on the basis of the national averages cited earlier, if about 40 percent of all reports are substantiated, and about 70 percent of those cases remain open for services, the share of cases substantiated and open would be 28 percent and the share substantiated and closed would be 12 percent. If all the unsubstantiated cases were closed, the share in the top of the first column would be 60 percent; if some unsubstantiated cases were kept open, these cases would move to the bottom of the first column and the share in the top left would be reduced accordingly.

In estimates for Boston as a whole, 61 percent of the cases are unsubstantiated: 50 percent are closed, and 11 percent—the ones that were already open with the agency for ongoing services before the latest report—are kept open. The next-largest group are substantiated and open for services, with only a small share substantiated and closed.

Another way to track outcomes is to ask where the child is at the conclusion of the investigation. Table 1.8 shows that only 5 percent of all reported children in the Boston sample are in placement; 42 percent

Table 1.8 Status of children at conclusion of investigation, Boston sample, (%)

Status	All reported children	Substantiated cases
At home, no open case	52.6	8.3
At home, case open	42.4	79.2
In placement	5.0	12.5

remain in their own homes but are receiving some protective supervision and services. Over half, then, are "filtered out" of the system and receive no services at all at the conclusion of the investigation. Even among those substantiated, the proportion in placement is fairly low, only 12.5 percent. However, nearly four-fifths of substantiated cases remain open.

Massachusetts in the 1880s

Some of the same characteristics can be seen in the annual reports and case records of the Massachusetts Society for the Prevention of Cruelty to Children (MSPCC) from a century ago.[43] Founded in 1878, the MSPCC was one of the earliest "child rescue" organizations in the nation. Like its counterparts elsewhere, the society received and investigated reports of children at risk of abuse or neglect. Although the MSPCC evolved into a statewide agency, initially the vast majority of its activities concerned children in the Boston or greater Boston area, with only 12–15 percent of its reports concerning children in other parts of the state during the 1880s.

A sample of cases reported to the MSPCC in the late 1880s presents several similarities to the cases seen in Boston in the 1990s.[44]

1. "Girl 8. Father intemperate. Mother sick in consumption."
2. "Five children, from 1 to 12. Mother intemperate and immoral. Disreputable men and women visit the house. Girl, 12, unruly; four other children in court as neglected."
3. "Eight children, from 2 to 16 years of age. Parents intemperate. House filthy. Children ragged and dirty. Parents warned, promised, but did not perform."
4. "Six children, from 2 to 12 years of age. Parents intemperate. Father ugly; once broke his wife's arm; has been in the House of Correction and the House of Industry. Mother did the best she could formerly. Children neglected, ragged, and dirty."

5. "Three children, from 8 to 14. Father dead. Mother has illegitimate child a few weeks old."

6. "Boy, 10. Parents intemperate and living in public institutions. One bed on the floor. No bedclothing, no fire, no food."

7. "Five children, from 3 to 16 years of age. Parents intemperate. Father loses work on account of drinking. Children not cared for."

8. "Two children, 9 and 3 years old. Parents intemperate. Mother immoral. Arrested twice in three months for drunkenness."

9. "Two children, 5 and 2. Father is a crank. Peddles from a wagon, and has taken the younger child out on his wagon, 'rain or shine,' before it was a year old. Has never been kind to his family, or properly provided for them. Lived in a shanty. Wife, worn out by his conduct, became insane, and was taken to an asylum. Child, when four years old, became sick and was taken to a hospital. Mother returned from the asylum, and husband had nothing to offer her to eat but bread and lard. She left, taking the older child with her."

10. "Two children by two husbands. Boy 7 and girl 5. Mother dead. Second husband intemperate and cruel to the step-son, who has been sadly neglected. House filthy, and everything in disorder."

11. "Five children, from 16 to 2 years. Neglected. Not in school. Parents intemperate and fighting. Took the pledge only to break it. House filthy. Not a bed fit to lie upon."

12. "Four children, illegitimate, from 11 years to 3 months old. Neglected. Parents intemperate."

Like those today, the cases seen by child protective services agencies in the 1880s and 1890s were predominantly ones of neglect. According to historian Linda Gordon, who analyzed records from the MSPCC along with three other Boston agencies, among the first 15 cases referred to the MSPCC in January 1881, nine (60 percent) concerned neglect rather than physical or sexual abuse or "stubborn children"; ten years later, the proportion of neglect cases in a monthly sample was 93 percent.[45] In the list of sample cases above, every one involves neglect.

Immigrants were twice as likely as native-born families to be reported to the MSPCC. In 1890, when immigrants made up 35 percent of Boston's population, they constituted 71 percent of the families reported.[46] Poverty was also extremely common. In 1880 over 40 percent of the families referred were poor; in 1890 the share was even higher, at over 60 percent. Moreover, many of the families who were not poor were not far above poverty.[47] The link between poverty and neglect was even stronger, with over 46 percent of neglect cases involving poor families in 1880 and over 70 percent in 1890.[48] The MSPCC was keenly aware of the connection between poverty and child abuse or neglect, and several of its annual reports addressed this issue.[49]

Single-parent families made up a disproportionate number of cases, particularly those involving neglect. During the years 1880–1910, when single-mother families represented 19 percent of the households in Boston, they constituted over 25 percent of the child abuse caseload and over 50 percent of the neglect caseload. Why were children in single-mother families so likely to be reported? One reason was the lack of child care while mothers worked. Fully 43 percent of the single-mother cases reported in these years involved "lack of supervision." A second reason was the tendency of single mothers to have men in their household. In 41 percent of the single-mother cases, it was alleged that the mothers were immoral on the grounds that they were having affairs with "boarders."[50] But probably the single most important reason for the high proportion of single mothers in the caseloads of MSPCC and other agencies was their poverty. Single-mother families were more likely to be poor, and poor families were more likely than nonpoor families to be reported to MSPCC or to refer themselves for assistance.

Single-father families were also a disproportionately high share of the caseload. As Table 1.9 shows, in the period 1887–1890 a larger share of children referred to MSPCC lived in single-father families than in single-mother families. Single-father families, like single-mother families, were reported for lack of supervision, immorality (especially intemperance), and poverty, but an important concern in these cases was also incest. Although we may think of awareness of sexual abuse as a modern development, cases involving sexual abuse represented some 10 percent of MSPCC cases in the 1880s.[51]

Cases came to the MSPCC through a variety of sources—not only from its own agents and from other charitable agencies, school teachers, police officers, and the like, but also, in surprisingly large num-

Table 1.9 Family structure of children referred to MSPCC, 1887–1890

Year	All children referred	Children without fathers	Children without mothers
1887	4,199	249	232
1888	4,079	448	532
1889	4,077	603	772
1890	4,244	599	837
Total	16,599	1,899	2,373

Source: Massachusetts Society for the Prevention of Cruelty to Children (MSPCC), *First Ten Annual Reports 1881–1890* (New York: Garland, 1987).

bers, from family members themselves. According to Gordon, family members made 34 percent of reports in 1880 and 61 percent of them a decade later.[52]

Not all the reports made to MSPCC were substantiated and kept open for services. In 1880 only 44 percent of reports were substantiated, and a decade later the rate was 35 percent.[53] These rates are quite comparable to modern-day substantiation rates, which average 40 percent or less nationwide. Of those cases that were substantiated, only 53 percent were kept open with the agency in 1880, a proportion that rose to just under 68 percent by 1893. The remainder were either closed with no action or were referred to other agencies for services or material aid.[54] These figures, too, are quite comparable to the estimated 70 percent or less of substantiated cases that are kept open for services today.

The fact that not all cases referred to the MSPCC were substantiated and opened for services raised concerns about the operations of the system, as it does today. The MSPCC addressed these concerns in its annual report for 1886, explaining that there were many reasons why not all reports would result in placement or other action:

Our powers are often misunderstood, and hence we are charged with failing to do the work expected of us. Earnest and kind people, finding children in a needy condition, apply to us to make an immediate removal, not realizing that we must act under the law or by consent of parents. We have no more authority to take children from parents, without legal process, than any citizen.

Under the neglect law we procure a warrant, and parents must submit. Often, of course, parents will yield, upon our recommendation that we shall resort to the legal process unless they voluntarily consent.

Often complaints are made when, upon investigation, we find that the suffering is the result of honest poverty of worthy parents. It would be cruelty on our part to forcibly remove children from such homes, and we must either get the consent of the parents or secure aid from some charitable organization or public authorities.

And when anonymous complaints are made, and we find them incorrect or the evidence insufficient, we cannot act, but are unable to report our reasons or ask for additional information.

The public may be assured that we do not neglect our opportunities.[55]

As in the Boston sample, a large number of cases referred to child protective services agencies were already known to those agencies. Table 1.10 shows that from 1881 to 1886, the share of referrals that concerned cases known to the MSPCC rose from 47 percent to over 64 percent. On average in these years, 59 percent of the cases investigated by the MSPCC were known to the agency, a figure that is strikingly similar to the 53 percent found in the Boston DSS sample in 1994. After 1886, perhaps in response to the rise in the number of re-referrals, the MSPCC changed the way it defined re-referrals, counting only re-referrals on cases known to the agency in the prior year or earlier. Because of this change, repeat referrals on cases first reported that calendar year—cases likely still to be open with the agency—were no longer recorded as re-referrals. Statistics from the four years following this change in recordkeeping, also shown in Table 1.10, suggest that on average 37 percent of the cases reported to MSPCC had been known to the agency before that calendar year and thus might involve closed as opposed to currently open cases. This figure, too, is remarkably similar to the 37 percent of reports that concern closed cases in the Boston DSS sample.

The picture that we obtain from both the modern-day Boston cases and those from a century ago is in sharp contrast to the image we get from newspaper headlines. A majority of children reported to child protective services today, as in the past, are victims of neglect, not of physical or sexual abuse. This pattern holds among substantiated cases as well. Moreover, today as in the past, children from poor, minority, and lone-parent families are disproportionately represented in the CPS population.

Table 1.10 MSPCC referrals and re-referrals, 1881–1890

Year	No. of cases	No. of re-referrals	% of re-referrals
	All cases previously known		
1881	712	641	47.4
1882	812	994	55.0
1883	885	1,295	59.4
1884	945	1,430	60.2
1885	891	1,620	64.5
1886	859	1,533	64.1
Total	5,104	7,513	59.5
	Cases open in prior year or earlier		
1887	2,355	1,644	39.2
1888	2,614	1,465	35.9
1889	2,674	1,403	34.4
1890	2,573	1,671	39.4
Total	10,216	6,183	37.2

Source: MSPCC, *First Ten Annual Reports.*

Note: Re-referrals in 1887–1890 do not include new reports on cases opened in the current calendar year. Thus, data from the two periods are not strictly comparable.

The data presented above lead to five general observations.

First, most of the children reported to child protective services are victims of parental neglect, not of abuse. They are also disproportionately likely to be poor, from racial and ethnic minorities, and from lone-mother families.

Second, very few of the cases reported to child protective services are ultimately substantiated and kept open for protective supervision and services. According to national statistics, by the time the various "filters" in the system have operated, only 28 percent of original referrals for abuse or neglect are substantiated and kept open for CPS monitoring and service delivery. In Boston the share is higher, 36 percent, with another 11 percent involving cases already open. Given these figures, it is hard to avoid the conclusion that the American child protective services system is investigating many families unnecessarily.

At the same time, however, CPS may be intervening too lightly and providing too few services to some families.

Third, many of the reports to child protective services are re-referrals of children who are already known to CPS, yet few of these cases are receiving services even after a second or subsequent referral. In these cases CPS seems to be failing to break the cycle of maltreatment.

Fourth, the statistics show that the system does not always intervene aggressively enough in very high-risk cases. The Boston sample includes several cases of serious abuse or neglect involving families previously known to DSS. In some instances, these cases had been closed; in others, the maltreatment occurred while the case was still open. Clearly, the existing system is unable reliably to prevent repeated abuse or neglect even when cases have been referred to it.

A fifth observation, highlighted by the case vignettes above, is that the system makes an important distinction between children in need of protection and children in need of services. For example, the case of the mother with the disturbed 3-year-old—who was banging his head and hitting himself—was closed because the mother had not crossed the line into full-blown abuse or neglect; she was only hitting the child with an open hand and not leaving marks. Another factor in the decision to close this case was that the mother acknowledged that she needed help with this child—particularly now that she had a newborn to take care of—and therefore was not neglectful. The agency decided to rely on the local health center's offer to provide help, although the center had been aware of the problem for some time and had so far done nothing. Another case, involving the 13-year-old girl who was taking drugs and running wild, was also closed because there were no protective issues involving abuse or neglect. Yet, clearly, if the report was true, this was a child who was heading for trouble. By focusing narrowly on the mandate to intervene in cases of child abuse or neglect, and only in those cases, the child protective services system is doing what it is meant to do, and it is also conserving precious resources. But we must wonder how well and how efficiently the system is protecting children in the long run if it is not intervening in cases such as these but rather waiting for them to escalate into full-blown abuse or neglect or other problems.

Most children reported to child protective services are unlikely to be substantiated for abuse or neglect or to receive any protective supervision or services beyond the screening or investigation of the report. Although this finding may indicate that many children who are reported do not in fact need protective services or supervision, inevitably we must worry that perhaps some of the screened-out or unsubstantiated cases do. Both national statistics and the Boston sample confirm that there are numerous cases in which children whose cases were screened out or unsubstantiated or closed for other reasons suffer further abuse or neglect. Nor does the system always do an effective job of protecting the high-risk children whose cases were opened for services. Clearly, the system is failing to protect some of the children referred to it.

The next chapters take a closer look at the children reported to child protective services and at the CPS system itself. To account for the very high reporting rates in the United States relative to those in other countries, Chapter 2 compares the 1994 Boston case-record sample with samples of reported children from Australia, Britain, and Canada. Chapter 2 also tracks outcomes over time for children reported to CPS. Chapter 3 surveys the evolution of the American child protective services system, the assumptions underlying it, and how well it is responding to the needs of children today. Chapter 4 examines how well the reporting, screening, and investigation components of the system are responding to children's needs and suggests improvements.

Chapters 5 through 8 spell out a new approach to child protection. Chapter 5 reviews and evaluates proposals to narrow the scope of child protective services. Chapter 6 presents a new paradigm for child protection—differential response—and draws upon examples of reforms in three states to illustrate some of its features and potential. Chapter 7 draws upon child protection reforms in Britain to illustrate other features of the new paradigm, in particular those that emphasize the collaboration of CPS agencies with other agencies, with community members, and with families themselves. Chapter 8 explores the practical implications of the differential response paradigm, again drawing upon examples of reforms under way in the United States and abroad.

Chapter 9 summarizes the case for reform, offers concrete steps that localities or states could take to move toward a differential-response approach to child protection, and identifies the benefits of the new approach for the various partners in child protection and, most important, for the children in need of protection.

Chapter 2

A Comparative Perspective

Data from the United States, Canada, Britain, and Australia provide a useful comparative perspective on criteria for child protection and the effectiveness of CPS systems. As we shall see, dramatic differences in indicators such as reporting rates provide some insights into the differences in outcomes for children.

In an ideal cross-country comparison, all characteristics of the countries would be the same except for the child protective services systems. Only then could we be reasonably confident about attributing differences in outcomes to features of the CPS systems and not to other factors. Clearly, however, no two countries are exactly alike, so the best we can do is to compare countries that are very similar.

A useful way to identify similar countries is to categorize them according to their political, institutional, and other structures. Political scientist Gosta Esping-Anderson groups industrialized countries into three main types: Anglo-Saxon or Anglo-American, Continental European, and Scandinavian.[1] The Anglo-American group includes Britain (which includes England, Scotland, and Wales) and its former colonies—the United States, Canada, Australia, and New Zealand. These countries share a common political and legal heritage. They also have similar welfare states, characterized by a fairly high reliance on means-tested public assistance programs, in contrast with the Continental European or Scandinavian models, which rely to a larger extent on universal social insurance programs. Despite important differences—

for example, Canada and Britain have universal health insurance while the United States does not—these countries are more similar to one another than they are to any in the other two groups. For this reason, the countries used in the comparative analysis are all from the Anglo-American group.

Operation of Child Protective Services

The United States has reporting laws in each state that require certain professionals to report suspected incidents of child abuse or neglect and require public CPS agencies to screen and investigate those reports in accordance with statutory definitions of abuse and neglect, procedural requirements for screening and investigation, and so on. Before passage of these mandatory reporting laws, many states lacked a formal public system to deal specifically with abused and neglected children and their families. In the colonial era, public concern for children's welfare was focused on saving them from poverty. The nineteenth century saw the founding of societies for the prevention of cruelty to children, beginning in New York City in 1874; by the 1920s more than 250 had been established across the nation.[2] These private organizations played the primary role in receiving and responding to reports of child maltreatment and in referring cases for court action in the nineteenth and early twentieth centuries.

By the 1930s, attention had shifted from a concern with child rescue back to a concern for poor children and child welfare. The Social Security Act of 1935 established a public welfare system for poor, fatherless children and a public child welfare system for "the protection and care of homeless, dependent and neglected children in danger of becoming delinquent." Child protection became part of a broader public child welfare mandate, and private agencies such as the societies for the prevention of cruelty to children no longer maintained primary responsibility for it.

The 1960s saw a heightened interest in child protection and the introduction of reporting laws. The primary impetus was the publication of an article by Henry Kempe and his colleagues on the "battered child syndrome" in 1962.[3] Soon thereafter the U.S. Children's Bureau issued a model reporting law, and states soon passed reporting laws of their own. The first federal legislation regarding child abuse, the Child Abuse Prevention and Treatment Act (CAPTA), was signed into law in

1974. CAPTA established uniform standards regarding the identification of and response to child maltreatment cases; created the National Center on Child Abuse and Neglect to conduct research on the incidence of maltreatment and to support state and local efforts to prevent and treat child abuse and neglect; and allocated federal money to states if they adopted mandatory reporting laws, created agencies to investigate child abuse allegations, and demonstrated that they had a child protective services system in place to respond to child abuse and neglect.

Canada, Britain, and Australia can similarly trace the origins of their present-day CPS systems to early efforts by private societies (in Canada these are called Children's Aid Societies; in Britain and Australia, as in the United States, they are called Societies for the Prevention of Cruelty to Children). The first local society in Britain was established in Liverpool in 1883; other local societies soon sprang up, and a national organization was established in 1890. In Canada, the first Children's Aid Society was founded in Toronto in 1891. In Australia, the Society for the Prevention of Cruelty to Children was formed in 1896. In all these countries, government has played an increasingly active role in child protection, and child welfare more generally, in the twentieth century, but the private societies continue to be active in child protection.[4]

Another similarity among the sample countries is that through the first half of the twentieth century, child protection was seen as part of the overall child welfare agenda. Not until the 1960s, with the publication of new medical studies on child maltreatment, was there a resurgence of interest in child abuse and neglect as a distinct condition requiring intervention by the state. Britain's Society for the Prevention of Cruelty to Children established a Battered Child Research Unit in 1967. Australia and Canada likewise concentrated their efforts on the "battered child." As in the United States, mandatory reporting laws were enacted in the Canadian provinces and territories (except the Yukon) and in two of the Australian states (New South Wales and Queensland).

Despite these similar histories, each country's CPS system operates a little differently. Table 2.1 highlights the key differences in the core functions of reporting, screening, and investigation.

In the United States, responsibility for child protection is at the state level, with some states further delegating responsibility to the counties.

Table 2.1 Reporting, screening, and investigation in the U.S., Canada, Australia, and Britain

Core characteristics	United States	Canada	Australia	Britain
Does CPS legislation vary by state or province?	yes	yes	yes	no
Does the legislation have a mandatory reporting clause?	yes	yes	no	no
Does the legislation permit any reports to be screened out?	yes	no	yes	yes
Are investigations conducted by public or private employees?	public	private	public	public
Is the substantiation decision mainly two-tier or three-tier?	two-tier	three-tier	two-tier	two-tier

All states have mandatory reporting laws and procedures in place for their CPS agencies to receive, screen, and investigate reports of abuse and neglect. In most states, the outcome of the investigation is a decision to substantiate or not substantiate the report of abuse or neglect; in some states, other decisions are possible (for example, a report may be indicated, or closed without a finding, or handled in some other manner).

In Canada, child protective services are organized at the provincial and territorial level, and each of the ten provinces and two territories has its own legislation. Ontario, the province analyzed in this chapter, was the first to pass a child protection law, the Act for the Prevention of Cruelty to and Better Protection of Children of 1893. Ontario's current child protection legislation is the Child and Family Services Act of 1984. This act is similar to the laws in U.S. states in that it has a mandatory reporting clause, but it is different in that it does not allow reports to be screened out. Thus, all reports made to CPS must be investigated. Another point of difference is that in Ontario investigations are the responsibility not of a public agency but of "semipublic" agencies, the private nonprofit Children's Aid Societies.[5] Like some U.S. states, Ontario uses a three-tier system for investigation decisions; reports may be founded, suspected, or unfounded.

Authority for child protective services in Australia is also at the state, rather than federal, level. For instance, each of the Australian states has its own policy regarding mandatory reporting. Western Australia, the state discussed here, has never instituted mandatory reporting, preferring not to disturb the "fine balance" that exists between professionals' role as helpers and as reporters of abuse and neglect.[6] Western Australia does allow screening, but the sample used here consists of screened-in reports only. As in the United States, those conducting the investigations are public employees. Like the United States, Australia uses a two-tier system for investigations; cases are either substantiated or unsubstantiated.

Unlike the United States and Canada, and like Western Australia, Britain has no mandatory reporting legislation. CPS investigations are handled by public employees, as in the United States and Australia. Reports are made to local authorities (a unit of government comparable to but smaller than the U.S. county), and, as in the United States, reports may be either screened out or screened in for investigation. At the conclusion of the investigation, decisions are made whether to substantiate the report, whether to take the case to a child protection conference, and whether to list the children on the child protection register.

Sample Data

Data for the United States come from a case-record sample of 188 children from 124 families, collected from a Boston, Massachusetts, CPS office in 1994 and, when possible, from national statistics.

The Canadian sample is from the Ontario Incidence Study, conducted by Nico Trocme and his collaborators in 1993.[7] Child abuse and neglect data in Canada are collected only at the provincial level. The Ontario Incidence Study is considered to be the best source of provincial data on children in need of protection in Canada. Indeed, it is now being used as a model for a Canadian National Incidence Study, which, it is hoped, will provide the first national database on children at risk of abuse or neglect. Another advantage of using the Ontario Incidence Study is that it was specifically designed to be comparable with U.S. data on abused and neglected children.

The Ontario research team gathered data on 1,898 families, with a total of 2,447 children, who were reported and investigated for abuse or neglect from March to June 1993. The sample was drawn from a random sample of 15 of the 54 Children's Aid Societies in Ontario. Trocme and his research team followed reported cases for 21 days.[8]

The Australian sample comes from a study conducted by David Thorpe for the Department for Community Services in Western Australia.[9] In this unique study, Thorpe and his research team read the case record of every child reported and investigated for abuse or neglect in Western Australia over a four-month period, from March 1 to June 30, 1987. This yielded a sample of 655 children from 277 families. The researchers followed the cases through the initial investigation and also checked the status of the cases one year after the report. The sample includes only the cases that were screened in and investigated.

There are two sources of data for Britain. One is a study undertaken for the national Department of Health by Jane Gibbons and her colleagues in 1991.[10] After surveying every local authority in England about its CPS procedures, they drew a case-record sample from eight local areas—four in inner London, two in outer London, and two in rural counties. The researchers sampled every child reported for alleged abuse or neglect in a 16-week period in 1991 across the eight local areas. Their sample includes 2,758 children from 2,015 families. Because the Gibbons study did not include Scotland or Wales, I also draw upon a small case-record survey conducted in one Welsh local authority in 1990.[11] This study was directed by David Thorpe and was designed as a replication of his Australian study. The Welsh study team collected data on all children reported to child protective services beginning in January 1990 and continued until they had a sample of 100 children. The Welsh study, following the Australian study design, includes only screened-in reports.

Criteria for Reporting

Table 2.2 shows the types of maltreatment reported in the United States, Canada, Australia, England, and Wales. Neglect is clearly the dominant category in the United States, but there is a gap between the share of reported cases of neglect in Boston and in the United States overall. However, since Boston does not use an "other" category and since most of the "other" cases at the national level (which account for 15 percent of the total) involve various types of neglect,

Table 2.2 Type of maltreatment reported (%)

Type of maltreatment	U.S., national	U.S., Boston	Ontario, Canada	Western Australia	England (8 areas)	Wales (1 area)
Neglect	45.0	60.2	29.8	47.0	45.0	33.0
Physical abuse	26.0	27.2	41.5	22.5	40.0	45.0
Sexual abuse	11.0	9.7	25.4	22.0	23.0	25.0
Emotional maltreatment	3.0	2.9	10.1	2.0	—	—
Other	15.0	—	2.1	6.5	—	4.0
Total	100.0	100.0	108.9	100.0	108.0	107.0

Sources: U.S., national: David Wiese and Deborah Daro, *Current Trends in Child Abuse Reporting and Fatalities: The Results of the 1994 Annual Fifty-State Survey* (Chicago: National Committee to Prevent Child Abuse, 1995), fig. 1; Ontario: Canada: Nico Trocme, Debra McPhee, Kwok Kwan Tam, and Tom Hay, *Ontario Incidence Study of Reported Child Abuse and Neglect: Final Report* (Toronto: Institute for the Prevention of Child Abuse, 1994), fig. 1; Western Australia and Wales: David Thorpe, *Evaluating Child Protection* (Philadelphia: Open University Press, 1994), tables 4.1, 4.2, England: averages calculated from data in Jane Gibbons, Sue Conroy, and Caroline Bell, *Operating the Child Protection System: A Study of Child Protection Practices in English Local Authorities* (London: Her Majesty's Stationery Office, 1995), table 3iii.

Note: U.S. data are from the National Committee to Prevent Child Abuse (NCPCA) rather than the National Center on Child Abuse and Neglect (NCCAN), because NCCAN does not track the type of maltreatment reported, only the type substantiated or indicated.

Note: Totals for Ontario, England, and Wales are greater than 100% because more than one type of maltreatment may be listed.

Note: Averages for the English data are unweighted; weighted averages are nearly identical (44.2% neglect, 40.3% physical abuse, and 24% sexual abuse).

the share of cases involving neglect is probably close to 60 percent nationally as well.

Neglect is also the dominant type of maltreatment reported in Australia and England. The reported frequency of physical abuse, however, is much higher in Canada, England, and Wales than in the United States. In England, nearly as many cases involve physical abuse as neglect, and in Canada and Wales the share is higher. Sexual abuse, too, constitutes a larger share of the caseload in the other countries. It seems, then, that the U.S. child protective services system is dealing with a somewhat different caseload, one that is characterized to a larger extent by concerns with neglect as opposed to physical or sexual abuse.

In some of the sample countries, case records identify whether specific risk factors are present. These records, summarized in Table 2.3, document a high coexistence of child abuse and domestic violence (abuse of a spouse or partner) and of child abuse and substance abuse (dependency on alcohol or other drugs). Where the type of substance is documented, drugs are more frequently mentioned in the United States, and alcohol in Canada, but in both countries many alcohol users also use drugs, and vice versa.

The case records also contain some limited information on the prevalence of criminal involvement, mental illness, and family history of abuse or neglect. These rates for domestic violence, substance abuse, and the other risk factors probably understate the true prevalence of the various risk factors, which in some cases might be unknown to the social worker and in others might be known but not recorded.

Among substantiated cases, the prevalence of these risk factors is even higher. In the Boston sample, domestic violence is documented in 20.8 percent of the substantiated cases, while substance abuse is a factor in 29.2 percent. This latter figure is consistent with national estimates that approximately one-third of substantiated cases involve substance abuse.[12] The proportion of Boston's substantiated cases in which an adult has a criminal record (10.4 percent) or history of

Table 2.3 Risk factors present in cases reported to child protective services (%)

Risk factor	U.S., Boston	Canada	England
Domestic violence	11.5	15.1	27.0
Substance abuse			
Alcohol	10.7	13.0	n.a.
Drugs	15.6	7.0	n.a.
Alcohol or drugs	20.5	14.3	20.0
Parent has criminal record	5.7	n.a.	13.0
Parent has mental illness	2.5	13.0	13.0
Parent was abused as child	—	—	12.5

Sources: Canada: Trocme et al., *Ontario Incidence Study,* table 6.9; England: Gibbons, Conroy, and Bell, *Operating the Child Protective Services System,* table 4iii.

mental illness (4.2 percent) is likewise higher than in the reported cases. This means that cases involving domestic violence, substance abuse, a criminal record, or a history of mental illness are more likely to be substantiated than the average reported case. This pattern holds for the most part in the Canadian sample, where cases involving substance abuse or mental illness are more likely to be substantiated than the average case; however, cases involving domestic violence are not more likely to be substantiated than other cases.[13]

The case-record data also allow us to look at the extent to which children from lone-mother families, minority families, and poor families tend to be reported more often than other children. Table 2.4 shows the percentage of reported children from one-parent and two-parent families. To place these figures in context, it is important to know something about the family structure of each country. In the U.S. sample, the proportion of children from single-mother families in cases reported to child protective services is considerably higher than their share of the population (25 percent); this result is consistent with the findings reviewed in Chapter 1.[14] In Canada, the share of cases involving lone-mother families does not seem high relative to the share

Table 2.4 Family structure of children reported to child protective services (%)

Family structure	U.S. Boston	Canada	Australia	England	Wales
Two parents	51.6	53.2	47.5	52.0	48.0
Biological parents	39.3	34.0	29.5	30.0	26.0
Parent & step-parent	12.3	19.2	18.0	22.0	22.0
Lone parent	43.4	41.3	49.1	36.0	48.0
Lone mother	41.0	35.7	42.1	–	44.0
Lone father	2.4	4.0	7.0	–	4.0
Substitute care	2.5	–	0.1	–	2.0
Other	2.5	5.5	3.3	12.0	2.0

Sources: Canada: Trocme et al., *Ontario Incidence Study,* fig. 10; Australia and Wales: Thorpe, *Evaluating Child Protection,* tables 4.7, 4.8; England: Gibbons, Conroy, and Bell, *Operating the Child Protective Services System,* table 4i.

Note: Parent/step-parent families include families in which a biological parent is cohabiting with a new partner.

in the United States but in fact is high relative to the population: over 41 percent of the Ontario caseload consists of single-parent families, who according to the 1991 Canadian census make up only 14 percent of the province's families with children.[15] In England and Australia as well, the share of single-parent families in the caseload is much higher than the share of families with children in the general population (no more than 20 percent in either country).[16] Thus, the tendency for single-parent families to be more likely to be reported to CPS is not a peculiarly American phenomenon.

Table 2.5 shows the breakdown of children reported to child protective services by minority racial or ethnic group. In the United States nationwide, where minority children constitute about a quarter of the population, they are a much larger share of the reported children. In the Boston sample, the share of minority children among reported children is not much different from their share of the population in the area. These results suggest that within neighborhoods, minority children may be no more likely to be reported than other children, and that what may account for their higher representation in CPS is their greater likelihood of living in neighborhoods where reporting rates for all groups are high.

Table 2.5 Racial or ethnic minority status of children reported to child protective services (%)

Minority status	U.S., national	U.S., Boston	Canada	Australia	England
Racial or ethnic minority	37.8	71.3	17.1	23.0	24.1
White (nonminority)	53.7	19.1	75.2	53.0	51.5
Unknown or missing	8.5	9.6	7.7	24.0	24.4

Sources: U.S., national: U.S. Department of Health and Human Services, National Center on Child Abuse and Neglect (NCCAN), *Child Maltreatment 1993: Report from the States to the National Child Abuse and Neglect Data System* (Washington, D.C.: U.S. Government Printing Office, 1995), fig. 2-12; Canada: Trocme et al., *Ontario Incidence Study,* table 6.6; Australia: Thorpe, *Evaluating Child Protection,* table 4.9; England: calculated from data in Gibbons, Conroy, and Bell, *Operating the Child Protection System,* table 3vi.

Note: Racial or ethnic minorities are defined as follows. U.S.: African-American, Hispanic, or Asian; Canada: Hispanic, Native Canadian, East Asian, South Asian, Southeast Asian, West Asian, North African, or Black; Australia: Aborigine; England: black, Asian, or biracial.

Minority children are a larger share of the CPS caseload than of the population in Australia, England, and Canada, as they are in the United States overall. In Western Australia, where Aboriginal children are 3 percent of the population, they constitute nearly a quarter of all reported cases, with another quarter of the cases of unknown or unidentified status. In the areas included in the English study, minorities, including those of mixed origin, make up 17 percent of the population but 24 percent of the reported cases, with another quarter of the cases of unknown or unidentified origin. In Ontario, where about 10 percent of children are Native Canadian or other minorities, minority children make up 17 percent of the caseload, with another 8 percent unidentified.[17]

Given the links between poverty and minority status, and the links between poverty and child abuse and neglect reports, it is likely that one of the factors that explains the high numbers of minority children reported to the system is the higher share of minority youngsters who are living in poor families and in poor neighborhoods. Although we lack income data for the U.S., Western Australian, and Welsh samples, the Canadian and English samples document families' economic status in some detail. The data that are available, summarized in Table 2.6, suggest that poor families are more likely than nonpoor families to be reported to the Canadian and English child protective systems. In both

Table 2.6 Economic status of children reported to child protective services (%)

Economic status	Canada	England
Employment		
No adult employed	38.2	36.4
Adult(s) employed	35.9	27.5
Unknown	25.9	36.1
Welfare status		
On welfare	36.4	33.9
Not on welfare	37.7	28.9
Unknown	25.9	37.2

Sources: Canada: Trocme et al., *Ontario Incidence Study,* table 6.7; England: calculated from data in Gibbons, Conroy, and Bell, *Operating the Child Protection System,* table 4ii.

Canada and England, well over one-third of families reported to CPS have no adult employed, and at least one-third are on welfare. If we exclude the cases for which data are missing, half of the Canadian sample is on welfare, a rate twice as high as the rate (23 percent) for all families with children in the province.[18]

Procedures after Reporting

The first decision point in the U.S. system is screening. On average in the United States, nearly half of all reports are screened out, but this share varies a great deal by jurisdiction. In Boston, over three-quarters of all reports were screened in. This is comparable to the rate for England, shown in Table 2.7. (As noted earlier, screening data are not available for the other countries, since all the reports included in the samples were screened in and investigated.)

The next decision point in the United States is substantiation. American substantiation rates are typically defined as the number of reports substantiated as a share of all reports received by the system. In the samples for Canada, Australia, and Wales, the substantiation rates are effectively the percentage of investigated cases that were substantiated. Thus, Table 2.8 calculates substantiation rates in two different ways, depending on whether the base is all reports made to the system or all reports investigated.

As a share of all reports made to the system, the U.S. rate of substantiation is notably lower than the English rate. As a share of the investigated cases, the substantiation rate for the Boston sample is somewhat higher than in Australia and Wales but lower than in England. The Canadian rate is not directly comparable because Ontario uses a three-tier system, in which a report may be substantiated, suspected, or unfounded. All we can be certain of is that the Ontario substantiation

Table 2.7 Screening rates (%)

	U.S., national	U.S., Boston	England
Screened in for investigation	53	78	74
Screened out	47	22	26

Sources: U.S., national: Wiese and Daro, *Current Trends in Child Abuse Reporting*, p. 2; England: Gibbons, Conroy, and Bell, *Operating the Child Protection System*, table 6i.

Table 2.8 Substantiation rates (%)

Reports substantiated/ reports received	U.S., national	U.S., Boston	England		
Substantiated	38.1	39.3	51.0		
Not substantiated	61.9	61.7	49.0		

Reports substantiated/ reports investigated	U.S., Boston	Canada	Australia	England	Wales
Substantiated	50.5	27.5	49.6	68.9	44.0
Suspected	—	30.5	—	—	—
Not substantiated	49.5	42.0	50.4	31.1	56.0

Sources: U.S., national: NCCAN, *Child Maltreatment 1993*, p. 3-5; England: Gibbons, Conroy, and Bell, *Operating the Child Protection System*, table 5i; Canada: Trocme et al., *Ontario Incidence Study*, table 3.1a; Australia and Wales: Thorpe, *Evaluating Child Protection*, tables 4.3, 4.4.

rate, in U.S. terms, is not higher than 58 percent and not lower than 27.5 percent.[19]

England's higher rate of substantiating investigated reports, as opposed to all reports, suggests that England may do a better job than the United States of screening out reports that are unlikely to be substantiated. However, as we saw in Table 2.7, England screens out only a slightly higher share of reports than Boston. This fact suggests that the low substantiation rate in the United States may be due in part to a larger number of cases that are unlikely to be substantiated being reported in the first place.

Although the comparison with Canada is not as informative as we would like, because of the difference in how substantiation decisions are categorized, it appears that the substantiation rate in Canada is probably not much higher than in the United States. If we assume that half the "suspected" cases in Canada would be substantiated and half would not, then the substantiation rate in Canada—defined as a share of investigated reports—would be about 43 percent, which is somewhat lower than in the United States. If we assume instead that all the "suspected" cases would be substantiated, the rate in Ontario rises to 58 percent, higher than the rate in Boston but not dramatically so.

Table 2.9 shows a great deal of variation across countries in the types of maltreatment substantiated—much greater than in the types

Table 2.9 Type of maltreatment substantiated (%)

Type of maltreatment	U.S., national (NCPCA)	U.S., national (NCCAN)	U.S., Boston	Canada	Australia	England	Wales
Neglect	49.0	55.2	70.8	35.9	28.0	19.3	4.5
Physical abuse	21.0	24.5	27.1	34.4	15.4	41.9	52.3
Sexual abuse	11.0	12.6	4.2	27.9	20.0	30.0	27.3
Emotional	3.0	4.5	0.0	7.8	3.1	—	—
"At-risk"	—	—	—	—	33.5	—	15.9
Other	16.0	14.4	—	2.7	—	8.8	—
Total	100.0	111.2	102.1	107.7	100.0	100.0	100.0

Sources: U.S., national (NCPCA): Wiese and Daro, *Current Trends in Child Abuse Reporting,* fig. 1; U.S., national (NCCAN): NCCAN, *Child Maltreatment 1995;* fig. 2-5; Canada: calculated from data in Trocme et al., *Ontario Incidence Study,* table 3.2; Australia and Wales: calculated from data in Thorpe, *Evaluating Child Protection,* tables 4.3, 4.4; England: calculated from data in Gibbons, Conroy, and Bell, *Operating the Child Protection System,* tables 6iv, 6v, 6vi.

Notes: Some totals exceed 100% because more than one type of maltreatment may have been substantiated.

of maltreatment reported. This outcome reflects a differential propensity to substantiate allegations of neglect. As a comparison with the figures in Table 2.2 shows, in England a report of neglect is much less likely to be substantiated than a report of physical or sexual abuse, while in the United States and Canada a report of neglect is more likely to be substantiated. In Boston, neglect rises as a share of the caseload when one moves from reports to substantiated cases. In Canada, too, neglect rises as a share of the caseload as one moves from reports to substantiated cases, but the share of neglect cases at the end of the investigation period is twice as high in the United States as in Canada because the U.S. share of neglect reports is so much higher to start with. In England, on the other hand, the share of cases involving neglect falls from 45 percent initially to under 20 percent by the time a substantiation decision has been reached. This pattern is seen to a lesser extent in Australia. Thus, by the end of the investigation, an even larger gulf opens up between the nature of the caseloads in the United States and in other countries, with the U.S. caseload much more likely to involve cases of neglect rather than physical and sexual abuse.

Table 2.10 Family structure of children substantiated for child abuse or neglect (%)

Family structure	U.S., Boston	Canada	Australia
Two parents	58.3	59.0	46.4
Biological parents	47.9	34.5	29.2
Parent & step-parent	10.4	24.5	17.2
Lone parent	35.4	37.3	51.4
Lone mother	33.3	30.9	44.0
Lone father	2.1	6.4	7.4
Foster family	2.1	—	—
Other	4.2	3.7	2.4

Sources: Canada: calculations from data in Trocme et al., *Ontario Incidence Study,* table 6.3; Australia: Thorpe, *Evaluating Child Protection,* table 10.13.

Since lone-parent families are more likely than other families to be reported for neglect, we might expect them to constitute a larger share of the substantiated caseload in the United States, relative to their share of the reported cases, than in the other countries, where neglect is a lower share of substantiated cases. Yet Table 2.10 shows that in the United States and Canada, lone-parent families constitute a lower share of substantiated cases than they do of reported cases. In Australia, in contrast, lone-parent families constitute roughly half of all reported cases and of all substantiated cases, even though neglect falls as a share of substantiated cases. The association of neglect with lone parenthood, then, seems not to be the primary reason for the disproportionate representation of lone-parent families in the system.[20]

The statistics in Table 2.11 indicate that minority children make up a larger share of children substantiated by CPS than of children reported to CPS (Table 2.5). Taken together, these data suggest that some factor associated with being African-American, Hispanic, or Asian in the United States, or Native Canadian, black, or other minority in Canada, or Aboriginal in Australia makes a family both more likely to be reported for abuse or neglect and more likely to be substantiated once reported. Although the small sample sizes preclude

Table 2.11 Racial or ethnic minority status of children substantiated for abuse or neglect (%)

Minority status	U.S., Boston	Canada	Australia
Racial or ethnic minority	78.7	20.9	32.0
White (nonminority)	15.7	74.3	48.0
Status unknown	5.6	4.8	20.0

Sources: Canada: Trocme et al., *Ontario Incidence Study,* table 6.6; Australia: Thorpe, *Evaluating Child Protection,* table 9.1.

more conclusive analysis of the relationship between minority status, reporting, and substantiation, this topic has received a good deal of attention in previous work on child protective services and clearly merits further analysis both in the United States and in other countries.

Differences in Outcome by Type of Reporter

The comparative data also shed some light on how families come to the attention of the CPS system and whether the source of the report affects what happens afterward. Information on the source of the report is available for the United States, Canada, and England. Although England does not have mandatory reporting laws, the majority of reports are made by professionals, as in the United States and Canada. Table 2.12 shows that the most striking difference is the larger share of reports made by informal sources such as family, friends, neighbors, and children themselves in Canada and the United States as compared to England. Another striking difference is the very low share of reports made anonymously in Canada (this may help explain the high rate of reports by informal sources there). The smaller share of reports made by teachers and other school personnel in the United States is also notable. (The low share of reports from teachers in the Boston sample relative to the U.S. share is due mainly to the fact that schools were not in session for part of the time during which the Boston sample was collected.)

National data from U.S. studies since the 1970s have indicated that

Table 2.12 Source of report (%)

Source	U.S., national	U.S., Boston	Canada	England
Health personnel	10.7	32.0	9.6	17.0
Social services	13.3	17.2	10.1	13.0
Police or probation	12.4	10.7	8.3	12.0
Teachers and school personnel	16.3	7.4	22.9	23.0
Informal sources	28.5	23.0	41.9	17.0
Family, friends, neighbors	27.1	19.7	38.1	n.a.
Child	1.4	3.3	3.8	n.a.
Anonymous	11.0	8.2	2.0	6.0
Other	7.8	3.3	5.2	12.0
Total	100.0	101.8	100.0	100.0

Sources: U.S., national: NCCAN, *Child Maltreatment 1993*, fig. 2-2; Canada: Trocme et al., *Ontario Incidence Study*, table 7.1; England: Gibbons, Conroy, and Bell, *Operating the Child Protection System*, chap. 3.

Note: Total for Boston sums to more than 100% because some cases were reported by more than one type of reporter.

reports from professionals are more likely to be substantiated,[21] and the Boston data in Table 2.13 clearly confirm this. On average, nearly half (48.8 percent) of reports from professionals are substantiated, as opposed to under a third (30.9 percent) of reports from nonprofessionals. As we shall see in Chapter 4, this result reflects professionals' greater accuracy in referring cases that meet the definitions of abuse or neglect, but it probably also reflects a tendency on the part of CPS to conduct more thorough investigations of reports that come from professionals. The gap in substantiation rates between professional and nonprofessional reporters is much lower in Canada than in the United States. This result is explained in part by the much lower frequency of anonymous reports in Canada.

A notable minority of reports in all countries are made by individuals such as ex-spouses, family members, or neighbors who might be involved in an ongoing conflict with one or both parents of the child. This share is just under 20 percent in Boston, 20 percent in Australia,

Table 2.13 Substantiation rate, by source of report (%)

Source	U.S., Boston	Canada
Health personnel	51.3	30.4
Social services	47.6	24.9
Police or probation	46.2	36.2
Teachers and school personnel	44.4	29.0
Informal sources	21.4	n.a.
Family, friends, neighbors	16.7	26.5
Child	50.0	31.0
Anonymous	10.0	10.0
Other	50.0	23.0
Average for professionals	48.8	29.7
Average for nonprofessionals	30.9	25.7
Average for all reporters	39.3	27.0

Source: Canada: Trocme et al., *Ontario Incidence Study*, table 7.1.

and 27 percent in Canada and Wales.[22] Cases in which a reporter might be in conflict with the family are much less likely to be substantiated than are reports made in nonconflictual situations, as can be seen in Table 2.14. Substantiation rates are especially low across all four countries for reports made by ex-spouses or ex-partners in situations of custody/access conflict; they also tend to be lower than average for reports made by neighbors. However, reports made by other family members, such as grandmothers, aunts, and uncles, are not necessarily less likely to be substantiated. This outcome makes sense, since these individuals typically would be close enough to have good information about the situation of a child but without being caught up in a struggle over custody or access. The U.S. and Canadian data also indicate that reports from children themselves have a higher-than-average substantiation rate; indeed, in the United States reports from children are as likely to be substantiated as reports from professionals.

Table 2.14 Substantiation rates for reporters who might be in conflict with the family, compared to other reporters (%)

Source	U.S., Boston	Canada	Australia	Wales
Ex-spouse or ex-partner	0.0	13.0	17.9	25.0
Neighbor	12.5	23.0	12.5	33.3
Other family member	33.3	32.6	36.8	66.7
Child	50.0	31.0	—	—
Professional	48.8	29.7	55.9	42.5
Average for all cases	39.3	27.0	49.6	44.0

Sources: Canada: Trocme et al., *Ontario Incidence Study*, table 7.1; Australia and Wales: calculated from data in Thorpe, *Evaluating Child Protection*, tables 4.5, 4.6.

Note: Substantiation rates for Canada, Australia, and Wales are as a share of all investigated cases. Substantiation rates for Boston are as a share of reported cases.

Outcomes

There are four possible outcomes at the conclusion of the investigation: a case may be substantiated and opened, substantiated and closed, unsubstantiated and closed, or unsubstantiated and opened. Table 2.15 presents the share of cases falling into these four groups for the Boston and Canadian samples. The fact that substantiation is defined differently in the two countries does not explain the much lower share of cases kept open in Canada at the end of investigation. In the Boston sample, nearly all the substantiated cases are kept open, in contrast to only about half in the Canadian sample. What happens to the remainder? About a third of the cases that are substantiated and closed are referred to other agencies; the remaining two-thirds are simply closed. Additional research comparing outcomes for these two samples may provide some answers about how long-term outcomes compare for the cases kept open, closed and referred, and simply closed.[23]

The English system is more complicated, incorporating two additional dimensions: referral to a child protection conference and listing on the child protection register. Only one-quarter of all the cases reported to CPS are considered serious enough to proceed to a child

Table 2.15 Case outcomes after investigation (%)

U.S., Boston	Unsubstantiated	Substantiated	Total
Closed	50	3	53
Open	11	36	47
Total	61	39	100
Canada	Unfounded or suspected	Substantiated	Total
Closed	59	14	73
Open	14	13	27
Total	73	27	100

Source: Calculated from data in Trocme et al., *Ontario Incidence Study.*

protection conference, where plans for service provision to the family will be made. Since about half of all reported cases are substantiated, this means that not all substantiated cases are referred for a conference, although they are much more likely to be referred than unsubstantiated cases. For cases of physical abuse, only 52 percent of substantiated cases reach a conference, along with 5 percent of cases that were not substantiated; for sexual abuse, the figures are 46 percent and 9 percent, respectively; and for neglect, the figures are even lower, 28.5 percent and 1 percent, respectively.[24] There is little evidence in the British data that too many low-risk cases were reaching the conference stage in 1991. On the contrary, there is some evidence that fairly serious cases, including many in which abuse or neglect was substantiated, were not reaching it.[25] Although there are alternative pathways for intervention in cases not reaching a conference (for example, in this sample, legal action was taken instead in about 5 percent of the cases), the British data nevertheless suggest that at the time of the 1991 survey some serious cases might have been closed prematurely.

Upon reaching the conference, cases may or may not be listed on the area's child protection register. A case is supposed to be registered if a child has been abused or neglected and is in need of services from more than one agency as a result of the abuse or neglect. Thus, not all children who have been maltreated should be listed (for example, a child whose abuser has left the home and who no longer needs services should not be listed), but most should be.[26] In practice, only 60 percent of cases reaching a conference are listed, even though the cases referred to conference tend to be serious.

Because many cases have been filtered out before this point and because not all cases that reach a conference are listed, only 15 percent of the original referrals to CPS are listed on a child protection register. Although all local authorities register a majority (between 57 and 82 percent) of the higher-risk cases discussed at a case conference, there is much variation (ranging from 21 percent to 71 percent) in their propensity to register the lower-risk cases.[27]

Substantiation does not automatically lead to provision of services in any of the sample countries. Moreover, most children seen by CPS, even those in substantiated cases of abuse or neglect, remain at home with their families, at least initially. (See Table 2.16.) In the United States nationally, as we saw in Chapter 1, only one in 20 children reported to CPS, and only about one in 7 of those investigated and substantiated, will end up in foster placement or some other type of placement by the end of the investigation. This is also the case in the

Table 2.16 Status of children at conclusion of investigation (%)

Population	U.S., Boston	Canada	Australia	England	Wales
All cases reported					
At home, no open case	52.6	66.1	62.9	58.0	63.0
At home, case open	42.4	26.9	27.3	31.1	30.0
In placement	5.0	6.0	9.8	10.9	7.0
All cases substantiated					
At home, no open case	8.3	51.0	25.2	—	17.8
At home, case open	79.2	33.7	55.1	—	66.6
In placement	12.5	15.3	19.7	—	15.6

Sources: Canada: Trocme et al., *Ontario Incidence Study,* table 5.2; Australia and Wales: calculated from data in Thorpe, *Evaluating Child Protection,* tables 4.10, 4.11; England: calculated from data in Gibbons, Conroy, and Bell, *Operating the Child Protection System,* chap. 6.

Boston sample: at the conclusion of the investigation, children had been removed from home in only one in 20 of the cases reported to CPS, and only one in 8 of the substantiated cases.

Figures from Australia, Britain, and Canada paint a similar picture, although children in the United States are somewhat more likely to be at home with an open case and less likely to be either at home with a closed case or in placement. In each of these countries, more than half the children reported to CPS (58–66 percent) are at home with no open case at the end of the investigation (as compared to 53 percent in Boston). Less than a third are at home with an open case (as compared to over 40 percent in Boston), and 6–11 percent (as compared to 5 percent in Boston) are in placement.

The four countries differ dramatically in the extent of linkage between substantiation and case opening. Because very few cases are substantiated and closed in the United States, the share of children in substantiated cases who are at home with no open case is much lower there than in the other countries, while the share who are at home with an open case is much higher.

Do reports trigger a response that protects children from further abuse or neglect? Or do children reported to CPS continue to suffer serious maltreatment as a result of being left home or having their cases closed in error, despite their having come to the attention of child protective services?

Although we have some evidence about the frequency with which children are abused and neglected again, we do not know how many children might have been abused and neglected again if not for CPS intervention. If we find, for example, that 25 percent of children reported to CPS are maltreated again in the next few years, we may conclude that in some sense the system failed to protect one-quarter of the children, but we may also conclude that the system may have protected 75 percent. We can put some bounds on the share protected—in this example, it is less than or equal to 75 percent—but we do not know whether it is greater than, less than, or equal to the share not protected. Nor can we judge the performance of the system by comparing the maltreatment rate of children reported with those not reported, because children who have been reported once are a select group who, all else being equal, are probably more likely to be abused or neglected in the future. For instance, Michael Wald and his collaborators, in their longitudinal study of abused and neglected children in

California, found that half of their sample of children who had been maltreated and were at high risk of placement but remained at home suffered further abuse or neglect in the two years following the initial report, a rate that is much higher than that found in the general population.[28] In another California study, Jill Duerr Berrick and her colleagues found that about 44 percent of young children who had been reported to CPS were reported again in the next three years; the rate of having a second report was highest—74 percent—for infants who had been reported for neglect.[29] These high rates of repeat maltreatment are not unique; most earlier studies have found that maltreatment recurs in one-third to one-half of cases and that recurrence is most likely in cases involving neglect or substance abuse.[30]

It is difficult, then, to set an absolute standard for the performance of a system in protecting children from further harm. Rather, we must compare the performance of systems at various points in time or in different locations to determine what might be a reasonable standard of performance.

Longitudinal studies tracking outcomes for abused and neglected children are fairly rare, but both the Australian and English studies followed the reported children for a short period—one year and 9–12 months, respectively. The Boston study tracked cases for nearly three years. The data from these three samples allow us to track repeat occurrences of abuse and neglect for the children originally reported to CPS.

In the Australian sample (Table 2.17), about 6 percent of all reported children suffered further abuse or neglect and had to be removed from home in the following year, after an initial decision that they could remain at home. Although these children were a small percentage of all those reported, they constituted over one-fifth (22 percent) of all children left at home after abuse or neglect was substantiated. At first glance this seems a fairly high failure rate, but in about half of these cases there was no further injury or harm to the child, only elevated risk of harm, and in most of the other cases the harm or injury was not serious.[31]

Another 3 percent of reported children were further harmed in the year after the report despite being open substantiated cases, but these were able to remain at home after the recurrence of abuse or neglect, so presumably the maltreatment was less serious. Nevertheless, these are children whom the system in some sense failed to protect. A

Table 2.17 Outcomes for Australian children in the year after initial report, as a share of all children originally investigated

Status of case and outcome	%
Substantiated & open	
Child at home suffered further harm/risk and was removed	6.1
Child at home suffered further harm but remained home	3.4
Substantiated & closed, then re-reported and substantiated	0.8
Unsubstantiated & closed, then re-reported and substantiated	4.3
Total	14.6

Source: Calculated from data in Thorpe, *Evaluating Child Protection*, chap. 11.

smaller group of children, less than 1 percent of the original number reported, were cases that had been substantiated and closed but were re-reported and substantiated during the year after the initial report. These children represented 7 percent of all those whose cases were closed after substantiation. Among the few cases re-reported and substantiated, the risk seems to have been very low: three were closed again after the investigation, while two were opened but for in-home services only. Finally, just over 4 percent of the children originally reported were re-reported and substantiated after a decision not to substantiate the initial report.

Altogether, then, of all the children reported to and screened in by CPS in the Australian sample, not quite 15 percent experienced further abuse or neglect in the following year. These statistics indicate that the Western Australian system did fairly well in protecting the children reported to it. Few children (at most about 10 percent of those reported) were left at home with insufficient protection after an initial substantiated report; a smaller number of cases suffered further harm after being unsubstantiated and closed; and even fewer suffered further harm after being substantiated and closed. These percentages are upper-bound estimates of the share of cases in which the agency made an error, since one cannot assume that all cases in which an agency failed to prevent future harm involved an error. Some instances of repeat maltreatment may have involved new situations that could not have been foreseen at the time of the initial referral. Moreover, none of the errors were grave ones, since no children sustained life-threatening injuries or were killed.

The English study included a one-year follow-up of the 399 children whose cases were brought to a child protection conference.[32] Because this follow-up did not cover outcomes for children whose cases were not brought to a conference, it is impossible to know how many potentially serious cases of abuse or neglect may have been missed. The children referred for a conference are all victims of fairly serious abuse or neglect, and only the most serious cases go on to be listed on the area's child protection register. Of the 399 children who were conferenced, 144 were never listed on the child protection register, 199 were listed and remained on the register, 45 changed registry status, and the status of another 11 was unclear. Listing made a big difference in the type of services that families received in the year after the initial report. Children who were listed were seen more frequently by social workers than children discussed at conference but not listed—about once every two weeks as compared to once every six weeks. They and their families were also significantly more likely to receive day-care services (16 percent versus 4 percent of nonregistered children), housing (16 percent versus 6 percent), mental health services (8 percent versus 2 percent), financial help (30 percent versus 15 percent), family aides (7 percent versus 3 percent), and educational help (6 percent versus 1 percent).[33]

Table 2.18 shows that over one-quarter of the children whose cases were brought to a child protection conference were reported again in the year following the initial report. Among the cases re-reported, the largest share (42 percent) concerned an incident of alleged abuse or

Table 2.18 Repeat reports 9–12 months after initial report for English children brought to child protection conference (%)

Status of child	Re-reported	Not re-reported	Total
Listed on register	18.6	41.4	60.0
Not listed	7.7	32.3	40.0
Total	26.3	73.7	100.0

Source: Calculated from data in Gibbons, Conroy, and Bell, Operating the Child Protection System, chap. 10.

neglect that was not serious; however, 38 percent concerned serious instances of abuse or neglect, including two fatalities (one of these as a result of the original injury, not a new one), while the remaining 20 percent of re-reports concerned risk only. Altogether, just under half of the new reports were substantiated.[34]

Table 2.19 summarizes the one-year outcomes for all children considered by a child protection conference. In 12 percent of the cases, new reports were substantiated. In about half of these cases, the maltreatment was serious enough to necessitate removal, with another 2 percent of the children removed from home for other reasons such as elevated risk of harm or family disruption. Altogether, 14 percent of the children suffered further abuse or neglect or other harm in the year following their child protection conference. These statistics suggest a moderate rate of further maltreatment—about the same as the rate seen in the Australian sample. However, the English follow-up sample contains more high-risk cases to start with; the Australian sample includes follow-up of all cases that were reported and investigated. Given that we might have expected more repeat occurrences of abuse and neglect in this higher-risk sample, the data suggest that the English system may be superior to Western Australia's in preventing further harm. However, because we do not know what happened to the children whose cases were not conferenced, we do not know how many cases of potentially serious abuse or neglect the English system missed.

Ideally, we would like more information in order to judge how many of the cases in which children suffered further harm were instances in which the system failed and how many were unavoidable recurrences or even new situations that could not have been foreseen

Table 2.19 Outcomes for English children brought to a child protection conference, 9–12 months after initial report

Outcome	%
Reported again, substantiated, but remained at home	6.0
Reported again, substantiated, removed from home	6.0
Removed from home for other reasons	1.9
Total	13.9

Source: Calculated from data in Gibbons, Conroy, and Bell, *Operating the Child Protection System,* tables 10iiA and 10iiB.

at the time of the initial referral. Nevertheless, we can conclude from the rates of further harm seen here that both among the conferenced cases in England and among the investigated cases in Western Australia, about 14–15 percent experienced repeat occurrences of abuse or neglect in the year after the initial report to CPS.

How do these rates of repeat maltreatment compare with those in the United States? Although data on this point are scarce, we can use the follow-up data from the Boston study, which tracked repeat reports and other outcomes for children for nearly three years.[35] To facilitate comparison with the Australian and British samples discussed above, let us first consider one-year outcomes, and then consider the fuller picture of outcomes after three years.

As Table 2.20 shows, 12.4 percent of the cases in the Boston sample were reported again within a year. At first glance, this rate of repeat reports appears to be much lower than the rate of 26 percent in the English sample (Table 2.18). However, the rates for the Boston cases that were substantiated or already open and for the English cases that had been conferenced and listed on the register for abuse or neglect are strikingly similar. As we saw in Table 2.18, 18.6 percent of the listed British children were reported again in the following year. In Boston, 17.5 percent of the substantiated or already open cases were re-reported in the following year. However, not all these new reports were substantiated.

Table 2.21 shows that nearly 10 percent of the cases in the Boston sample were substantiated for further abuse or neglect in the first year after the original report. Another 9 percent, though not substantiated for abuse or neglect, were at high enough risk that the children were removed from their homes by CPS. Altogether, then, about 19 percent of the children suffered further harm or were removed by CPS in the first year.

The Boston data also track some other adverse outcomes, in addi-

Table 2.20 Repeat reports for Boston children in the year after initial report

Population	Re-reported	Not re-reported	Total
All children	12.4	87.6	100
Children substantiated or already open with CPS	17.5	82.5	100

Table 2.21 3-year outcomes for all children reported in Boston sample (%)

Outcome	1-year follow-up	2-year follow-up	3-year follow-up
Substantiated for further abuse or neglect	9.7	22.1	23.9
Not substantiated, but removed by CPS	8.8	8.0	8.8
Not substantiated, removed by another agency	4.4	4.4	2.7
Total experiencing further harm or removal	22.9	34.5	35.4

Note: Figures in rows are cumulative and represent the share of children experiencing a given outcome by the 1-year, 2-year, or 3-year follow-up. Children are counted only once; for example, a child experiencing a further report of substantiated abuse or neglect is not counted among those removed by CPS or by another agency. Therefore, the share of children counted as experiencing removal falls over the 3-year follow-up as some are substantiated for further abuse or neglect.

tion to reports of abuse or neglect and placements by CPS. These data indicate that another 4.4 percent of children were removed from home within a year for other reasons (such as delinquency or psychiatric illness). If these children are included, then the share of cases experiencing further harm or removal rises to nearly 23 percent.

Table 2.21 also shows cumulative outcomes for children at the end of the second and third years. These statistics reveal that the share of children experiencing further harm or placement rose dramatically in the second year after the report before stabilizing in the following year.[36] The share of cases substantiated for further abuse or neglect rises to 22 percent by the end of the second year and to 24 percent by the end of the third year, while the share substantiated or placed by CPS or by another agency rises to about 35 percent by the end of the second year and remains at that level in the third year.

How do these rates of repeat reports of abuse and neglect, and of further placement, compare to those in the English and Australian samples? Even if we exclude the share of children experiencing other adverse outcomes, since these children are not counted in the English and Australian follow-ups, the rate at which children experienced further harm or placement by CPS in the first year after the report—19 percent—is somewhat higher in the Boston sample than the rate of 14–15 percent in the samples from England and Australia. However, these samples are not exactly comparable, since the Australian follow-up includes only cases that were screened-in and investigated, while the English sample includes only those that were conferenced and listed.

Table 2.22 shows one-, two-, and three-year outcomes for children in the Boston sample according to their status at the time of the original report. If we compare the first group in the table—which includes only cases that were screened in and investigated by CPS or were already open with CPS—with Table 2.17, we find that the rate of further harm or removal in the first year is notably higher in the United States (where 20.6 percent of cases suffer further harm or removal by CPS, with an additional 4 percent removed by other agencies) than in Australia (where 14.6 percent of cases suffer further harm or removal). By the end of year two, 24 percent of the investigated or already open Boston cases are substantiated for further abuse or neglect, and 36 percent are either substantiated or placed; these figures rise to 25 percent and 37 percent by the end of year three.

The second group in Table 2.22—which includes only cases that were screened in and substantiated or were already open with CPS—provides information on the sample of high-risk Boston cases that is most nearly comparable to the high-risk cases included in the English follow-up and shown in Table 2.19. Again the rates of repeat harm or removal are notably higher in the United States: 24.6 percent of the Boston cases are substantiated or placed by CPS by the end of the first year, compared to 14 percent of the English cases. Indeed, if we include all the children who were further harmed or removed (including the 5 percent placed by other agencies), the share of high-risk children experiencing adverse outcomes in the Boston sample is twice as high as that in the English sample. The statistics for the high-risk Boston children in years two and three are even more disturbing: by the end of year two, one-third are substantiated for further abuse or neglect, and 47 percent are either substantiated or placed; by the end of year three, these figures rise to 35 percent and 48 percent, respectively.

The Boston data also allow us to track outcomes for the cases judged to be lower-risk at the time of the initial report. Outcomes for the third and fourth groups in Table 2.22—showing cases that were screened in and investigated but not substantiated at the time of the original report, and cases that were screened out and were not already open with CPS at the time of the original report—suggest that CPS investigators are for the most part making good decisions at the point

Table 2.22 3-year outcomes for children in Boston sample, by original status (%)

Status and outcome	1-year follow-up	2-year follow-up	3-year follow-up
Cases screened in and investigated or already open (N = 97)			
Substantiated for further abuse or neglect	10.3	23.7	24.7
Not substantiated, but removed by CPS	10.3	8.2	9.3
Not substantiated, removed by another agency	4.1	4.1	3.1
Total experiencing further harm or removal	24.7	36.0	37.1
Cases screened in, investigated, and substantiated, or already open (N = 57)			
Substantiated for further abuse or neglect	12.3	33.3	35.1
Not substantiated, but removed by CPS	12.3	10.5	10.5
Not substantiated, removed by another agency	5.3	3.5	3.5
Total experiencing further harm or removal	29.9	47.3	48.1
Cases screened in and investigated but not substantiated (N = 40)			
Substantiated for further abuse or neglect	7.5	10.0	10.0
Not substantiated, but removed by CPS	7.5	5.0	7.5
Not substantiated, removed by another agency	2.5	5.0	2.5
Total experiencing further harm or removal	17.5	20.0	20.0
Cases screened out and not already open (N = 16)			
Substantiated for further abuse or neglect	6.3	12.5	18.8
Not substantiated, but removed by CPS	0.0	6.3	6.3
Not substantiated, removed by another agency	6.3	6.3	0.0
Total experiencing further harm or removal	12.6	25.1	25.1

Note: Figures in rows are cumulative and represent the share of children experiencing a given outcome by the 1-year, 2-year, or 3-year follow-up. Children are counted only once; for example, a child experiencing a further report of substantiated abuse or neglect is not counted among the children removed by CPS or removed by another agency. Therefore, the share of children counted as experiencing removal falls over the 3-year period as some are substantiated for further abuse or neglect.

of substantiation: the rates of repeat reports for the unsubstantiated cases in the third group are much lower than for the substantiated cases in the second group.

The picture is worse for the 16 cases that were screened out and were not already open with CPS at the time of the original referral. One in eight of these cases is substantiated or placed by another agency within the first year, and the share rises to one in four by the end of the second year. Although the overall share substantiated or placed remains stable from year two to year three, the share reported to and substantiated by CPS rises steadily over the three-year period. For this small sample of cases, the CPS screening process seems to have simply postponed intervention; within three years one-quarter of the screened-out cases have returned to CPS and been either substantiated or placed by CPS. This is an even higher share than for the screened-in but unsubstantiated cases, one-fifth of which are substantiated or placed by the end of year three.

Are these high rates of repeat maltreatment and placement typical? Earlier longitudinal studies of CPS cases in the United States have found varying rates of repeat maltreatment, with estimates ranging from about 10 percent to 74 percent, depending on the age of the child, the type of maltreatment originally reported, the length of time the child was followed, and the way in which repeat maltreatment was tracked.[37] Most studies find that one-third to half of children suffer repeat maltreatment.[38] A study of cases in New York City, conducted in 1996 just before the CPS reforms there, found that 43 percent of children in substantiated cases were abused or neglected again in a six-month period.[39]

Thus the rate of recurrence in the Boston sample, with 24 percent of the entire sample substantiated again in the following three years, is probably low by U.S. standards. In this regard it is useful to recall that the Boston office chosen for the study was considered to be one of the stronger offices in Massachusetts, and that Massachusetts is generally considered to have one of the best CPS systems in the country.[40]

Why Are U.S. Reporting Rates So High?

The U.S. reporting rate—45 per 1,000 children in 1993—is more than twice as high as in Canada (21 per 1,000 in 1993), and higher still in relation to England's (under 18 per 1,000 in 1991). Nico Trocme and his collaborators provide some evidence that neglect cases account for much of these differences.[41]

My own estimates for the United States, Canada, and England, shown in Tables 2.23 and 2.24, confirm that neglect almost entirely explains the higher rates of reporting and substantiation. Table 2.23 shows that the frequency of each specific category of reported maltreatment does not vary a great deal by country, with the exception of neglect, which is reported two to three times more frequently in the United States than in Canada or England. This effect is even more pronounced for substantiated cases, as we can see in Table 2.24.[42]

Why is neglect so much more likely to be reported and substantiated in the United States? One possibility is that the United States simply has a better-developed system for reporting abuse or neglect in general, as a result of mandatory reporting legislation and heightened awareness of abuse and neglect issues. However, the data from Canada and England refute this explanation, since neglect is the only type of maltreatment more likely to be reported and substantiated in the United States. Another possibility is that the United States defines neglect differently from other countries and hence finds and substantiates more cases of it. Yet criteria for neglect in the various countries, summarized in Table 2.25, show strong similarities; if anything, the

Table 2.23 Comparative rates of reported maltreatment per 1,000 children

Type of maltreatment	U.S., national 1993	Canada 1993	England 1991
Neglect	20.25	6.26	8.10
Physical abuse	11.70	8.72	7.20
Sexual abuse	4.95	5.33	4.14
Emotional abuse	1.35	2.12	—
Other	6.75	0.44	—
Total	45.00	22.87	19.44

Sources: calculated from data in Table 2.2 and published reporting rates. Reporting rate for U.S. (45 per 1,000 in 1993): Wiese and Daro, *Current Trends in Child Abuse Reporting,* table 1; for Ontario (21 per 1,000 in 1993): Trocme et al., *Ontario Incidence Study,* table 3.1a; for England (17.5 per 1,000 in 1991): Gibbons, Conroy, and Bell, *Operating the Child Protection System,* chap. 2.

Note: Totals for Canada and England exceed the published reporting rates because more than one type of maltreatment may have been reported.

Table 2.24 Comparative rates of substantiated maltreatment per 1,000 children

Type of maltreatment	U.S., national 1993 (NCPCA)	U.S., national 1993 (NCCAN)	Canada 1993	England 1991
Neglect	8.33	9.22	2.15	1.74
Physical abuse	3.57	4.19	2.06	3.77
Sexual abuse	1.87	2.18	1.67	2.70
Emotional abuse	0.51	0.84	0.47	n.a.
Other	2.72	2.35	0.16	0.79
Total	17.00	18.78	6.51	9.00

Sources: Calculated from data in Tables 2.8 and 2.9.

Note: For the U.S., the NCPCA substantiated case rate is 15 per 1,000 (Wiese and Daro, *Current Trends in Child Abuse Reporting,* table 1, report that there were 45 reports per 1,000 children in 1993 and that 33 percent of these were substantiated); the NCCAN rate is 16.77 per 1,000 (NCCAN, *Child Maltreatment 1993,* p. 3-5, reports that there were 43 reports per 1,000 children in 1993 and that 39 percent of these were substantiated or indicated). For Canada, the substantiated case rate is estimated to be 5.78 per 1,000 (Trocme et al., *Ontario Incidence Study,* table 3.1a, reports that there were 21 reports per 1,000 children in 1993 and that 27.5 percent were substantiated). For England, the substantiated case rate is estimated to be 8.93 per 1,000 (I estimate that there were 17.5 reports per 1,000 children, on the basis of data in Gibbons, Conroy, and Bell, *Operating the Child Protection System,* chap. 2, who report that 51 percent of these are substantiated).

Note: Totals for the U.S., Canada, and England exceed the estimated substantiated case rates per 1,000 because more than one type of maltreatment may have been substantiated.

definitions in Australia and Britain seem to be broader than they are in the United States.

Another possibility, given that all four countries apparently define neglect in much the same way, is that the United States simply has more cases of it. Given the well-documented association between poverty and reports of neglect, one plausible explanation is the greater numbers of children in poverty in the United States. Poverty figures for our sample countries indicate that the United States has by far the highest child poverty rate (21.5 percent in 1991, compared with 13.5 percent in Canada, 14 percent in Australia, and 9.9 percent in Britain).[43] As we saw earlier, in the United States poverty is strongly linked to the likelihood that a child is reported. An-

Table 2.25 Criteria for reporting neglect in sample countries

United States:	The most common reported type of neglect is physical neglect, such as inadequate food or clothing, or dangerous or unsanitary housing. Other types include lack of supervision, educational neglect, medical neglect, emotional neglect, and abandonment.
Canada:	The most commonly reported types of neglect are failure to supervise and physical neglect. Other types include medical neglect, emotional neglect, permitting criminal behavior, abandonment, and educational neglect.
Australia:	Neglect is broadly defined as any serious omission or commission by a person having the care of a child that, within the bounds of cultural tradition, constitutes a failure to provide conditions essential for the healthy physical and emotional development of a child.
Britain:	Neglect is broadly defined as failure to provide care that a reasonable parent would provide for the child concerned.

Sources: U.S.: Peter Pecora, James Whittaker, and Anthony Maluccio, *The Child Welfare Challenge: Policy, Practice, and Research* (New York: Aldine de Gruyter, 1992), pp. 192–194; Canada: Trocme et al., *Ontario Incidence Study*, pp. 50–51; Australia: Thorpe, *Evaluating Child Protection*, p. 205; England and Wales: Department of Health, *An Introduction to the Children Act* (London: Her Majesty's Stationery Office, 1989), p. 6.

other possibility, considered further in Chapter 7, is that more children may be referred to CPS in the United States because fewer alternative sources of services exist for them here than in other countries.

In comparing reporting rates across countries and in assessing the performance of CPS systems, it is important to take into account the extent to which cases reported to CPS are new or already known to the system. In the Boston sample, over half (53 percent) of the families reported to CPS were already known to the agency: about 16 percent were currently open with CPS, while 37 percent had been reported to CPS in the past. This finding suggests that a large share of the reports made to CPS are "duplicates," in the sense that the same children may be reported more than once. Thus, the true incidence of reportable child abuse and neglect may be much lower than the number of reports per 1,000 children.

As far as can be determined with available data (shown in Table

2.26), however, this is also true in Canada, where nearly half of all reports involve cases known to the agency, and in England, where an even higher proportion involve cases known to the agency. Thus, the high rate of repeat reports in the U.S. caseload is unlikely to explain the much higher rate of reports in the United States as compared to Canada or England.

These high rates of reports on cases already known to the system, taken together with the low rates of service delivery to reported cases even when substantiated and the high rates of further abuse or neglect in reported cases, have important implications in terms of the efficiency of the system. If a report to CPS is meant to be a trigger that releases a set of services to protect a child, then this mechanism is not working very well. Many children who are referred are already known to the system, many of those referred will never receive services that they might need, and some of those referred will suffer further abuse or neglect. It is hard to escape the conclusions that, as the system currently operates, too many children are being referred unnecessarily, and that some children who are referred don't receive the help they need. Moreover, although other countries such as Canada and England are certainly not immune, these problems appear to be more acute in the United States than elsewhere.

The comparative data from the United States, Canada, Australia, and Britain allow us to consider in what ways children in need of protection in the United States are different and in what ways the problems seen in the United States are universal. Several conclusions emerge.

Table 2.26 Cases reported to CPS, by whether they were already known to CPS (%)

Status of case	U.S., Boston	Canada	England
Known to CPS	53	48	65
Open case	16	—	21
Past case	37	—	44
Not known to CPS	24	52	35
Not specified at time of referral	23	0	0

Sources: Canada: Trocme et al., *Ontario Incidence Study,* table 7.3b; England: Gibbons, Conroy, and Bell, *Operating the Child Protection System,* chap. 4.

First, neglect reports dominate the caseload in the United States more than elsewhere. Furthermore, neglect case are much more likely to remain open in the United States. Many of these families are low-risk and might not need full-blown CPS intervention; on the other hand, intervention is not always effective in protecting neglected children from further harm.[44] The fact that other countries keep fewer neglect cases open after investigation, without incurring dramatically higher rates of further harm (indeed, their rates of repeat maltreatment seem to be lower), indicates that we might be able to learn something from other countries about alternative approaches to protecting children in lower-risk cases of neglect. Providing a non-CPS pathway for lower-risk neglect cases could be beneficial to those families, if it spared them heavy-handed and adversarial CPS intervention. It might also benefit high-risk children remaining in CPS by freeing more resources for them.

Second, high-risk cases are not necessarily well served by child protective services in any of the sample countries. The Australian and British systems appear to filter out some high-risk cases, and some low-risk cases may be inappropriately kept in. In the United States, fewer than half of the cases reported to CPS are opened for services. The share in England is under one in five. However, the scope of the problem is larger in the United States simply because a larger share of families is referred to the system in the first place. Moreover, the follow-up data from the Boston case-record sample suggest that the system may not be doing as good a job of protecting the children referred to it as the systems in the two other countries for which we have follow-up data.

Finally, the comparative data confirm the impression that many cases may fall through the cracks because the system is overwhelmed with the sheer volume of cases coming to its attention. Again, this problem is more acute in the United States because the share of children reported to CPS is so much larger in the first place and because a larger share of those children are kept open in the system for investigation and for intervention thereafter. However, re-reporting does not explain the higher rates of reported abuse and neglect seen in the United States in comparison to other comparable countries. Rather, the data presented here provide some indication that poverty may play a role in explaining the higher rate of child maltreatment seen in the United States.

Chapter 3

The Current Child Protective Services System

Although the American child protective services system is relatively young, a consensus is forming, among those with firsthand knowledge and among observers across the political spectrum, that it is in need of drastic reform. This chapter reviews the scope and origins of the current system, its underlying assumptions, and assessments of its effectiveness by current practitioners, scholars, and other observers. This perspective reveals a set of problems that have implications for a new paradigm for child protective services.

Scope

In 1996 more than three million reports were made to CPS concerning children who were possible victims of abuse and neglect—an enormous increase in reports, and reporting rates, over the past few decades. (See Table 1.1.) It is unclear how much of this dramatic rise is due to a true increase in child maltreatment and how much is due to reporters' greater awareness and knowledge of what constitutes reportable abuse and neglect. Nor is it clear what the trend is likely to be in the future. Projected cutbacks in welfare and related social programs may trigger a new, and steeper, increase in reports of child maltreatment, particularly in referrals for poverty-related neglect such as inadequate housing, food, and clothing.

Funding for CPS comes from a mix of federal dollars, which primarily fund out-of-home care and some supportive services for intact families; state dollars, which fund the bulk of staff salaries; and a small amount of local dollars. Although the federal contribution is extremely important, states generally provide more than half the funding for CPS activities.[1] Federal programs currently include both entitlements (for example, Title IV-E funding for out-of-home care) and block grants (for example, Title XX funding for a range of social services).

In every state and the District of Columbia, responsibility for child protective services rests in a public agency; depending on the state, these agencies are state-administered or state-supervised and county-administered. These public agencies are staffed by social workers with varying levels of qualifications, ranging from entry-level staff who might not have a college degree on up to senior clinicians with master's degrees in social work or related fields.[2] As public employees, many social workers are represented by unions, and issues such as caseload size are often hotly contested. Guidelines from national bodies such as the Child Welfare League of America suggest that social workers should be responsible for no more than 20 families at any one time and that those with responsibility for investigating reports of abuse and neglect should carry even fewer cases. Few jurisdictions are able to meet these guidelines, however, and it is not uncommon for social workers to be carrying two or more times the recommended number of cases. Social worker safety is also a major concern for those working in child protective services. Social workers are routinely called upon to enter dangerous neighborhoods and homes, and there is always the fear that a parent who has been reported for abuse and neglect, or whose child is being removed, may react by assaulting a social worker.

Most states make fairly extensive use of private nonprofit and for-profit agencies in their CPS programs. Private agencies are particularly likely to be involved in providing placement services such as foster care, group care, residential treatment, and adoption. Private agencies are also used in the provision of supportive services for intact families, such as day care, homemaking assistance, and respite care. In some jurisdictions, private agencies also are involved in the provision of casework services for at least some cases. Thus, private agency involvement might entail provision of a specific purchased service while a public agency social worker maintains overall responsibility for the case; in some instances, the private agency might assume casework responsibility as well.[3]

What happens to a report of child maltreatment depends, of course, on the nature of the abuse or neglect, but the response also varies a great deal by jurisdiction. CPS agencies are guided not just by federal law but also by state law. To operationalize the federal and state mandates and to clarify requirements in areas not covered by federal or state legislation, CPS agencies promulgate regulations, policies and procedures, and standards of practice. They also conduct training for their staff, usually both pre-service and in-service. However, how a social worker handles a case is not necessarily consistent within states or counties. To the extent that community conditions and norms vary and to the extent that CPS procedures allow for worker discretion, practice can vary by local office and even by social worker or supervisor. Thus, the steps outlined below provide only a general description of how the current CPS system generally responds to reports of abuse and neglect.[4]

Upon receiving a report of abuse or neglect, the public agency responsible for CPS conducts an initial screening to determine whether the report falls within its mandate. If the report does concern suspected child maltreatment (or if the state's laws require an investigation of all reports without the opportunity to screen some out), a social worker from the public agency conducts an investigation. The nature of the investigation (such as the number and range of "collateral" contacts made with other professionals) varies by jurisdiction, but typically the investigator visits the family, sees the reported children, and interviews other sources of information, including the original reporter, to determine whether the child has been abused or neglected and whether the child can safely remain at home. Typically an investigation must be initiated within a day or two of the report and be completed within a week or a month (depending on the state); a swifter response is required in cases of emergency.

If a situation is particularly likely to involve criminal activity (for example, sexual abuse), in many jurisdictions law enforcement might participate in the CPS investigation or might even conduct the initial investigation in place of CPS. In fact, in criminal cases, the initial report might be made directly to law enforcement, who would then ask CPS to become involved in order to assess the child's situation and/or to make arrangements for care of the child.[5]

Even when law enforcement does not participate, the initial investigation can feel intimidating to the family. The investigator, after all, is informing family members about allegations, reading a statement of their rights, and/or warning them of the possibility of court action to remove the child from the home. Although the investigator may also be trying to assess the family's situation and need for services, the primary purpose of the investigation is to determine the safety of the child victim and the likely identity of the adult perpetrator. The final phase of the investigation includes a decision as to whether the allegations in the report are "substantiated" or "indicated" or "founded." A decision is also made as to whether the case should remain open with CPS and, if so, what the immediate plan of action should be.

What happens after the investigation depends on the family's situation and on the jurisdiction. At one extreme, more than 70 percent of all reported cases nationwide are closed, either because there was no credible evidence of abuse and neglect, or because there was too little evidence to compel a family to participate involuntarily.[6] Even with evidence of abuse or neglect and parental willingness to cooperate, a case might be closed because, with only limited resources available, it is considered lower risk and hence a lower priority for services than other cases in the system.

At the other extreme, in a minority of cases (less than 10 percent of the original referrals, or less than 20 percent of cases kept open for investigation) the risk of severe maltreatment is so high that the case is taken to criminal or, more likely, civil court.[7] In civil proceedings (typically held in a family, probate, juvenile, or district court), the CPS agency initiates action to remove the child from the parental home and ultimately, if the situation is not rectified, to terminate the parent's rights. In criminal proceedings, the focus is on prosecuting the adult perpetrator, and civil court action (whether in family, probate, juvenile, or district court) might still be necessary in order to make provisions for the care of the child.

The remainder of the cases, some 20 percent of those originally referred or 40 percent of those investigated, stay open with the public CPS agency or with a private agency under contract to CPS, for "ongoing treatment" or "supervision." Typically, an assessment of the family's situation is conducted, and a service plan developed. For some families, ongoing treatment involves an intermittent visit or call from a social worker; for others, the service plan includes some support services (such as day care for a young child) in addition to a social worker's visits.

In cases in which a determination is made that a child cannot stay safely at home, the child may be placed in some form of substitute care (such as a foster home or group home). Some jurisdictions place a much higher proportion of their caseload than others. Most such placements are intended to be temporary, with children either returned to an improved parental home or placed in a new permanent home in a timely manner, but in practice many children linger in foster care. Although other factors, especially court delays, are also responsible, the tendency toward "foster care drift" has probably been exacerbated by the increase in other pressing priorities—in particular, the need to respond to an ever-increasing number of reports in a timely manner. Passage of major child welfare reform legislation in 1980 reduced the foster-care population for a few years. However, as Table 3.1 shows, by 1987 the number of children in placement equaled the number in 1980. At last count, in 1996, more than 7 children per 1,000 were in placement nationwide.[8]

As this overview shows, the current CPS system is primarily concerned with using public authority and funding to protect children from abuse and neglect. To that end, the system focuses on identifying and responding to child victims and adult perpetrators. The initial contact with the family is reactive and investigative, concentrating on gathering information to confirm or disprove the allegations made by the reporter. Investigators and families are also keenly aware that the information being collected during the investigation might be used as evidence in future court proceedings. To the extent that parents are seen as perpetrators, it is assumed that they are part of the problem, not part of the solution. It is also assumed that many parents will not cooperate without the use or threatened use of state authority. Thus, the model for CPS operations, particularly at the investigative stage, is adversarial: it is reactive, investigative, suspicious of parents, and authoritative. This paradigm is, to a large extent, a legacy of the history of child protective services.

Table 3.1 Children in foster care, 1980–1996

Year	No.	No. per 1,000 children
1980	302,000	4.5
1981	274,000	4.0
1982	262,000	3.9
1983	269,000	4.0
1984	276,000	4.1
1985	276,000	4.1
1986	280,000	4.2
1987	300,000	4.5
1988	340,000	5.0
1989	383,000	5.6
1990	400,000	6.2
1991	414,000	6.5
1992	427,000	6.6
1993	445,000	6.7
1994	468,000	7.0
1995	483,000	7.2
1996	507,000	7.6

Sources: U.S. House of Representatives, Committee on Ways and Means, *1994 Green Book: Background Material and Data on Programs within the Jurisdiction of the Committee on Ways and Means* (Washington, D.C.: U.S. Government Printing Office, 1994), pp. 639–640; Toshio Tatara, "U.S. Substitute Care Flow Data and the Race/Ethnicity of Children in Care for FY 95, along with Recent Trends in the U.S. Substitute Care Population," VCIS Research Notes, No. 13 (American Public Welfare Association, Washington, D.C., 1997); Toshio Tatara, *Child Substitute Care Flow Data for FY 96* (Washington, D.C.: American Public Welfare Association, 1998).

A Brief History of CPS

The first organized group of "child-savers," the New York Society for the Prevention of Cruelty to Children (SPCC), was formed in 1874 in response to the well-publicized case of "Mary Ellen," who was the victim of severe physical abuse by her stepmother. Taking its model (and name) from the animal welfare movement founded in England 50 years earlier, the SPCC's focus was on rescuing children from cruel and abusive treatment. The child rescue movement arose at a time when children were first coming to be seen as priceless and vulnerable individuals and when women were finding their voices as uniquely qualified advocates for children and families.[9] Soon there were chapters in other states, along with new local and state agencies to address the problem.

From the outset, the child protective services system faced three defining issues: the primacy of parents vis-à-vis the child protection system, the scope of government intervention, and the nature of government intervention. The original child protection movement (in conjunction with the early child welfare and public welfare systems) had resulted in the separation of large numbers of children from their families and the placement of those children in predominantly institutional settings.[10] In many communities, the child-savers came to be feared. Indeed, some clients in Boston referred to the local chapter of the SPCC as "The Cruelty."[11]

Early in the twentieth century, child protection programs shifted their stance on these issues in a way that was consistent with the philosophy of the nascent Progressive era. The new system reflected a consensus that children were better off with their own parents whenever possible, a preference for minimal government intervention, and the view that agencies should deliver services in a familylike rather than institutional setting if at all possible. The new system did not redress all the problems of the old one. Children from poor and ethnic minority families continued to be disproportionately likely to be placed, and in many instances the new familylike placement settings were not much of an improvement over the old institutional ones. Nor were the three defining issues of the system—the degree of family autonomy, the scope of government intervention, and the nature of government intervention—resolved once and for all; indeed, they continue to be debated today.

The federal government established a Children's Bureau in 1912, but child abuse was not high on its agenda and remained primarily a state and local issue for the next 50 years. This is not to say that there was no federal activity related to child protection in those years. The Social Security Act of 1935 provided federal funds for services to abused and neglected children as well as dependent children, and the amendments of the early 1960s emphasized the expectation that states would implement programs for abused, neglected, and dependent children.

Henry Kempe's identification of the battered child syndrome in 1962 placed child protection on the national agenda.[12] Kempe's article sparked tremendous interest among medical professionals, groups such as social workers and lawyers that had traditionally been concerned with child protection, and the general public. Organizations such as the American Humane Association and the Child Welfare League of America stepped up their lobbying for more federal involvement. The contemporaneous civil rights movement also was conducive to an increased emphasis on children's rights.[13]

The burgeoning interest in child protection had dramatic results: the issuance of a model reporting law by the Children's Bureau in 1963; the adoption of mandatory reporting laws by all 50 states by 1968; and the passage of the first national child protection legislation, the Child Abuse Prevention and Treatment Act (CAPTA), in 1974. Barbara Nelson offers three reasons for the swift movement on this issue. First, child abuse is a valence issue; that is, the proposition that children should not be abused or neglected is not a controversial one. Second, the issue was narrowly framed; although the CAPTA definition included both abuse and neglect, the primary focus in the public and legislative debate was on battered children (as opposed to, for example, all children with less than optimal homes). Third, the issue appeared to have a simple and inexpensive solution: requiring physicians and other professionals who had frequent contact with children to report instances of abuse and neglect to the proper authorities.[14]

Since 1974 Congress has reauthorized and extended CAPTA several times, most recently in 1996. During this period Congress has become increasingly involved in shaping, rather than just mandating, child protective services. Five key pieces of legislation enacted from 1980 to 1997 illustrate this trend.

The first piece of legislation, the Adoption Assistance and Child

Welfare Act of 1980, established new requirements for CPS agencies to make reasonable efforts to prevent placement and to provide service plans and case reviews for children in placement. The aims were to prevent unnecessary placements and to end "foster care drift" for children in placement by promoting "permanency." Depending on the specific case, permanency might mean reunification with the biological family, adoption, guardianship, or independent living. This legislation led to the overhaul of agency policies and procedures as states complied either voluntarily or, increasingly, pursuant to litigation.

The second legislative initiative, the 1984 "Baby Doe" amendments to CAPTA, changed the definition of child abuse and neglect to include the withholding of medical treatment from "medically needy" newborns. Hospitals were required to post notices encouraging the filing of such reports, and state child protection agencies were required to accept and investigate them. Generally seen as a socially conservative piece of legislation, the intent of Baby Doe was to address concerns that hospitals and parents might be allowing severely handicapped newborns to die rather than making extraordinary efforts to prolong their lives.

The third piece of legislation, the Child Welfare Services, Foster Care, and Adoption Assistance Reforms of 1993, created the Family Preservation and Support Services Program, which provided funding for family preservation and support services, to be administered by the state child protective services agencies but to be delivered in conjunction with community agencies. This legislation not only encourages family preservation and provides a preventive service—family support—but also mandates a role for private agencies in their delivery. Private agencies, which have historically played an important role in child protection, had been eligible for federal funds since the Social Security amendments of 1967, but this was the first time that public CPS agencies were required to include community agencies in their planning and service provision as a condition of receiving federal funding.

The fourth law, the Multiethnic Placement Act of 1994, addressed the sensitive issue of interracial adoptions. By barring agencies from discriminating against prospective foster or adoptive parents solely on the basis of race, color, or national origin, the act was intended to make it easier for white families to adopt African-American or other minority children. Because the law included language about considering the child's needs with regard to his or her cultural or racial identity, however, it was not clear whether the law would in fact ease interracial adoptions if agencies did not want to pursue them.

The fifth piece of legislation, the Adoption and Safe Families Act, passed at the close of the legislative session in November 1997, revisited several of the issues addressed by the Adoption Assistance and Child Welfare Act of 1980 and made two major changes. First, the 1997 law specified types of cases in which efforts to prevent placement need not be made. Second, the 1997 law pushed even further in the direction of permanency planning, tightening the timeline for disposition from 18 months to 12 months. The 1980 law had been widely seen as an effort to balance child rescue and family preservation; the 1997 law could only be seen as a step back in the direction of child rescue.

Clearly, the issues of the primacy of the family, the scope of government intervention, and the nature of that intervention have yet to be resolved, and the federal government is playing an important role in the continuing debate. The primacy of the family versus the child's need for a safe and permanent home is the central concern of both the 1980 and the 1997 laws, as well as the 1993 family preservation and family support legislation. The "Baby Doe" legislation of 1984 expanded the scope of government intervention. And the family preservation legislation addressed the nature of government intervention in specifying the type and role of agencies to be involved.

The political concerns also remain the same. All things being equal, Congress still demonstrates a preference for valence issues that are narrowly defined and that appear to have simple remedies. For example, ending "foster care drift" was a patently good idea, and case planning and periodic review were obviously simple and sensible solutions. But in the area of child abuse and neglect, simple solutions are increasingly elusive. Family preservation, for example, which harkens back to the Progressive era's preference for the family and would seem to be a readily shared goal, is in fact by no means noncontroversial; analysts sometimes disagree about which families should be preserved and for how long. Nor is permanency planning as straightforward as it might at first appear, as evidenced by the long debate over, and the conflicting language in, the interracial adoption bill, and by the continuing debate over topics such as kinship care.

Today child protective services coexist, and often overlap, with two other closely related systems: child welfare and public welfare. Child welfare is the set of public and private agencies that provide a whole range of social services to children and their families.[15] The domain of child welfare includes residential services such as foster care and adoption but also services provided to children living in their own homes, such as day care, respite care, homemakers, parent aides, and counseling. Public welfare refers to the set of agencies and programs that provide financial assistance, including food and health assistance as well as cash assistance, to poor families.

Clearly, child protective services are much narrower in their focus than child welfare and public welfare. Yet at the federal, state, community, and private agency levels, distinctions in their mandates are often blurred. At the level of service delivery, all three systems were often housed in the same office or agency. This practice ended in the early 1970s, when a federal directive mandated the physical separation of social services and financial assistance services and resulted in the creation of new social services agencies distinct from the old public welfare offices throughout the country. Some states and counties went one step further and also separated child protection from other social services functions. One goal of these separations was to improve the quality of services delivered to children and families in the child protection system, by establishing a separate and professional cadre of child protective workers. A related goal was to uncouple the eligibility determination process for Aid to Families with Dependent Children (AFDC) from the client's decision about using social services, in order to avoid the perception that a client might somehow have to accept unwanted social services intervention as a condition for receiving financial assistance. Another goal was to extend access to social services and child protective services to individuals and families who were not poor but who needed services. Fifteen years later, service integration reformers seek to reverse this trend and to unite disparate services such as child protection, child welfare, and financial assistance.

Nevertheless there is still considerable overlap of client populations, with low-income families served by the public welfare system, for example, disproportionately likely to be involved with the child protection system.[16] Thus, the response made by government to individuals and families is closely tied to the evolution of the child welfare and public welfare systems.

Like the CPS system, the child welfare and public welfare systems began with local and state initiatives that eventually culminated in action at the federal level. Here, too, tensions existed from the start over the role of the family, the role of government, and the nature of government intervention. This history has been well documented by others.[17] For understanding the linkages among the systems, the key elements of the story are as follows.

The American response to families in need of financial or other assistance has always been to a large extent locally determined by agents such as charitable organizations, town administrators, and state legislators. Nevertheless, three distinct phases are common across localities. In the first phase, following the English poor-relief system, the American public welfare system (that is, the system designed to respond to narrowly defined situations of financial need) relied upon poorhouses. This approach was seen as preferable to the alternative of giving assistance to families in their homes, known as outdoor relief, which it was feared would erode work incentives. Another feature inherited from the English was that the system attempted to distinguish between the deserving and nondeserving poor, again because of concerns about adverse incentives.

Toward the end of the nineteenth century, a concern for children's welfare launched a second phase, marked by a campaign to remove children from poorhouses. This phase resulted in an increase in family breakups, as poor adults continued to have no alternative but the poorhouse from which their children were now banned. Children of indigent parents were increasingly likely to be separated from their parents and placed, initially in large orphanages, although over time more familylike settings such as foster homes and small group homes came to be preferred. Not all these placements were involuntary; it was not uncommon for parents to relinquish their children voluntarily so that they could be in a home that offered better food, clothing, education, and opportunity.

In the third phase, beginning in the early decades of this century, poor relief evolved into a system of financial assistance closer to what we think of as public welfare, as state after state enacted laws to provide cash grants, known as mothers' pensions or widows' pensions, to needy women to enable them to keep their children at home. This campaign for mothers' pensions was spearheaded by two women's groups, the General Federation of Women's Clubs and the National Congress of Mothers, supported by a diverse coalition including juvenile court judges, editors of women's magazines, leaders in the settlement house movement, and trade unionists.

The chronology is truly breathtaking. The inclusion of mothers' pensions in the platforms of the National Congress of Mothers national conference in 1911 and the General Federation of Women's Clubs national conference in 1912 inspired women activists to push through legislation in 20 states by 1913 and another 20 by 1920.

Mothers' pensions by no means redressed all the ills of the local poor-relief system. First, since funding was often inadequate, the new system did not entirely replace the old one, as many needy families were wait-listed or received grants too small to live on. Second, because the new program continued to distinguish between the deserving and nondeserving poor, recipients were subject to scrutiny and monitoring as well as sometimes arbitrary rules and denials.[18]

The first federal public welfare legislation, the Economic Security Act of 1935, established the program that was to become AFDC, the main cash assistance program for single-mother families until 1996, when it was replaced by Temporary Assistance to Needy Families (TANF).

As defined in the Economic Security Act, child welfare services were designed for the "protection and care of homeless, dependent and neglected children and children in danger of becoming delinquent." This definition justifies the provision of child welfare services for several very different but possibly overlapping populations: children who need services by reason of poverty (the homeless and dependent); children who need services for protective reasons (the neglected); and children who need services in order to prevent future bad outcomes (the pre-delinquent). In theory, income is not relevant except in defining dependency, but in practice, federal child welfare mandates and federal reimbursement for services to implement them have tended to be divided on the basis of financial versus nonfinancial need. For income-eligible families (those with incomes low enough to qualify for AFDC), child welfare services such as foster care and day care were funded by Title IV-A of the Social Security legislation beginning in 1961 (for foster care) and 1962 (for day care); day care and other social services for income-eligible families were later consolidated under Title XX, and foster care for income-eligible children was subsequently moved to Title IV-E. For families in need of social services without regard to income (for example, those with runaway children or pre-delinquent children), child welfare services such as foster care and group care were provided under Title IV-B.

The child protection system is also linked financially with the larger child welfare and public welfare systems. Thus, reductions in housing assistance from the public welfare system or in child care from the child welfare system may create greater demand for services from the child protection system.[19] In the 1980s, for example, there were concerns that increasing numbers of children were being placed in foster care by the child protection system solely for reasons of homelessness. Today, too, CPS may be called upon to take care of children whose parents are no longer able to provide for them. The time limits and sanctions associated with welfare reform, while prompting some families to move into employment, will move others into deeper poverty.[20] Given what we know about the relationship between poverty and reports of child abuse and neglect, we can anticipate that at least some of these families will be referred, or will refer themselves, to CPS.[21] The impact on the system could be serious; if only one in five of the 1.1 million children moved into poverty as a result of welfare reform was placed in foster care or kinship care, the number of children in foster care or kinship care would rise by 220,000, an increase of nearly 50 percent over the 450,000 children already in care in 1994.

Underlying Assumptions

How have the origins of the CPS system shaped our current thinking about child protection? And are those assumptions still valid?

Protecting children as an end in itself has been an explicit goal for more than a century. Today the risks facing children seem to be expanding exponentially. Sexual abuse accounts for 12 percent of child abuse cases nationwide, and the harms produced by substance-abusing parents extend far beyond our statistics on alcohol- and drug-affected newborns. Without timely and appropriate intervention and treatment, abused and neglected children are at elevated risk of problems later in life, including the possibility that they will repeat the cycle with their own children.[22] We may disagree on the precise definition of what constitutes child abuse and neglect, but as citizens we share the goal of wanting to protect children from (what we perceive as) abuse or neglect. We also share an interest in wanting to prevent today's victims from becoming tomorrow's perpetrators.

In the context of child protection, the three chief issues continue to be the role of the family, the scope of government intervention, and the nature of government intervention. Addressing these issues requires establishing criteria and standards that specify when and how the family's and government's respective roles and responsibilities change as the child's and family's circumstances change. In this task beliefs and assumptions play a critical role.[23]

Our strongest convictions relate to families. We believe that families are and should be the primary childrearers, on the grounds that families are best positioned and motivated to advance their children's best interests. We believe that families should be free of unwarranted government or other institutional intrusion, on the grounds that such intervention would interfere with their liberty and could actually do damage, by undermining parental authority, by introducing inappropriate values, and the like. We do acknowledge, however, that some families (although people do not necessarily agree on the definitions) fail to protect their children, that is, abuse or neglect them.

We also believe that many families will not come forward on their own to request help and will not accept help on a voluntary basis, whether to prevent abuse and neglect or to seek help after it has occurred. Thus, the current paradigm for child protection takes as given that intervention for the purposes of protecting children from abuse and neglect must often be coercive, that is, must carry with it the use or threat of state authority in the form of criminal or civil action to compel parents to accept services or to take other actions against their will.

These beliefs about family constitute the first underlying assumption of the current CPS system: *a family should be free of coercive government intervention unless that family has crossed the line into what we have defined as abuse and neglect.* The drawing of the line, by child abuse and neglect statutes, is an important and necessary role for government but also one that will reflect society's values. Hence, we would expect that the line would move over time, as our values shift and as different political forces become dominant. We would also expect that the line might fall unequally across populations, if, for example, childrearing practices and norms differ across populations and if these differences are not reflected in the statutes. Intervention into the family is regarded as a "second-best" course of action: it is undesirable because it interferes with family autonomy and liberty but is justified since the family has demonstrably failed in its responsibility to protect the child. Thus, intervention is a coercive and intrusive act that is warranted only if the family has violated the norms. It is also by construction, and by its links to the criminal justice system, punitive, because its goal is not just the protection of children but also the punishment of perpetrators.

This stylized description of a dividing line between "good" and "bad" families presents the family as autonomous and inviolate unless it crosses the line, at which point it is expected to be compliant and subject to government and institutional authority. This is an accurate description of how society views the dividing line from afar and, in many instances, of how families view their experience with the system up close. But the child protective services system is, of course, more nuanced than this. In each CPS system, there are multiple forms of intervention along the continuum from least intrusive to most intrusive—from screening in a report to substantiating allegations to opening a case for ongoing intervention to placing a child in substitute care to obtaining a court order that permanently terminates parental rights. In principle, then, the degree of autonomy of the family depends not only on whether the family has crossed the line into the child protective services system but on where within the system it stands and on how serious the situation is. To the extent that CPS workers and agencies vary, the family's status might also depend on who is doing the intervening; families with identical profiles could receive very different treatment by worker X and worker Y, or by the commonwealth of Massachusetts and the state of New York. Nor is the family necessarily unitary from the viewpoint of the child protection system. A family may be able to provide adequately for one or more children but fail to protect others, or, particularly in situations of domestic violence or sexual abuse, one parent might be a danger to the child while the other parent still fulfills the protective role, or could if given adequate supports.

The second and third assumptions of the current CPS system, regarding the role of government and the nature of its intervention respectively, are inextricably bound up with the first. Since we see the family as primary unless it deviates from defined norms of child protection, the second assumption naturally follows: *coercive government intervention into family life should be used as a last resort and should be minimized to the extent possible.* And, since we see the intervention as identifying and remedying instances of violated norms, the third assumption also follows: *the agencies that do the work of child protection should have as their focus the identification of abuse and neglect and the protection of children from abuse and neglect, whether by remedying the situation in the home or by removing the children from the home.*

These latter assumptions are also not as clear-cut as they at first appear. Although coercive government intervention is seen as undesirable because it intrudes on family autonomy and liberty, it is also seen as helpful for the children involved. This child welfare perspective helps explain why, although much of the emphasis in the child protective services system is on investigating and assigning blame for injuries to children, in most jurisdictions this function is carried out not by police or prosecutors but rather by social workers, members of a "helping" profession.

Thus there is a fourth assumption underlying the current child protection system: *government intervention by agents such as social workers can and should be helpful to children and families.* We expect the intervention to help not only in assuring the child's safety, but also in promoting permanency for the child and both the child's and the family's well-being. In this respect the goals of CPS resemble those of the child welfare system,[24] although in child protective services the primary focus is clearly child safety, with the other two outcomes important but subordinate. Thus, if a child is being abused or neglected, we want CPS to stop the maltreatment but also to provide services to address other needs the child might have for medical care, therapy, or educational help, and we want CPS to make sure that its plan for the child meets the child's need for a permanent family. However, if a child has not been abused or neglected, our response to the family is not consistent. A struggling family's cry for help is grounds for intervention in the child welfare system but not necessarily in the CPS system, where the provision of "voluntary" services varies by jurisdiction and over time. At the same time, we believe that society's limited resources should be targeted to deserving families who meet established criteria.

These assumptions and the CPS system that has developed to implement them contain several inconsistencies and contradictions. It is time to consider these.

A Critical View of the System

Recently increasing numbers of practitioners, policymakers, clinicians, and scholars who have had years of experience and day-to-day contact with the child protection system and with children and families at risk have spoken out about the need to reform CPS. Looking at the system and its underlying assumptions from their perspective not only clarifies the problems with the current system but also generates an alternative set of assumptions.

Knowledgeable practitioners and observers of the current child protection system can readily cite its shortcomings:

> I think we do too little, too late. I think we have an investigation driven system, and we don't deliver the treatment and remediation resources that families need. I am extremely concerned, as I look at how we deliver service, that there has been an erosion of basic intervention skills, by line workers . . . We used to talk about casework. Now we talk about case management.   (Former child protective services worker)
>
> I don't want a child protective services system that is the only door to child welfare . . . A family that needs housing shouldn't have to come through the CPS gate to get it, with all of the stigma and labeling that gets attached to that, if housing is the only problem.   (Former child protective services administrator)
>
> It's unfair for the state, whatever arm of the state it is, to intervene in a family and disrupt the family, if the state doesn't have the capacity to offer treatment in return . . . I don't want a system that allows us to intrude in a family, or a child's life, without some assurance that it's going to help, that the family somehow is going to be better off.   (Child protective services administrator)[25]

These comments reflect a broad dissatisfaction with the current system. This dissatisfaction can be seen not only in newspaper headlines about mishandled cases but also in the sprouting of parents' rights groups (such as VOCAL, Victims of Child Abuse Laws), foster parent groups, and foster children's groups; and in the prevalence of lawsuits against state child protection agencies, with important sectors of the child welfare community (such as child advocates, social worker associations, and human service worker unions) often joining forces with aggrieved parents or children.

Parents and social workers, in fact, share many of the same concerns about the system, as can be seen in the following comments.

We are just so overwhelmed. My counselors are servicing between 80 and 100 children each . . . All you're doing is crisis intervention, you're not really providing the families with what they need.   (Social work supervisor)

Most of us are on AFDC and food stamps. You just can't afford the bus, and taxis. They have to work with us as much as they want us to work with them—give and take—instead of demanding. It's very hard, they just don't understand.   (Parent, Florida)

It is a shock, you get into the system and you find out, I can't get you a pair of shoes, I can't pay that electric bill, I can't get him a bed to sleep in, I can't get him into day care. I can't get you that job training . . . here I am but I'm not able to help you but I've invaded your presence, invaded your home, separated your family, and there is nothing here for you. (Social worker, Missouri)

The time they give you is good, but it really isn't enough time. They get you to the point where you want to live . . . once they find out your situation, it shouldn't be such a quick pull-out . . . It is just not enough time because you still haven't accomplished the goals you want to accomplish.   (Parent, Missouri)

My biggest concern is the emphasis on getting in and out too fast. (Social work supervisor, Missouri)[26]

These comments from parents, social workers, and observers of the child protective services system are also reflective of deep concerns within the child protection and child welfare communities. In 1988 the National Association of Public Child Welfare Administrators issued a call for a new, more narrowly focused CPS, which would be part of a three-tier system along with an expanded voluntary/preventive family support system (an improved version of the child welfare system) and an adequately funded child well-being system (including public welfare, education, health, and early childhood education).[27] In the same year, a collaborative effort by the American Bar Association, the American Public Welfare Association, and the American Enterprise Institute produced a set of recommendations to overhaul child abuse and neglect reporting and investigation. Chief among these were a recommendation to provide better guidance to reporters about what to report and what not to report, and a recommendation to develop tighter criteria for screening reports.[28] In 1989 Sheila Kamerman and Alfred Kahn's multistate study of child protection and child welfare services concluded that the states were overwhelmed by their CPS responsibilities and were increasingly unable to provide either quality child protection or child welfare. Kamerman and Kahn's study called for major reforms within CPS and a strengthening of the child welfare and child well-being systems, as did a study by the Center for the Study of Social Policy.[29] In the early 1990s the American Public Welfare Association and the U.S. Advisory Board on Child Abuse and Neglect also issued calls for reform.[30] This growing consensus that the CPS system was in need of overhaul was the impetus for the convening of the Harvard Executive Session on Child Protective Services in 1994. This group, too, concluded that CPS was in need of major reform.[31]

Five distinct criticisms of the current child protective services system emerge from these and other groups that have considered the current state of CPS. These concerns are shared to some extent by observers of the child protective services system, clients, social workers, advocates, and other child welfare professionals and scholars.

The first problem is *overinclusion:* some families who are currently in the system shouldn't be there. This is a widespread complaint, but there is wide divergence of opinion as to which families are being inappropriately referred. Parents' rights groups, for example, are organized around the principle that the current abuse and neglect statutes and practices result in intervention where it may not be warranted. Both parents and CPS agencies worry about vindictive reports made in the context of ongoing custody disputes, fights with neighbors, and the like. Child protection professionals also express concerns about the apparent overrepresentation of poor and minority families and the heavy representation of "neglectful" (often vaguely defined) as opposed to abusive families.

There is a real tension in the system between a desire to avoid inappropriately labeling families as needing protective services and a desire to provide services to families that don't meet strict abuse and neglect criteria. Reflecting that tension, advocates in the community report their frustration with a system that forces them to refer families to CPS just to get services such as day care or therapy for a child, even though being in the system is no guarantee of receiving any services. Uniting these disparate groups is the common concern that the child abuse and neglect definitions and reporting and screening criteria as currently drawn may inappropriately place some families on the wrong side of the dividing line between family autonomy and coercive intervention. This is a problem for the families inappropriately included, who are unnecessarily exposed to a coercive and investigative system. It is also problematic for the children who are at serious risk, since they may get less attention than they deserve, and may thus be inadequately protected, because of the sheer volume of cases in the system.

The second problem has to do with *capacity:* the number of families involved with the child protection system far exceeds the capacity of the system. This is not a new problem, but it is an increasingly severe one. In jurisdictions across the country, the system is overwhelmed and overloaded. The number of child abuse and neglect reports has grown tremendously over the past 20 years, and the reported cases seem to have become tougher, in that they involve higher levels of drug use and family stress. As a result, even the best-funded systems have been unable to keep up with the increased caseload. Although it is not clear whether the remedy is to reduce the demand for child protective services and/or to increase the capacity of CPS to meet that demand, there is consensus that the system is at or near the breaking point. As caseloads soar, lawsuits become a popular remedy because it is relatively easy to document instances in which agencies are out of compliance with federal and state mandates. Meanwhile the risks to children are less likely to be addressed, and the array of services available to a typical family becomes fewer.

The third problem, paradoxically, is *underinclusion:* some families who should be receiving child protective services aren't. Even the best reporting and screening systems will miss some abusive families who should be subject to intervention. There are some families who could be referred but are not, because potential reporters know that the capacity to serve them is nonexistent. But the underinclusion problem as seen by child welfare professionals and community advocates is different. The issue from their perspective is that families who voluntarily contact child protection to ask for help (or who would accept help on a voluntary basis) will more likely than not be denied that help unless they have already crossed the line into abuse and neglect. Excluding families who voluntarily come forward to ask for help but who perhaps have not crossed the line into abuse or neglect is problematic for several reasons. First, in many jurisdictions, some services such as day care or therapy are available only to children in the child protective system. Second, many within the child protection system see their role as a dual one, with both child protection and child welfare components; thus, it makes no sense to them to turn away needy

families asking for their help. Third, because practitioners and scholars share a belief that prevention and early intervention are cost-effective, they resist the notion that families should be turned away until
their problems reach reportable levels of abuse and neglect. The remedy is not necessarily inclusion in the CPS system; these families' needs
could be met by inclusion within another system (for example, the
child welfare system or a broader child well-being system) if that system had the capacity to serve them and had services to offer.

The fourth problem has to do with *service delivery*: families in the
child protection system, even if they do get in appropriately and do get
services, do not necessarily receive the right type of services. In some
instances, the needed service is identified but simply not available; in
other instances, service needs are misdiagnosed or misread; and in
others, it is not clear what service might be effective. Service delivery
tends to be uneven across communities, with particular shortages of
services that are delivered in the client's language and by agencies and
workers that are knowledgeable about and respectful of the client's
culture. An overarching service delivery issue, not unique to child protection, is that families often have multiple and overlapping problems
while services for them tend to be fragmented, delivered in separate
locations by different professionals. This has led service integration
reformers to explore ways to improve coordination of the entire package of services a family needs.[32]

The fifth problem has to do with *service orientation*: the basic orientation of the child protection system may not be right for some families in the system. The CPS system is predicated on the notion that
families involved with it by definition lose a great deal of autonomy
and that it is the job of the child protection agency to investigate and
remedy the abuse and neglect in an authoritative way. At the same
time, the preferred option is always to keep the family together whenever possible.

This dual mandate to protect children and preserve families can lead
to tensions within the system, and debates outside it, about which goal
is and should be preeminent. The family preservation movement, as its
name suggests, argues that the current CPS system does not do enough
to keep families together. Family preservation is predicated on the
belief that most abusive or neglectful families are still the best resource
for their children until proven otherwise, and that it is the job of the
family therapist to work in partnership with families and to build

upon families' strengths. This has a range of implications, for the relationship between the worker and the family, the types of services delivered, and the expected outcomes, which would fundamentally change the workings of the child protection system. The evidence is not all in on the effectiveness of family preservation programs.[33] However, many now argue that CPS has gone too far in the direction of keeping families together, at the expense of child protection.[34] There are some families, from this perspective, that are so irredeemably broken down (by substance abuse, violence, and the like) that they are beyond preserving and whose children therefore would be better off in alternative settings, whether that means foster care or other residential alternatives.[35] Other critics are concerned that family preservation will deny or usurp funding for specialized residential treatment services for children, particularly adolescents, who have repeatedly failed in family settings and for whom placement in any family setting, including their own, would be a recipe for disaster.[36]

But the apparent dichotomy between family preservation and child protection is in some ways a false one. One important unifying theme underlying the core concerns of family preservation and child protection advocates alike is that CPS tends to overreact in the direction of either family preservation or child protection, and then to swing back too far in the opposite direction. A second, related theme is that CPS tends to adopt a "one-size-fits-all" approach, whereas both family preservation and child protection principles emphasize the need for a more nuanced, dynamic, and individualized approach to assessment and case planning. The families coming to the system's attention are a varied group, whose needs change over time, and the system's response must take their different, and changing, needs into account.

Implications for a New Paradigm

This critique of the current system produces several alternative assumptions for a new paradigm for child protection. These assumptions, in turn, have direct implications for practice.

First, on the assumption that families are and should be the primary protectors of their children, services for even those who have crossed the line into abuse and neglect, but who are not yet irretrievably broken down, would place more emphasis on family resources and responsibility. Because the current CPS system is designed to detect family weaknesses rather than to identify family strengths, families may not be forthcoming with the social worker, and even if they are, important family resources may be overlooked. Placing more emphasis on family resources and responsibility requires a fundamental change of attitude and practice, but many CPS agencies have already taken some steps in this direction, as a result of the push toward placement prevention and family reunification. In the past, once a child was placed in foster care, the CPS agency, in the person of the social worker and/or the foster parent, assumed virtually all parental responsibilities, from authorizing school field trips and arranging routine medical care to signing off on special education plans and arranging for major surgery. In many agencies, parents now retain these responsibilities or share them with the agency while the child is in foster care. This approach makes sense, since parents of children in foster care need to be preparing to resume full parental responsibility, unless and until their parental rights have been terminated. Another source of inspiration and ideas for agencies wanting to move in this direction is, of course, the family preservation movement, which focuses on recognizing and building on families' strengths, listening to families' perspectives, and working with families as partners in protecting children.

Placing more emphasis on the primacy of the family does not mean that CPS should treat all families as primary or that it should neglect its child protection mission. CPS should not attempt to preserve families that are beyond repair. And CPS must continue to act swiftly and authoritatively in situations in which children are at imminent risk.

Second, on the assumption that government should intervene in the most effective way possible, we should explore the promise of shifting the timing of service delivery from reaction and intervention after abuse and neglect have occurred to early warning and prevention, to the extent possible. If we knew with certainty which children were going to be abused or neglected and what it would take to prevent this from happening, we could simply identify these children and intervene with the right preventive services before the abuse occurred. Failing that, however, we need not simply wait for abuse and neglect to come to the attention of child protective services. Several specific changes could be made. First, CPS (or another agency) could respond to a family's request for help even if the family had not abused or neglected the children. Second, CPS (or another agency) could respond to a concerned third party's referral even if the family had not crossed the line of reportable abuse and neglect. One possibility might be to use a "consultation," that is, a noninvestigative visit to consult with the family about their children's well-being and to ensure that the family knew about services in the community available on a voluntary basis.

More generally, we could do a much better job than we do currently of understanding and evaluating the relationship between the risk factors for specific types of abuse and neglect and preventive services designed to ameliorate those risk factors. The home visiting movement has made great strides over the past decade or so to identify newborns who are at high risk and whose families could benefit from a program of supportive home visiting.[37] Such programs are spreading rapidly throughout the country, although the evidence on their effectiveness remains inconclusive.[38] In fact it is hard to think of a single early intervention program that has convincingly demonstrated its effectiveness in preventing later and more expensive CPS intervention. Yet surely effective preventive programs can be developed. For example, it is well documented that cocaine addiction, particularly in combination with other risk factors, creates substantially heightened risk of abuse and neglect, yet many CPS staff (and others) are not convinced of the effectiveness of early intervention services (such as drug treatment for pregnant women and new mothers) in ending drug dependency and preventing subsequent abuse and neglect.[39]

Third, on the assumption that government should intervene as a partner rather than as an independent agent, service delivery should emphasize family support and collaboration. Here, successful models abound. Community-based family support centers providing comprehensive services to families on a voluntary basis now exist in many localities. Many of these family centers are sited at schools or collocated with other community agencies such as health centers or day care centers. Thus, they often combine the virtues of family support with the well-documented benefits of "one-stop shopping," or integrated service delivery.[40]

Some communities also have made great strides in promoting collaboration among service providers. Although here successful models are fewer, collaborations that break down barriers between agencies and create the climate for flexible uses of their services do exist, and there is no reason to believe that their success could not be replicated in other communities. Agencies commonly report that once they start talking with each other, they find that barriers come down relatively quickly.[41] These collaborations are critical, since more often than not the problem is not the lack of services but rather "turf battles" over which families are to receive services and which agencies are to pay the costs.

Another benefit of service collaboration is that agencies often discover hitherto unknown or untapped resources. A service provider who has pioneered the development of wrap-around services tells the story of an interagency group planning services for an emotionally disturbed child who would need transportation to a special school and afterschool program as an alternative to an institutional residential placement. The group was prepared to use flexible discretionary funds to purchase a van until one of the agency representatives mentioned that a transportation service (which none of the other agency representatives had ever heard of) already existed and had the capacity to serve this child. In this instance, collaboration alone provided a better service package for the child, without spending any of the new flexible funds that were available for that purpose, and of course at a substantial savings over the alternative residential program. In other instances, collaborative efforts can identify the need for new services, create the impetus for their development, and oversee their implementation.

Fourth, on the assumption that government can and should respond to families who are asking for help and need help according to defined criteria, a struggling family's request for help would be heeded, whether or not the family had technically crossed the line into reportable abuse and neglect. That is, if a family asked for help, the CPS system or perhaps a new parallel system (discussed below) would seek to determine not only whether abuse or neglect had occurred but also whether the family wanted and needed help. Again, this would not be an entirely new function. Many child protective agencies used to handle voluntary requests for services (in fact, some still do), so there are some policies and procedures to draw upon in developing this kind of response. And this need not be a function for which CPS assumes primary responsibility. Rather, child protective services could develop a system to screen and refer such families to child welfare or "child well-being" services, or a family could apply directly to such services, whether located in the same agency, another public or private agency, or in the community.

If we are to allocate resources responsibly to families who are asking for and need help, criteria should be developed that spell out which families should be helped and how. Two types of families, in addition to those currently served by the CPS system, might be given priority. First, families who are asking for help and who demonstrate known risk factors for abuse and neglect (such as substance abuse, domestic violence, or history of abuse as a child) should be given priority for "preventive services." Second, families who are asking for help and who are struggling with a problem that we agree requires help (such as a severely disabled child, a runaway child, or a child on the verge of delinquency) should be given priority for "voluntary services."

Who would deliver these preventive and voluntary services is not a simple issue to resolve. There are at least three alternative scenarios. Their respective strengths and weaknesses can be assessed along the three dimensions of organizational capacity, goals and values, and political support and legitimacy. These dimensions form the three legs of what has been called the "strategic triangle," because a policy strategy must work on all three dimensions in order to be successful.[42]

Under one scenario, these services could simply become part of an improved child protective services system, which would serve both its traditional protective population and these new preventive and voluntary families. In theory, CPS could, given the resources, develop the capacity to serve these families. Serving preventive families would be consistent with its goals and values. The voluntary families would fit less well into a narrowly defined CPS but could fit into an integrated child protective and child welfare system. Whether this scenario is politically viable is hard to judge: CPS does have some credibility with the public and legislators, but this credibility derives to a large extent from the perception that the CPS mission is narrowly defined and focused on child protection.

Under a second scenario, the child protective services system would identify such families and then refer them to a parallel, voluntary system specially designed for them. This parallel system, which would replace and go beyond the traditional child welfare system, might be called a preventive or family support system. It could be public, private, or mixed. Organizational capacity is an issue here, as this scenario relies on the ability of CPS to identify and screen these families and on a new system's ability to serve them. From the perspective of goals and values, there would be advantages to having a new system, with new goals and values, to carry out this new mandate. Justification for such a system would have to be documented to the public's and legislators' satisfaction.

Under the third scenario, families asking for services would be able to go directly to the parallel system, although they could also be referred by CPS or by others in the community. The parallel system would be responsible for prioritizing among the preventive and voluntary applicants. This scenario shares many of the disadvantages of the others, but it also appears to have distinct advantages. First, it does not involve building a new capacity within CPS. Second, it presents the fewest conflicts in terms of goals and values, since in principle the new system would be designed specifically to serve preventive and struggling families and thus would incorporate our goals and values for those families. Finally, in terms of political viability, this new program could be piloted or started in a small way, perhaps in conjunction with the federal family preservation and support initiative or with other state or local child and family services reform initiatives. The political disadvantage, of course, is that more than the others, this might be seen as a new open-ended entitlement that could lead to out-of-control spending down the line. That is why defining strict criteria for the families to be served, though very difficult to do, would be critically important.

The cost implications of such reforms need to be explored. While many practitioners take it as given that the provision of early community-based services will prevent more expensive full-blown CPS intervention at a later date, more extensive and more careful documentation on this point is needed. We must consider questions such as the following. How many families currently in CPS could have been served earlier if preventive and voluntary services had been available? What are the costs, and cost savings, associated with these types of families? If voluntary and preventive services did exist in the community, what percentage of the families served would be diverted from CPS intervention? Equally important, what percentage would not, either because they nevertheless went on to abuse and neglect their children or because they were never at high risk for abuse and neglect in the first place?

The concerns voiced by parents, social workers, and others with experience and knowledge of child protective services, and their implications for a new paradigm for child protective services, pose an enormous challenge.

One clear message is the need to change the criteria for entry into the CPS system and perhaps a parallel family support system from the one dimension of abuse and neglect to a multidimensional matrix incorporating the family's desire and need for services in addition to society's judgment as to the presence or absence of abuse or neglect. A second implication is the importance of changing government's response to families, from a "one-size-fits-all" model that is investigative and coercive to a capacity for differential response depending on individual families' situations. And finally, the service delivery system must intervene in a way that is more responsive to the needs of families and better integrated from the perspective of families.

To implement these changes for families who have crossed the line into abuse and neglect would require fundamental changes in philosophical orientation, social work practice, and service delivery within CPS. To serve in addition families who have not crossed the line but who are asking for help and, according to established criteria, need help would demand even more far-reaching changes, because it would require new capacity within CPS or a parallel system.

The feasibility of such fundamental changes is a legitimate issue. Indeed, there are a number of critical issues involved in making a new paradigm a reality. Chief among these are political concerns about the public and legislatures' willingness to embrace a new paradigm; questions about the prospects for systemic reform within child protective services; and concerns about what it would really take to build a new preventive or family support system, whether within the existing CPS system or within the community. But before addressing these issues, we must examine the CPS system of reporting, screening, and investigations. This "front end" sets the tone for all CPS operations and necessarily affects all families referred for child protective services. Any effort to reform CPS must first come to grips with the problems there.

Chapter 4

Entry into the System

Society has long relied on the assumption that parents should be responsible for the welfare of their children and that they should be allowed wide latitude in how they meet this responsibility. Despite this general presumption, however, there are always cases in which parents either cannot or will not meet standards that society implicitly or explicitly sets for them. Some of these cases become visible—to relatives, friends, neighbors, or others who have contact with the family. Some of the cases that become visible are reported. In that moment, something private becomes, in some important sense, public. It becomes public in the sense that the witnesses discuss it with one another or the parents, and families are informally referred to services or chastised for their conduct. It also becomes public in the sense that it becomes the focus of official governmental action.

How much abuse and neglect becomes public in this sense is partly a function, then, of some kind of reporting system. Throughout most of the history of child protection efforts this system was largely informal. Fairly recently, however, formal reporting laws were established. These laws, and the media campaigns that followed, focused an unprecedented amount of public attention on child abuse and neglect, leading to a dramatic increase in the number of cases reported. In addition, the laws mandated a formal bureaucracy for receiving, screening, and investigating these reports that remains a cornerstone of the current child protection system. In assessing the current state of

CPS, it is therefore essential to evaluate the reporting, screening, and investigation system.[1]

History of the Reporting Laws

The First State and Federal Laws

In 1963, soon after the publication of a widely read article on the "battered child syndrome," the federal Children's Bureau drafted a model statute for the reporting of child abuse.[2] It and the statutes that followed are frequently referred to as "mandatory" reporting laws because they required certain professionals (such as physicians) to report child maltreatment to a public agency; the laws also established public agencies to respond to such reports.

By the end of 1963, 13 states had enacted reporting laws, and by 1967 every state and the District of Columbia had passed statutes requiring reporting by health care professionals. The problem was narrowly defined, and the solution seemed straightforward: the problem was the physical abuse of children, and the solution was to require physicians and other health care providers to report suspected maltreatment while protecting them from liability for reporting in good faith.[3]

The Child Abuse Prevention and Treatment Act (CAPTA), passed in 1973 and signed into law in 1974, provided financial incentives for states to adopt mandatory reporting laws and to establish formal child protective services systems. States received federal money if they adopted mandatory reporting laws, created agencies to investigate child abuse allegations, and demonstrated that they had a CPS system in place to respond to child abuse and neglect. This law also formalized public concern about child maltreatment by establishing a National Center on Child Abuse and Neglect (NCCAN) in the U.S. Department of Health and Human Services to conduct research on the incidence of maltreatment and to support state and local efforts to prevent and treat child abuse and neglect.

Reporting was expected to have two benefits: it would lead to the early detection of abuse and neglect and the prevention of more serious injuries and fatalities. It would also have a deterrent effect, as the fear of being reported might stop some people from maltreating their children.

Both the federal and the state reporting laws emphasize mandatory rather than voluntary reporting. This feature reflected a concern that many people might not report if they were not required to do so. This concern may have been based on the relatively small number of reports made prior to the passage of the mandatory reporting laws. It may also have been based on the discovery of children with evidence of prior serious injuries (such as broken bones) that had gone unreported even though they were treated by medical professionals.

There were also good reasons to assume that well-intentioned adults, even if they were professionals, might not report all the instances of child maltreatment they observed.[4] First, reporters might not know what constituted abuse or might not recognize its symptoms. The "battered child syndrome" was not discovered until the 1960s, after all, and child sexual abuse was not widely recognized until the 1980s. Reporting laws would help promote awareness and knowledge of what constituted abuse and neglect and how to recognize it. Second, reporters, even if they recognized maltreatment, might be afraid of liability associated with reporting. Mandatory reporting laws addressed this concern by imposing a positive mandate to report, establishing penalties for failure to report, and/or guaranteeing immunity to all those who reported in good faith. Third, some professionals, in particular therapists, might hesitate to report for fear of breaching confidentiality and damaging the therapist-client relationship or because they might feel that some cases of abuse or neglect could be better addressed by them than by the public child protection system; from this perspective, reporting would not be in the best interests of the child. Further, some might fear that reporting would only result in agency inaction or in unnecessary family disruption. Mandatory reporting laws in principle addressed these concerns as well, in that they provided a clear imperative to breach client-patient confidentiality, but they did not resolve the issues of which system was best positioned to provide treatment to abused children and their families and of whether CPS intervention would in fact be helpful to children and families.

Changes since the Passage of CAPTA

Since 1973 there have been frequent revisions to the state laws; the definitions have been broadened, and new categories of reporters have been added. What began as a fairly small system that would respond to physicians' reports of battered children has evolved into a much larger system that accepts reports from a range of professionals and nonprofessionals concerning children alleged to be suffering from various types of maltreatment.[5]

Across the nation, the definitions of abuse and neglect have been broadened. For example, 49 states now include sexual abuse in their definition of child maltreatment, and 41 include emotional abuse, although neglect and physical abuse still account for most maltreatment.[6] (See Table 1.2.) The categories of mandated reporters have also been broadened. In most states, virtually all professionals who come into contact with children (mental health professionals, teachers, day-care workers, law enforcement officials, and so on) are required to report. Some 17 states also require nonprofessionals ("any person" who suspects child abuse or neglect) to report. Moreover, all states accept reports from nonmandated reporters (such as family members, friends, or neighbors), and many states accept reports made anonymously.

The Reporting, Screening, and Investigation System

The Intake System

The intake system for child protective services consists of three stages. Stage 1, reporting, involves a definition of what constitutes reportable abuse and neglect; a set of potential reporters; a set of inducements for reporting; and a process by which reporters file reports, the CPS system receives them, and potential reporters and CPS workers can interact with each other. Reports are typically made by telephone; in some instances, a written report may be made as well.

Stage 2, screening, involves a process by which the child protective services system can elicit sufficient information by speaking on the telephone with the reporter and by checking its own sources (such as a registry of prior reports) to determine the current location of the child, the extent and type of risk to the child, the history of prior abuse or neglect, and the credibility and motivation of the reporter, in order to (a) determine the appropriateness of each report for investigation by CPS and (b) prioritize reports in terms of the need for an emergency response.

Stage 3, investigation, involves a process for seeing the reported child and other children in the family; interviewing the child's parents and/or caretakers; contacting other collateral sources of information such as teachers, doctors, as well as the reporter; and taking immediate steps to protect the child, including removing the child and/or taking court action if deemed necessary. It also involves a process for concluding whether a report is substantiated or unsubstantiated, according to the definitions of what constitutes abuse and neglect and the standards for deciding whether a particular case meets those definitions; and a process for deciding what further action, if any, child protective services will take to protect the child and provide services to the family.

Evaluating Current Performance

The primary goal of the mandatory reporting laws was to reduce the number of missed cases of maltreatment. It was assumed that mandatory reporting would lead to accurate as well as relatively complete reporting. Because underreporting was considered to be the problem, little thought was given to the possibility that too many cases might be referred. As the definitions and categories of reporters were broadened, however, the potential for overreporting grew as well. Thus, in evaluating the current operations of the system, we want to know both whether the laws have had the intended effects and also whether they have had any unintended negative consequences. Are people now more likely to report suspected maltreatment? Have the laws reduced underreporting? Have the laws in some instances increased overreporting? Is the reporting, screening, and investigation system achieving its goal of protecting children?

To evaluate the current performance of the CPS intake system, ideally we would want data on all three stages of the system: the number of reports filed, the number screened in, and the number substantiated. Often, however, data on one or more of these stages are missing. Typically, we have data on the number of reports substantiated and either the total number of reports or the number of screened-in reports. This means we can calculate a substantiation rate (expressed as a percentage of total reports or screened-in reports) but not a screen-in rate. Another extremely important limitation is that although we can make projections from survey data, we do not know with certainty the number of true cases of child maltreatment. Thus, we cannot calculate the percentage of cases missed.

In using data on reporting rates and substantiation rates, we need to be careful about how we interpret these measures. The substantiation rate is particularly problematic. Although a higher substantiation rate is commonly interpreted as evidence of more accurate reporting, this is not the only possible interpretation. A higher substantiation rate could also reflect better sorting at the level of screening and/or better decisionmaking at the level of investigation. Conversely, less accurate reporting is not the only possible cause of a lower substantiation rate. If a CPS agency is overwhelmed with reports, it may attempt to reduce the number of cases by screening out or unsubstantiating appropriately reported cases.[7] Moreover, the fact that a case was unsubstantiated does not always mean that the allegations in the report were false.[8]

The reporting rate is also an imperfect measure. Because all states have expanded their definitions and categories of reporters over time, it is difficult in interpreting changes in reporting rates to sort out the effects of the changes in law from possible changes in underlying rates of child maltreatment.

Another issue to keep in mind is that the front end of CPS is not merely engaged in finding cases. Reporting, screening, and investigation are also interventions in themselves. How a case is reported, screened, and investigated may have a dramatic impact on the family and implications for the effectiveness of any subsequent intervention. When the CPS intake system works well, the intervention can make a dramatic difference in the life of a child and family, helping to resolve an immediate crisis and laying the groundwork for continued therapeutic intervention. Done badly, the intake process risks rupturing relations within the family, between the family and the reporter, or between the family and CPS. Thus, in thinking about how the intake system should operate, we cannot evaluate the system only in terms of the numbers of accurately identified cases, missed cases, and inaccurately identified cases. We must also pay attention to the impact of the information-gathering process on the present and future prospects of the family.

Intended Consequences

Under the informal reporting system in place before passage of the reporting laws, many cases of abuse and neglect never came to the attention of the authorities, and even after passage of the first state reporting statutes, reporting remained low. For instance, in a 1968 study in Rochester, New York, 10 percent of children under 5 years of age who were treated in the emergency room fell into the "battered child syndrome" category and another 10 percent had been neglected, yet it is unclear whether any of these cases would have been reported had the study not been conducted.[9] Similarly, a 1970 study in Auburn, New York, revealed that 13 percent of emergency room cases involved children with serious injuries that should have been reported, yet none of them were.[10] Nationwide in 1967 there were only 9,563 abuse reports, a rate of 0.14 per 1,000 children, and in 1968 there were only 10,931 reports, a rate of 0.15 per 1,000.[11]

The primary goals of the reporting laws were to raise reporting rates and to reduce the number of missed cases of abuse and neglect. The first question to be considered then, is whether reporting rates increased after the adoption of state reporting laws and the passage of CAPTA in 1973. The available data (shown in Table 1.1) indicate that in the years immediately following the passage of CAPTA the reporting rate more than doubled, from 294,796 reports (4.5 per 1,000 children) in 1975 to 669,000 (10 per 1,000 children) in 1976. In no other two-year period did reporting rates increase as much. Some of this increase probably reflects the imposition of legal requirements to report and the creation of systems to receive reports. There may also have been an improvement in the recognition of abuse and neglect by reporters because of training or education pursuant to the laws, or because of increased national attention to the issue.[12]

But the causal linkage between the reporting laws and reporting rates is not straightforward. Even in the 1970s, the laws might not account for all the increase in reporting rates, and clearly the passage of laws in the 1970s cannot account for the dramatic increase in later years. Some of the increase in reports may reflect an increase in the actual level of child maltreatment, as appears to have happened with the introduction of crack cocaine in the 1980s. Similarly, higher reporting rates may reflect more stringent societal definitions of abuse and neglect such that actions or behaviors that once were considered acceptable discipline are now considered abusive. Thus, although the reporting laws probably caused reports to rise in the 1970s, we cannot attribute all the increase in those years to the effect of the laws, and we must look to other factors to help explain the increase in more recent years.[13]

Data from California are particularly helpful in this regard. Vicky Albert and Rick Barth show that substance abuse was an important factor behind the rise in reports in that state in the 1980s.[14] Drug-related arrests in California rose sharply in the late 1980s, from 5,700 per month in January 1985 to a high of 12,000 per month in August 1989; arrests then tapered off to 7,500 in December 1990. Child abuse and neglect cases handled by CPS followed a similar pattern, beginning at a level of about 25,000 per month in 1985, rising steeply to about 45,000 per month in 1989, and then rising more slowly to 46,000 per month in 1990. Analysis of the time-series data for 1985–1990 indicates that the rise in the number of arrests for drug-related offenses was correlated nearly one to one with the rise in abuse and neglect cases investigated by CPS: for every 100 new drug arrests, there were an additional 99 children reported for abuse and neglect. Not surprisingly, there was also a fairly strong relationship between drug arrests and placement rates, with an estimated 66 additional children placed in foster care for every 100 additional adults arrested for drug offenses.[15]

Pennsylvania data provide further evidence on the reasons for the increase in reports in the 1980s. Pennsylvania had the lowest reporting rates in the nation in the 1980s, a reflection of its narrow definitions (which were not broadened until 1993). However, even this state saw big increases in reports over the decade, suggesting that factors other than changes in reporting laws were responsible for the increased rate of reporting. When David Gilgoff and I analyzed the data for Pennsylvania's urban counties, we found the same pattern seen in California: the increase in the rate of drug-related arrests over the 1980s in Pennsylvania's urban areas was an important predictor of the increase in abuse and neglect reporting rates in those areas.[16]

Let us now turn to the second question about intended consequences. Did the reporting laws result in fewer missed cases of abuse and neglect? This is a difficult question to answer in the absence of accurate data on the true rates of child maltreatment, but there are two sources of data that can be used.[17]

One source is incidence data, gathered by surveying professionals who are likely to know about cases of abuse and neglect. Three national incidence studies have been conducted to date.[18] These studies track, among other things, how many cases of suspected maltreatment identified by outside agencies were not known to the formal CPS system, whether because these cases were not reported to CPS or, if reported, were subsequently screened out or closed. Although these

Table 4.1 Suspected cases known to professionals but not to CPS, 1980–1993 (%)

Type of professional	1980	1986	1993
Hospitals	44	0	60
Mental health	69	18	61
Police departments	58	22	55
Social services	69	71	75
Schools	87	74	84
Public health	74	74	97
Probation and courts	76	77	83
Overall average	79	65	79

Source: Andrea Sedlak and Diane Broadhurst, *Third National Incidence Study of Child Abuse and Neglect: Final Report* (Washington, D.C.: U.S. Department of Health and Human Services, National Center on Child Abuse and Neglect, 1996), table 7-5.

figures overstate the number of cases that were missed as a result of underreporting, since they also include some cases that were reported but were screened out or unsubstantiated, they provide some information as to the share of cases reaching CPS. As shown in Table 4.1, on average, 79 percent of cases known to professionals were not known to CPS in 1980. The rate fell slightly, to 65 percent, in 1986, but this change was not statistically significant. Comparing the data for 1986 and 1980, then, suggests that little progress was made in the 1980s, 10 years after CAPTA, in lowering the rate of cases missed by the formal CPS system.

Data from 1993 suggest that, if anything, the rate of missed cases may have gone up again since 1986. However, the data do not tell us what accounts for the lack of progress. Reporting rates may have fallen, or they may have remained constant or even gone up but been counteracted by increased rates of screening out reports.[19]

A second way to track missed cases is to use fatality data to determine the percentage of children who died from abuse or neglect who were not known to CPS before their deaths. The higher this percentage, presumably, the more likely it is that extremely serious cases of child maltreatment have been missed by the system (although some of these missed cases may have been reported but subsequently screened out or unsubstantiated).

Interpreted in this way, a lower percentage of child fatalities not known to CPS represents progress, although we could also interpret this statistic in a different way. If the system were operating at optimal effectiveness, we might expect to see no child fatalities among the cases known to CPS. Thus, the fact that an increasing percentage of child fatalities is known to CPS is not necessarily an indicator that the system as a whole is performing well. Rather, it is merely an indicator that the reporting system is doing a good job of bringing cases at high risk of fatal child abuse to the attention of CPS.

Unfortunately, we do not have many data on the share of child abuse–related fatalities known to CPS. The only consistent time series available is for the period 1990–1993.[20] In these years, as shown in Table 4.2, the percentage of child fatalities not known to CPS fell from 67 percent to 55 percent. This decline coincided with an increase in the reporting rate (and relative stability in the child fatality rate), which gives us some hope that as reports were rising, perhaps fewer serious cases were being missed. Nevertheless, it is concerning that in 1993, two decades after the passage of reporting laws, over half of the children who died from abuse or neglect were not known to CPS until it was too late. Seen from another perspective, it is also concerning that half of the child fatality victims were known to CPS agencies who were evidently unable to protect them from fatal maltreatment.

Incidence data and fatality data, then, point in the same direction but are not conclusive. There is some indication in the incidence data that the reporting laws may have led to fewer cases being missed (although the most recent incidence data point in the other direction), but the rate of missed cases, including some extremely severe cases, is still disturbingly high, as is the child fatality rate. In this regard, the reporting laws have not been as great a success as we had hoped.

Unintended Consequences

If the laws led to a greater number of reports, are they appropriately identified cases? The data suggest that the system is not working as accurately as we assumed it would. Although more cases are being reported, the cost apparently is a large number of inappropriately identified cases. Furthermore, while as a society we may decide that it

Table 4.2 Abuse-related fatalities not known to CPS, 1990–1993

Year	Reports per 1,000	Fatalities per 100,000	% not known to CPS
1990	40	1.78	67
1991	42	1.92	65
1992	45	1.73	57
1993	45	1.81	55

Sources: Karen McCurdy and Deborah Daro, *Current Trends in Child Abuse Reporting and Fatalities: The Results of the 1992 Annual Fifty-State Survey* (Chicago: National Committee to Prevent Child Abuse, 1994), table 3; David Wiese and Deborah Daro, *Current Trends in Child Abuse Reporting and Fatalities: The Results of the 1994 Annual Fifty-State Survey* (Chicago: National Committee to Prevent Child Abuse, 1995), table 3; and Ching-Tung Wang and Deborah Daro, *Current Trends in Child Abuse Reporting and Fatalities: The Results of the 1995 Annual Fifty-State Survey* (Chicago: National Committee to Prevent Child Abuse, 1996), table 3.

is worth the cost of investigating some inaccurate reports if it means we are catching more cases that would otherwise be missed, that outcome is not necessarily being achieved either: a large number of cases, including some very serious ones, still never come to the attention of the authorities.

The customary measure of the accuracy of reporting is the substantiation rate, which is the number of reports determined to meet the threshold for abuse and neglect at the conclusion of an investigation divided by either the number of reports made to the formal CPS system or the number of reports screened in by the system. As noted earlier, the substantiation rate is not a pure measure of accuracy of reporting, since it may be affected by other factors such as capacity and funding constraints and since children in unsubstantiated cases may nevertheless have been harmed or may need services to prevent harm. But it is the best measure of the accuracy of reporting that we have.

The most consistent finding when we look at substantiation rates is that they tend to be low. Further, substantiation rates apparently have been low for quite some time. The American Humane Association, the National Committee to Prevent Child Abuse, and the National Center on Child Abuse and Neglect (NCCAN) all report that substantiation rates have been roughly 40 percent since the late 1970s.[21]

On average, then, considerably more than half of reports are unsubstantiated. Does this mean that the substantiation rates are too low? A debate in the journal *Public Welfare* focused attention on this issue in 1990. Douglas Besharov argued that rates were indeed too low, indicating that too many cases were being referred to CPS. David Finkelhor agreed that rates were low, but argued that low rates were inevitable, given the difficulty of proving abuse or neglect to the exacting standards demanded by most statutes. Another point of disagreement was the time-series trend in substantiation rates. Besharov cited evidence that rates had fallen from 1986 to 1988, although the decline was small, but Finkelhor countered with evidence that on the contrary there was no clear trend over the period 1976–1986.[22]

Data from NCCAN, shown in Table 4.3, show a clear downward trend in substantiation rates since tracking began in 1990. After holding steady from 1990 to 1992, the average rate of cases that were substantiated or indicated fell to 38 percent in 1993. At last count, in 1996, the national average had fallen a bit further, while both the rate of unsubstantiated cases and other dispositions had risen.[23] Part of the recent decline in substantiation rates is due to the increased use of alternative outcomes in states such as Florida and Missouri that are

Table 4.3 Substantiation rates, 1990–1996 (%)

Year	Reports substantiated or indicated	Reports unsubstantiated or intentionally false	Other disposition or closed without a finding
1990	44	53	3
1991	43	54	3
1992	43	51	6
1993	38	54	8
1994	37	56	6
1995	36	58	6
1996	34	59	7

Sources: U.S. Department of Health and Human Services, National Center on Child Abuse and Neglect (NCCAN), "National Child Abuse and Neglect Data System Summary Data Component Data Tables, 1990–1994" (Washington, D.C., 1996), pp. 1990 SDC-4, 1991 SDC-4, 1992 SDC-4, 1993 SDC-4, 1994 SDC-4; *Child Maltreatment 1995: Reports from the States to the National Child Abuse and Neglect Data System* (Washington, D.C.: U.S. Government Printing Office, 1998), p. 2-3.

pursuing CPS reforms. However, these statistics confirm that substantiation rates continue to be low and perhaps are falling further.

If we are now persuaded that substantiation rates are too low, we need to ask what our ideal substantiation rate would be. Reporting laws require reports to be made on the basis of "suspicions of, reasonable suspicions of or cause to believe or suspect child maltreatment" and thus encourage people to err on the side of overreporting. These laws reflect society's decision that it is worth incurring the costs and risks associated with investigating more cases if it means we may be able to protect more children from abuse. Clearly, we would not expect the substantiation rate to be 100 percent; but 34 percent seems too low. What would be a reasonable target? Several experts have suggested 50 percent.[24] Is this figure attainable?

There is a great deal of variation in substantiation rates across states. Data from NCCAN indicate that states' substantiation rates in 1993 ranged from about 14 percent to 96 percent.[25] Some of this state-level variation may be due to differences in how the substantiation rate is calculated, but some probably reflects real differences in cases and in operations across systems. What does the distribution of state substantiation rates suggest about the possibility of achieving higher substantiation rates? Of the 47 states for which substantiation rates can be calculated based on the 1993 NCCAN data, only 8 (17 percent) have substantiation rates above 50 percent, 11 (23 percent) have rates between 40 and 50 percent, 19 (40 percent) have rates between 30 and 40 percent, and 9 (20 percent) have rates below 30 percent.[26] Since the vast majority (83 percent) of states currently have substantiation rates below 50 percent, raising the average rate to 50 percent would represent real progress; raising the rate much above 50 percent is likely to be an unreasonable target, at least in the short run.

The reporting laws imposed a specific obligation on particular professionals, the so-called mandated reporters. Therefore, it is important to look at the substantiation rate of cases referred by mandated reporters as compared to those referred by others. If, in the extreme case, we found that the substantiation rate for mandated reporters' reports was near 100 percent, then they could not be responsible for the low substantiation rates we see overall. Conversely, if mandated reporters did no better than others at accurately identifying abuse and neglect, we might want to reconsider the special mandate we have imposed on them to report. We need to be careful here, however. Very high substantiation rates for mandated reporters may mean that they do a very good job of identifying true cases of abuse and neglect, or it may mean that the CPS system gives their reports higher credence, because it trusts their professional judgment or for other reasons, or it may mean that it investigates their reports more aggressively because of the professionals' involvement.[27]

In general, CPS receives about an equal number of reports from mandated and nonmandated reporters. Data from the American Association for the Protection of Children (AAPC) indicate that from 1976 to 1982, roughly half of the reports received by CPS agencies came from professionals.[28] The remainder came from nonprofessionals such as parents, neighbors, and friends, and from anonymous reporters. The AAPC also tracked reporters by specific professions over the period 1977–1980. As shown in Table 4.4, the data suggest that the percentage of reports from mandated as opposed to nonmandated reporters rose slightly, while the breakdown by type among mandated reporters held fairly constant. Since 1980 the share of reports made by mandated reporters has remained about the same, as has the breakdown by category of professionals. Among nonprofessionals, nearly half the reports come from within the family. In 1995 family members (victims, parents, and other relatives) made nearly one-fifth of all reports. The most striking change from 1980 to 1995 is the increase in

Table 4.4 Sources of reports, 1977–1980 and 1995 (%)

Source	1977	1978	1979	1980	1995
Professionals	46.8	47.4	51.5	52.0	52.9
Medical	11.9	11.7	11.2	11.0	11.1
School	11.6	12.4	12.1	13.0	15.4
Social service	10.2	10.0	15.9	15.0	11.9
Law enforcement	11.5	11.6	10.9	11.0	12.8
Child care	1.6	1.7	1.4	2.0	1.7
Nonprofessionals	38.4	40.1	35.8	39.0	28.3
Other/Anonymous	14.8	12.5	12.7	9.0	18.8

Sources: American Association for the Protection of Children (AAPC), *Highlights of Official Child Abuse and Neglect Reporting—1980* (Denver, 1981), and earlier years; NCCAN, *Child Maltreatment 1995*, fig. 2-1.

the share of reports made anonymously, which grew from 9 percent to 19 percent. Since the share of reports made by nonprofessionals fell by about the same amount, it appears that nonprofessionals are more likely now than they were in the past to make reports anonymously.

Are mandated reporters more accurate reporters, and has their accuracy improved over time? In general, professionals do tend to have higher substantiation rates than nonprofessionals, while anonymous reporters have the lowest rates.[29] As Table 4.5 shows, substantiation rates for reports from all sources increased from 1977 to 1985, then declined to an even lower point in 1995, but at all three points in time professionals' reports were more likely to be substantiated.

In a detailed study of New York state, John Eckenrode and his colleagues found that this gap in substantiation rates between professional and nonprofessional reporters varied by type of abuse. The differential in substantiation rates was highest (26 percentage points, with substantiation rates of 39 percent versus 13 percent) for neglect reports, next highest (23 percentage points, 48 percent versus 25 percent) for physical abuse reports, and lowest (11 percentage points, 41 percent versus 30 percent) for sexual abuse reports.[30]

Although professionals generally have higher substantiation rates, there is large variation within groups, and some nonprofessionals have substantiation rates equal to or higher than those of some profession-

Table 4.5 Substantiation rates by source of report, 1977–1995 (%)

Source	1977	1985	1995
Law enforcement	60	72	52
School	52	64	37
Medical	48	62	48
Social service	42	56	44
Child care	45	53	36
All professionals	50	61	44
Nonprofessionals	34	46	28

Sources: 1977 and 1985: AAPC, *Highlights of Official Child Abuse and Neglect Reporting—1977* (Denver, 1977) and *Highlights of Official Child Abuse and Neglect Reporting—1985* (Denver, 1986); 1995: NCCAN, *Child Maltreatment 1995,* table D-1.

als. In Massachusetts, for example, substantiation rates for nonprofessionals range from 13 to 39 percent, while those for professionals range from 25 to 51 percent.[31] Among nonprofessionals, mothers living in the house have about the same substantiation rate as professionals on average, as do child victims and other household members such as siblings.[32]

These and the earlier data on reporting rates indicate that some professionals are particularly effective reporters. Police and sheriff departments, for example, have both high rates of reporting (indicating few missed cases) and high rates of substantiation (indicating few inappropriate reports). Mental health agencies, in contrast, have high rates of reporting but low rates of substantiation.

The reporting, screening, and investigations system appears to be biased with respect to class, race, and ethnicity. Research on reporting suggests that professionals in particular are more likely to report cases of suspected maltreatment among lower-income families.[33]

The high percentage of inaccurately identified cases is problematic for families and for the CPS system. Investigations of inappropriate reports disrupt the lives of families unnecessarily and may have adverse consequences for both children and parents. These investigations also divert precious resources from families who are truly in need.

This problem is related to the second unintended consequence, which is that the system appears to be overwhelmed by the sheer volume of cases. The consequences of the overload are seen at all levels. At the reporting stage, many callers find it difficult to make reports because CPS agency phone lines are often busy. At screening, reports that warrant investigation may instead be put into a "hold" pile or screened out altogether. At investigation, caseworkers carry many more than the recommended number of cases and therefore do not make enough contacts with the family and with collateral sources of information, including the reporter. Throughout the system, because limited resources are being stretched to cover so many cases and because so much of the system's efforts are being devoted to intake, many families do not receive the services they need. These apparent problems of overinclusion and overcapacity have led many observers to conclude that if there were fewer cases in the system they could be served better. Improvement in this direction, however, might come at the cost of missing more cases.

Reforming the Intake System

It is clear that in thinking about reforming the CPS intake system, we must improve the system's capability to achieve a balance between bringing in too few reports and bringing in too many. It is also clear that the issue is not volume per se, but rather getting the right cases brought to CPS attention. If we reduce the overall volume of reports without improving the accuracy of reporting, we will surely be missing more cases of child maltreatment. If, on the other hand, we allow the overall volume to continue to rise without improving the accuracy of reports, we will be conducting more inappropriate investigations.

How can we reform the intake system of CPS to achieve both fewer missed cases of child maltreatment and fewer inappropriate reports? The options discussed here are not meant to be an exhaustive list of possibilities but to present the most promising ones.

Changing or Clarifying Definitions

Reportable conditions of child abuse and neglect can be defined along five dimensions:

1. Severity. Maltreatment can be defined along a continuum ranging from less serious to more serious.
2. Risk versus actual occurrence. Another continuum ranges from a situation of risk of future harm to an injury that has already occurred.
3. Type of maltreatment. Many different types of child maltreatment (for example, physical abuse, sexual abuse, emotional abuse, and neglect) may be reportable.
4. Type of caretaker. Other perpetrators beyond parents and guardians (for example, parents' boyfriends or girlfriends, babysitters, relatives, neighbors, and institutional caretakers such as teachers) may be reported.
5. Burden of proof. The level of certainty required of the reporter ranges from subjective impressions to objective evidence.

One option for reform is to limit the number of cases coming into the system by narrowing the definitions along one or more of these dimensions. Several groups have recently recommended narrowing along the dimension of severity, so that only cases in which a child is the victim of, or is at risk of, serious maltreatment would be accepted by CPS, with the less serious cases referred for other services available on a voluntary basis in the community. In principle, narrowing—which we consider further in the next chapter—seems to be a sensible way to improve the likelihood that the system is not missing serious cases and yet is not intervening in nonserious ones. Given the goals of reform, it also makes more sense than other possible reforms of the definitions. Eliminating reports based on risk, for example, would rule out reports in which no harm has yet occurred even if a child is in an extremely dangerous situation. Limiting the types of maltreatment presents the same problem; ruling out neglect, for example, would eliminate many less serious cases but would also mean missing some life-threatening cases. Narrowing along the fourth dimension, the type of perpetrators that may be reported to CPS, would certainly help reduce the volume of cases in the system, but it is not clear that it would affect the balance between missed cases and inappropriately referred cases. Further, eliminating certain categories of perpetrators (such as teachers) from CPS jurisdiction would most likely mean moving both their cases and the resources to handle them to another system, so the net effect on CPS might well be zero. Narrowing along the fifth dimension, that of burden of proof, may be a way to target CPS intervention, but this option needs further study. (For further discussion of these issues, see Chapter 5.)

In practice, however, making any change in the definitions will not be simple. At a minimum, it would mean changing reporting laws and related statutes. It would also mean notifying mandated reporters and members of the public, retraining CPS staff, and coordinating with other agencies whose clients or programs might be affected. Changing definitions also leaves unsolved the issue of what would happen to the less serious cases no longer coming in to CPS. As we shall see in Chapter 6, states such as Florida and Missouri are currently experimenting with or considering differential response reforms that would provide an alternative track for these less serious cases.

Another option is clarifying the definitions, whether we stay with the existing ones or change them. Reporting laws should clearly specify what constitutes reportable abuse or neglect, what should be looked for, and what counts as evidence. Current laws typically do not accomplish this. If reporters were more aware of what constitutes child abuse and neglect and what constitutes a reportable condition of it, they might be better able to decide when to report. Thus, clarifying definitions might help us achieve the more accurate reporting we desire.

Changing the Types or Behavior of Reporters

One extreme proposal for limiting the number of cases entering the system is to eliminate mandatory reporting.[34] The rationale is that if the reporting laws have been responsible for the drastic increase in the number of cases entering the system, then perhaps eliminating mandatory reporting would help return the system to a lower, and more manageable, level of cases. This proposal makes some sense if the goal of reform is simply to reduce the volume of reports and hence cases in the system. Mandated reporters do, after all, make some 50 percent of all reports, and some of these reports presumably would not be made at all if not for the requirement to report. Many, however, would be made even in the absence of mandated reporting laws, because professionals are now aware that child maltreatment exists in the populations they see and that a public agency, CPS, is there to respond to it. But the goal of reform is not simply to reduce the volume of cases. Rather, we want to reduce the number of inappropriate reports without at the same time raising the number of missed cases.

Is eliminating mandated reporters the right way to achieve this goal? The evidence reviewed above suggests just the opposite. Mandated reporters are, as we have seen, on average better reporters than nonprofessionals in that they are more likely to report cases that CPS subsequently determines to be genuine cases of child abuse and neglect. We have no evidence that mandated reporters are less likely than nonprofessionals to file appropriate reports. Therefore, we have no reason to believe that eliminating the mandate to report would reduce the number of inappropriate referrals.[35] It might, however, have the undesirable effect of raising the number of missed cases, because some professionals might not report suspected cases even of serious maltreatment without the protective cover of the legal obligation to report.

Another alternative would be to try to reduce reports from those who tend to be bad reporters—that is, those with typically low substantiation rates. Since reports made anonymously are particularly likely to be unsubstantiated, it might be worthwhile to consider no longer accepting anonymous reports. Another, more extreme, option would be to refuse to accept reports from nonprofessionals on the grounds that they have such low substantiation rates, although certainly we would want to make an exception for victims and household members, who have substantiation rates as high as professionals. An even more extreme option would be to accept reports only from certain categories of professionals, such as the police and hospitals, who have proved over time to be the most accurate reporters of abuse and neglect. These options would undoubtedly reduce the number of inappropriate reports but at a cost in terms of missed cases that would probably be unacceptably high. Imagine the consequences, for example, if CPS refused to accept a report on a child because it was made by someone who wasn't the right type of reporter (say, only a relative or a day-care teacher) and if subsequently the child was severely injured or died. Limiting the categories of reporters, then, is unlikely to be a prudent way to reform the system.[36]

If we cannot limit the types of reporters, could we change the behavior of reporters to reduce both the number of inappropriate referrals and the number of missed cases? One option might be to increase the penalties for false reporting and for nonreporting. Before undertaking this type of reform, however, it would be helpful to do more research on how current sanctions seem to be affecting reporter behavior. It would be interesting to know, for example, whether any states have experimented with raising the penalty for malicious false reports and whether this has been effective in reducing reports from estranged ex-spouses or in-laws. It would also be interesting to know whether states that have higher penalties for nonreporting do in fact have lower rates of missed cases.

A second option for changing the behavior of reporters is providing more training. We could put resources into training mandated reporters so that they have a clearer sense of issues such as what types of cases to report, what type of evidence is needed to substantiate abuse or neglect, and what happens to cases after they are reported. Such training might help close the gap between reporters and CPS, enabling reporters to provide better information to CPS and allowing CPS to make better screening and investigation decisions.

Another proposal is to give professionals some discretion in deciding which cases to report. The idea behind discretionary reporting is that some children who are indeed victims of abuse or neglect may nevertheless not be appropriate for mandatory reporting to CPS, because the mandated reporter could without CPS intervention ensure that the children and their families receive the services they need, either by providing them directly or by referring the family to another social service agency. The assumption is that discretionary reporting would reduce the number of reports entering the CPS system by lifting the requirement to report children if they do not in the judgment of a professional need CPS intervention. In order for discretionary reporting to work, mandated reporters and CPS would need to reach agreement about exactly which cases (in terms of type and severity) would be candidates for it; this agreement would have to be supported on an ongoing basis with training and frequent consultations.[37]

The dangers here are clear: cases might easily fall through the cracks. But discretionary reporting is worth further consideration. Professionals are only reporting about a third of the cases they suspect, leaving open the question of what happens to the other two-thirds. Many professionals report that they handle the cases themselves, by intervening directly or by referring the family for other services. If so, what are these non-CPS professionals doing with these abusive and neglectful families? How do outcomes for the children who are not reported compare with outcomes for children who are? Understanding the fate of such cases and the operations of non-CPS networks used to handle them would help us to determine whether and when discretionary reporting or other alternatives to CPS intervention might work.

Expanding the Extent and Scope of Screening

Proposals for reforming the intake system in CPS often skip the screening stage entirely, but this is in fact an area in which improvements could be made. Screening is the CPS system's first opportunity to weed out inappropriate reports; it is also the stage at which cases can be prioritized (for example, emergency cases can be flagged for immediate response).[38] We consider two types of reforms here: expanding the extent and the scope of screening.[39]

Although it may seem obvious that all reports should be screened, in fact some CPS agencies do not allow their hotline workers to do any screening. Even among the jurisdictions that do screen, screen-in rates range widely, from a low of 20 percent to a high of 85 percent.[40] Routinely accepting every, or nearly every, case reported to CPS is inefficient in several respects. It means that some investigations will be conducted unnecessarily, wasting agency resources and needlessly disrupting families' lives. It also means lost opportunities to educate reporters about how abuse and neglect is defined and what constitutes a reportable condition.

CPS agencies could also do a more thorough job of screening. A first step would be to put better-qualified and better-trained staff into these jobs. Some states, in fact, assign some of their best staff to screening, on the grounds that the screening decision is one of the most important that CPS will make. Others see screening as purely a clerical function and expect staff merely to transcribe reports as they are called in. It would be interesting to see how this variation in screening staffing is reflected in subsequent substantiation rates. Notes Doug Besharov: "Agencies that carefully screen calls have lower rates of unsubstantiated reports and expend fewer resources investigating inappropriate calls."[41]

If more staff resources were devoted to screening, it might be possible to ask screeners to do more. Screeners talk with the reporter while receiving the report, but they do not routinely call others who know the family, although they could. Similarly, screeners may check for the existence of prior reports or case records, but they do not necessarily check the contents. Screeners also vary in the extent to which they do outreach and education with reporters and other members of the community, yet they are particularly well-positioned to do this because of their ongoing contacts with reporters and their knowledge of what types of reports are coming into the system. Expanding the scope of screening would require more resources, but this might be a prudent investment if it reduced the number of inappropriate cases making it into the system. Investigation is a costly intervention, from the viewpoint of both the agency and the family, so spending more up-front to reduce unnecessary investigations might be worthwhile.

Improving screening might also require changes in agency operations. For example, many states currently have centralized screening, which is helpful in that one statewide hotline number can be used; it also can be helpful in terms of assuring uniform and consistent treatment of all reports. However, statewide screening does not facilitate the enhanced screening described here, in which a screener might do more thorough work on individual cases and more outreach and education in the community. Statewide screening also does not allow screeners to develop a relationship with regular reporters and a working knowledge of other services available in the community, which would be essential in implementing some of the other reforms to the reporting system (such as discretionary reporting) considered above.

Improving the Investigations

Among the many proposals to improve investigations by CPS, what we are interested in are reforms that might help reduce the number of inappropriate cases in the system and the number of cases missed by the system; we are also interested in reforms that would minimize the harm done by inappropriate investigations. Most of the reforms that might help us attain this goal would have to occur at the level of reporting or screening, but there are three notable options at the level of investigation.

One possible reform is to improve the thoroughness of investigations. States vary a great deal in the extent to which they invest in sufficient numbers of well-qualified and well-trained staff. As a result, investigators all too often do not do a thorough job: they do not always interview all the family and household members who might be involved in or have information about the abuse or neglect, nor do they always talk with collaterals such as doctors or teachers who know the family and are well positioned to assess the level of risk to the children. Failing to do so can result in the most tragic type of missed case: a case in which a child in real danger was reported to the system and investigated, but in which the system failed to recognize that danger.

A second possible reform is to improve the quality of investigations so that they are a more helpful intervention for families and children. One step in the right direction would be for CPS to provide a more customized response to families, rather than approaching all families with a one-size-fits-all investigative model that may be appropriate and necessary only in the most serious of cases. One option would be to shift to an assessment, as opposed to an investigative, model for the initial contacts with many if not all families. This shift would change the way parents are viewed (from alleged perpetrators to potential partners in child protection) and the way families experience the intervention.

A third possible reform at the investigation stage is to increase communications between investigators and reporters. There are two types of communication that should virtually always occur between investigators and reporters and yet commonly do not. First, the investigator should talk with the reporter early in the investigation to gather more information about the report and to find out what if anything has changed since the report was filed.[42] Second, the investigator should tell the reporter, at the conclusion of the investigation, what the outcome is and what if any further action the agency will be taking. This is an important part of the feedback loop that provides information to reporters about the appropriateness of their reporting. Communication with reporters is also important in terms of children's safety, particularly in those instances in which CPS will not be taking further action on a case. Yet not all jurisdictions require notice to reporters, and even in those that do, notice is not always provided.

The available data indicate that the current reporting, screening, and investigation system is probably more successful than the previous informal system in terms of reducing the number of cases of abuse and neglect missed by the system. The reporting laws have resulted in more public awareness and more reporting, but unfortunately the reporting is not always accurate. The result is that too many cases enter the system, many inappropriately.

The challenge is how to reduce the number of inappropriately identified cases without increasing the number of cases missed by the system. Several of the reforms discussed above might help us achieve this goal. Many of these options need further study, but at this point the most promising and most deserving of further consideration are: improving reporting by changing or clarifying the definitions, changing the incentives for reporters, and exploring the option of discretionary reporting; expanding the extent and scope of screening; improving the thoroughness of investigators' work with families and collaterals; improving the quality of investigations as a helpful intervention with families; and enhancing communications between investigators and reporters.

Chapter 5

Narrowing as a Strategy to Improve Child Protection

A common theme among critiques of the child protective services system is that the mandate of CPS has become too broad and should be narrowed, although critics are not unanimous in what they mean by "narrowing." There is also widespread support among observers of CPS for building an alternative child and family services system to serve families for whom CPS intervention is not appropriate. But uncertainty remains about whether such a system can actually be built and about what form it might take. This chapter examines the case for narrowing the mandate of CPS and analyzes its feasibility as a strategy for improving child protection.

The Case for Narrowing

A key element of the argument for narrowing is that CPS has become the only way for families to access services, crowding out less coercive, more family-friendly services and unnecessarily exposing families that are at low risk for abuse and neglect to an intrusive and sometimes punitive system. To those who counter that CPS functions as a social safety net for children and families, advocates of narrowing point out that many families involved with CPS receive grossly inadequate or inappropriate services or none at all. On average, only 28 percent of all families reported to CPS in the first place receive any services.[1] In most states, even a case kept open for services typically receives little

more than "case management," involving an infrequent visit by a social worker who may be supervising anywhere from 20 to more than
100 other families at the same time. Although other services such as
day care or a parent aide may be prescribed, availability is uneven
across communities, and in virtually all communities the current level
of resources is inadequate to meet the demand. As one observer commented, the problem is not just that CPS is the only door; it is also that
CPS is "a door to an empty room." Another characterized CPS as "a
system that allows us to intrude in a family, or a child's life, without
some assurance that it's going to help."[2]

Other observers point out that the current system is not only inefficient but also inequitable; poor children, racial and ethnic minority
children, and children from lone-parent families are disproportionately likely to be represented in the system. Today as a century ago,
lone motherhood and especially poverty are critical factors in determining whether or not a child is reported and removed.[3]

Defenders of the status quo argue that for many needy families,
CPS is better than nothing despite its shortcomings. Some families
receive useful counseling services, either from a CPS social worker or
from an agency to which CPS refers them. Others receive more tangible assistance, such as a child-care place, a parent aide, or a homemaker. Advocates of narrowing, however, argue that as long as the
CPS mandate is overly broad, the system will be unable to deliver
adequate services. Although narrowing would exclude some families,
advocates contend that CPS is so stigmatizing and punitive and offers so few services that some of the excluded clients would be better
off without it. Those remaining in the system, on the other hand,
would have better access to resources because the system would be less
overloaded.

What Would "Narrowing" Mean?

In 1994 experts participating in an executive session on child protective services at Harvard's Kennedy School of Government offered a
range of views about what narrowing of the system might mean. The
following comments are typical.

> My vision is . . . [to] establish preventive and early intervention services
> in the normative institutions that serve children, at different points in

their lives, the health care system, the school system, in community centers . . . Given that kind of scenario, I would see child protection services
as a much narrower system . . . in terms of whom it serves—because I'm
assuming that families would get the services they need before they are in
crisis—but that is also a quality system.

. . . instead of investigation being the only gateway to services for
families in need of some kind of attention, there [would] be some kind of
early warning system.

. . . we would downsize child protective services. We would create a
much narrower focus for them to intervene, only as the last remaining
viable option for families, and . . . CPS would become the system of last
resort and not first resort.[4]

These comments reflect widespread sentiment that CPS agencies are
overwhelmed by the current caseload. In response, a broad range of
observers have advocated a narrowing of the CPS mandate, usually in
tandem with an expansion of non-CPS services. In 1988 the American
Bar Association, the American Public Welfare Association, and the
American Enterprise Institute jointly recommended clearer guidelines
for reporters along with stricter criteria for screening reports, with the
aim of narrowing the range of families coming into the CPS system.[5]
In the same year the National Association of Public Child Welfare
Administrators (NAPCWA) issued a proposal to narrow CPS and to
expand the provision of non-CPS services. Under the NAPCWA plan,
a more narrowly focused CPS would form part of a three-tier system,
alongside an expanded voluntary/preventive family support system
and an adequately funded child well-being system (including public
welfare, education, health, and early childhood education).[6] In an in-
fluential report in 1989, social policy experts Sheila Kamerman and
Alfred Kahn called for reforms within CPS and for an expansion of
services outside the system so that families would not have to be referred to CPS to get services.[7] In 1993 Elizabeth Hutchison recommended limiting CPS intervention to the most severe cases, involving
serious physical injury, risk of imminent harm, or sexual abuse, so
that these children could be better protected while other families
would be spared having to deal with the intrusive and punitive CPS
system.[8] In 1996 the Child Welfare League of America proposed a
comprehensive reform of the child protection system in which CPS
intervention would be limited to the most severe but noncriminal cases

of abuse or neglect, with criminal cases handled by the police and nonsevere cases of child maltreatment handled by a non-CPS social services system.[9]

Others would limit CPS intervention to cases in which a criminal act has been perpetrated against a child. Leroy Pelton, for example, recommends that criminal child abuse be reported to the police and prosecuted in the criminal justice system, and that social workers focus on cases of noncriminal neglect.[10] Duncan Lindsey also proposes that child abuse be redefined as criminal assault and handled as a police matter.[11] Although some social workers would still be involved in child abuse cases, since they could be hired by police departments to help with their investigations, most of the social workers who are currently engaged in CPS investigations would be freed to provide services to needy families instead. In Pelton's and Lindsey's models, the CPS system as we know it today would wither away, to be replaced by a police system for criminal cases of child maltreatment and a child welfare system for needy families.

In an interesting variation on these models, Lela Costin, Howard Karger, and David Stoesz propose the establishment of Children's Authorities with overall responsibility for both the police function and the family support function, along with other functions related to the protection of children.[12] Under this plan the police involved in child protection would operate under the rubric of child protective services. Costin, Karger, and Stoesz cite two advantages to linking what Pelton calls the investigative/coercive/child removal role and the helping roles under one overarching authority.[13] First, it offers an opportunity for better coordination across what are now separate agencies that have historically done a poor job of sharing information and resources. Second, it provides a mechanism for improved accountability if the system fails to operate as it should.

While all these proposals recommend that CPS handle only the most serious cases of abuse or neglect, they differ about where to draw the line. Some would use criminal definitions as the dividing line, but most would not. And some do not specify what would happen to cases no longer handled by CPS.

For a narrowing strategy to succeed, advocates must reach consensus on what they mean by narrowing and must formulate a strategic plan to build the alternative service delivery system that they envision.

As we shall see in the following analysis, a narrowing strategy alone cannot bring about the improved protection of children that we as a society desire.

Evaluating the Case for Narrowing

Most of those who advocate narrowing envision the creation of an alternative system that will better meet the needs of families who are at risk of abuse or neglect or of disruption (for example, families with a severely disabled child or a runaway child). Such proposals involve what I call a "narrowing plus" scenario, in which the role of CPS would be narrowed and an alternative system or subsystem developed to provide services to those excluded from CPS. Both the existence and the capacity of an alternative system would depend on the public's willingness to authorize and pay for it. Under another scenario, which I call minimalist, CPS would be narrowed, but no provision would be made for offering services to families no longer included in CPS. In evaluating the feasibility of a narrowing strategy, this distinction is crucial.

In Chapter 3 we saw that five problems are most frequently identified in critiques of the current CPS system:

Overinclusion: Some families are inappropriately included in CPS.

Capacity: The number of families involved with CPS far exceeds the capability of the system to provide adequate child protection.

Underinclusion: Some families who should be receiving services from CPS, including some who are low-risk and some who are high-risk, are not included in the system at all.

Inadequate service delivery: Some families in the CPS system receive no services, while others receive neither the right type or amount of services.

Inappropriate service orientation: CPS has a one-size-fits-all, coercive, and investigative approach that is not appropriate for some families in the system.

Clearly, a narrowing strategy would solve the problems of *overinclusion* and *capacity*. But the effect on *inadequate service delivery* is less straightforward. If the focus of CPS was narrowed and the level of resources held constant, each case, on average, would have access to greater resources. But it is more likely that resources for CPS would be cut back in response to its narrowed scope. At the same time, the average case left in CPS would be much more serious and more difficult to handle than previously. The result might be a system even more resource poor than before. Alternatively, if resources were allocated in proportion to the severity of the caseload and if the narrower scope led to a greater sense of obligation to provide services, the outcome might be a system with more resources to offer children and families. The impact of a narrowing strategy on service delivery also crucially depends on whether and to what extent an alternative service delivery system would be funded, and on how much of its funding would come from existing CPS budgets.

Narrowing the focus of CPS might help solve the problem of *service orientation*. If only "hard-core" abusive families were left in the system, service planning might become more individualized, and service delivery might feature more intensive and more integrated services better suited to the complex and multiple needs of the most troubled families. Another possibility involves orienting services more toward protecting the child victim and punishing the adult perpetrator, linking CPS and criminal justice efforts or even moving a narrowed CPS into the criminal justice system. This approach raises a whole host of questions about the compatibility of the criminal justice system with the service orientation of CPS, the needs of families served by CPS, and the professional orientation of CPS staff.

The value of narrowing as a remedy for *underinclusion* is less immediately apparent. A narrowed focus that resulted in families' being less likely to come to the attention of CPS would clearly exacerbate the problem, especially for families who have not crossed the line into serious abuse or neglect but who nevertheless need services to prevent abuse or neglect or family disruption. Some of these cases are missed by the CPS system today; others are screened out or closed after an investigation. Narrowing CPS would almost certainly worsen the situation of these families unless the more narrowly focused CPS was accompanied by an expanded preventive system.

Policy analysts have identified three dimensions that any policy strategy must satisfactorily address if it is to be successful:[14]

The *mission* of the agency or agencies that will carry out the policy
The *operational capacity* of the agency or agencies
The *political mandate* for the agency or agencies

Together, these dimensions provide a consistent analytic framework for evaluating alternative policy strategies.

The Current System

MISSION

The mission of the current CPS system can be broadly defined as follows: to protect children, using the authority of the state (or the threat of such authority), by providing a comprehensive program of child protective services, beginning with the screening and investigation of reports, to children and families in cases in which it is alleged that a child has been harmed or is at risk of harm as a result of abuse or neglect by a parent or other caretaker. This protective mission encompasses a broad range of families.[15]

At one extreme are the "tougher" cases, in which a child has been very seriously harmed or is at risk of serious harm and in which intervention is warranted to protect the child even if the parents will not agree to it voluntarily. Some of these cases, involving death, sexual assault, or grave bodily injury, require intervention by the criminal justice system. These serious and criminal cases represent about 10 percent of the current caseload, although obviously this percentage varies a great deal by jurisdiction and over time.[16]

There is another group of cases that are also serious but do not require criminal justice intervention. This category includes cases involving extreme corporal punishment; lack of supervision of a very young child; or grossly inadequate provision of food, clothing, or attention to medical needs, often as a result of parental addiction to crack cocaine or other drugs or alcohol. Let us assume for the purposes of discussion that these cases represent about 40 percent of the current caseload, although again there will be a great deal of variation.

I refer to these serious cases—both the criminal and the noncriminal—as the "authoritative protective" end of the spectrum because they are so serious that society sanctions the use of authority if necessary to protect these children from further abuse or neglect. This is not to say that all families, and all family members, at this tougher end of the spectrum are unwilling to cooperate. Nor does it mean that case workers should not try to engage the parents and work with them cooperatively to the extent possible. However, if the parents are not willing to cooperate, society is willing to use authority to override their wishes in order to protect the children.

At the other end of the spectrum are the cases in which a child is at lower risk of serious harm and a parent may be willing to work with an agency to secure needed services. Typically, these cases involve less serious physical abuse (for example, a single, minor injury such as a bruise or a scratch) or less severe neglect (such as parental drug or alcohol abuse but with no other apparent protective issues, dirty clothes or a dirty home, lack of supervision of a school-age child, missed school or medical appointments). Many of these lower-risk neglect cases are poverty-related (for example, inadequate housing or inappropriate child-care arrangements while a parent works). But some of them might escalate into more serious maltreatment, and a report of a seemingly low-risk situation or incident might actually signal a case of serious and chronic abuse or neglect.[17] Let us assume that these cases account for the remaining 50 percent of the current CPS caseload.

Whether this lower-risk, "protective/preventive" end of the spectrum warrants authoritative intervention is the issue at the heart of the narrowing debate. If authoritative intervention is appropriate for these cases, then they are appropriately included in CPS. But if the protective issues are not severe enough to warrant compulsory intervention, these cases should be excluded from CPS, and any services they are to receive should be offered on a voluntary basis.[18]

OPERATIONAL CAPACITY

How does the breadth of the mission affect the extent to which CPS agencies are equipped to do the job? Typically the "authoritative protective" cases take a disproportionate share of resources, leaving the protective/preventive end of the spectrum with inadequate resources. The tougher protective cases also set the tone for agency operations, which can result in an inappropriately investigative and punitive service orientation.

The breadth of the mission—and the combination of investigative and helping roles—may also adversely affect casework with families. On high-risk cases, social workers may place too little emphasis on protecting children because they are trying to help the family as a whole. On lower-risk cases, the agency may err by not allowing a social worker to work with a family who needs and wants help unless that family is actively abusive or neglectful. The resulting tension can lead to role conflict for CPS workers. It can also jeopardize the capacity of CPS agencies to fulfill their child protection mandate.

POLITICAL MANDATE

Legislators and the public continue to support intervention on the tougher cases despite perceived operational shortcomings. Even when budgets for other services are being cut back, it is not uncommon to see increased appropriations for CPS. But the depth of support for government intervention at the lower-risk end of the spectrum is much less certain. To some extent, this is because CPS work with the lower-risk families is a well-kept secret. When CPS officials ask legislators for additional funding, they emphasize their most serious cases, not the protective/preventive ones. Thus the extent of potential support for an alternative protective/preventive system remains an open question, to which we shall return shortly.

A New, Narrowed CPS

MISSION

In a new, narrowed CPS, the scope of the mandate would be scaled back to cover only the "authoritative protective" part of the spectrum, and the criteria for entry into the system would be more precisely defined. For example, the new mission might be defined as follows: to protect children, using the authority of the state (or the threat of such authority), by providing a comprehensive program of child protective services, beginning with the screening and investigation of reports, to families with children where there is reasonable cause to believe, on the basis of a report by a credible, named reporter, that a child has been seriously harmed or is at risk of serious harm as a result of physical abuse, sexual abuse, or negligence by a parent or guardian.

This sample mission statement narrows the child protective mandate in several ways. First, it narrows along the dimension of severity, by requiring that the harm to the child be serious. Second, it narrows along the dimension of type of abuse, by excluding categories such as emotional abuse and replacing the general term "neglect" with the more precise legal term "negligence."[19] Third, it narrows along the dimension of burden of proof, by using the standard of reasonable cause to believe (although one could establish an even higher standard, such as a preponderance of evidence). Fourth, it narrows along the dimension of type of caretaker, by excluding cases of abuse or neglect by nonparental caretakers. Fifth, it narrows along the dimension of type of reporter, by requiring reporters to be "credible" and by disallowing anonymous reports.

Narrowing along other dimensions would be more controversial. For example, narrowing along the dimension of risk versus actual occurrence, by excluding cases in which a child has not yet been harmed but may be at risk of harm, would leave too many children at high risk with no prospect of intervention. Narrowing the mission by restricting involvement to the "front end" (intake and investigation), and moving cases to another agency or agencies for treatment after investigation, would still expose an unacceptably large number of families to, and use a disproportionately large share of resources for, investigations of low-risk cases.

OPERATIONAL CAPACITY

The ability of a new CPS to meet its mission would depend critically on the level of resources available after narrowing was implemented. Excluding some 50 percent of the current caseload would still leave the toughest half behind. If resources were reduced by half too, CPS would probably have less capacity to provide adequate and appropriate services for those cases.

Operational capacity would also depend on the ability of CPS to define its mission precisely, communicate that mission to the community and other agencies, and enforce it. Restricting CPS to only 50 percent of its former caseload would have major consequences not only for those accustomed to referring cases to CPS but also for CPS staff. On the positive side, it might help resolve some of the ambiguity about and conflict between roles discussed above. It might also help CPS to develop services more appropriate to its client population. On the other hand, it might drive the helping professionals out of the CPS agencies, leaving behind a core of more prosecutorially oriented workers. Would these workers have the skills and the orientation to assess children and families' needs and to provide services to meet those needs?

An important operational issue concerns the relationship of a narrowed CPS to the criminal justice system. There is already a fair amount of overlap and coordination on selected cases; in many jurisdictions, cross-reporting of potentially criminal acts of abuse and neglect is required by statute. Law enforcement agencies commonly have some responsibility for investigating the most serious child abuse complaints and also receive referrals from CPS after an initial CPS investigation. Conversely, law enforcement agencies frequently refer families to CPS for assessment and treatment. If the scope of CPS responsibility was restricted to the tougher cases, this type of interaction would become more common. For example, if the criminal justice system was typically involved with the toughest 5–10 percent of the CPS caseload, and if CPS restricted its scope to the toughest 50 percent of its previous caseload, then in the absence of any other changes, the proportion of CPS cases involved with criminal justice would rise from 5–10 percent to 10–20 percent. This increase in turn might generate other changes. Some jurisdictions might come up with new configurations, separating responsibility for the investigation and the treatment phases and/or building in mechanisms for smoother referrals between CPS and the criminal justice system. Or the investigative function might be moved to criminal justice altogether, as envisioned by reformers such as Pelton and Lindsey. Such an outcome again raises questions about the system's capacity to respond to children's and families' needs for services.

POLITICAL MANDATE

Presumably a new, narrowed CPS would enjoy strong political and public support. However, if the new agency was perceived to be working with "hard-core" perpetrators only, public support for traditional functions such as treatment and family support services might decline. On the other hand, to the extent that CPS was increasingly linked with criminal justice, it might pick up some of the public support for funding that system.

An Alternative System

MISSION

In the "narrowing plus" scenario, an alternative system would pick up some of the families dropped from the current CPS system.[20] For example, the mission of the alternative system might be defined as follows: to protect children and to prevent child abuse and neglect by providing a range of family support services available on a voluntary basis to families at risk of abuse and neglect or family disruption.

This type of a mission statement is clearly broader than in even the most expansive CPS systems today, reflecting the belief that providing better protection to children requires providing a greater array of preventive services on a voluntary basis. Ideally, this system would be an improvement in three ways. First, it would meet the needs of children and families who need services but are not currently included in the CPS system. Second, it could better meet the needs of some children and families that are ill served in the current CPS system by reaching families earlier, and in a more helpful way. Third, it might prevent some families from ever needing authoritative CPS intervention, ultimately reducing the pressures on the new narrowed CPS system.

In the minimalist scenario, no public funding for an alternative system would be provided; families excluded from the new narrowed CPS would have to rely on existing resources, whether formal or informal. Over time there might be indirect effects on other agencies' missions if families excluded from CPS placed increased demands on other agencies. For example, emotionally disturbed children currently referred to CPS might increasingly be referred to mental health departments for institutional placements.

OPERATIONAL CAPACITY

In the "narrowing plus" scenario, the operational capacity of the new alternative system, like that of the new CPS, would depend critically on the resources allocated to it. Beyond resources, important questions must be resolved with regard to a new system's ability to precisely define and adhere to its mission, to prioritize clients, and to provide the right mix of services. Those advocating a "narrowing plus" scenario emphasize the need for community involvement in the operations of the alternative system, but such community involvement is still relatively new and untested.

Operational capacity in the minimalist scenario depends on the ability of existing supports to meet the needs of at-risk families who no longer meet the criteria for CPS. It is generally agreed that CPS has long functioned as the "social safety net" for families and children who are not served by other formal or informal resources. It is an open question whether in the absence of that safety net, other resources would prove sufficient to meet those families' needs. For example, if schools could no longer refer cases of poverty-related neglect to CPS, might schools discover that they or someone else in the community in fact have the capacity to address those children's needs, or would those children's needs simply go unmet?

POLITICAL MANDATE

The political mandate for a new protective/preventive system is uncertain. Because our ability to identify families at risk is so poorly developed, it would be hard to demonstrate that an alternative system would be a more cost-effective way of dealing with families at risk of abuse and neglect. Moreover, if the new system served not only families formerly seen in CPS but also other families who are now being identified or coming forward voluntarily for services, there would inevitably be concern that building a new system would amount to a costly expansion of the overall child and family services system. Given the current trend to reduce federal funding for social programs and to replace entitlement programs such as welfare and child nutrition with capped block grants to the states, the political will to support an alternative system seems absent.

Reforms such as the federal welfare reform legislation enacted in 1996, even in the absence of any reforms to the CPS system, will clearly have an effect on CPS. It is generally agreed that the safety net for children whose families cannot provide for them is the child welfare system, including foster homes, group homes, or some other form of residential care. To the extent that reductions in cash assistance and food stamps increase the number of families who cannot provide for their children, such reforms are likely to increase the number of families referred to CPS. Thus, even as CPS agencies were trying to define their mission more narrowly to exclude lower-risk cases (such as poverty-related neglect), they might receive more referrals as a result of families' deteriorating economic circumstances. These referrals would impede efforts to narrow the criteria for entry into CPS, and would exacerbate the existing problems of capacity and overinclusion. Because so many more children are on welfare than are in CPS, the children affected by welfare reform could swamp the child protective services system, especially if they have to be placed in foster care or other out-of-home care. It is estimated that 1.1 million children will be made poor as a result of the welfare reforms.[21] Placing one in five of those children in out-of-home care would add 220,000 children to the pre–welfare reform foster-care population of some 450,000 and constitute a nearly 50 percent increase in the foster-care caseload.

Recent congressional proposals would reduce overall funding for

CPS and child welfare and replace the entitlement (Title IVE) with a block grant. Enactment of this legislation would render CPS unable to meet current demand for its services, let alone an increased demand for investigations and placements resulting from cuts in welfare and child nutrition. A second proposed reform is to replace a series of categorical programs (such as child abuse and neglect prevention and family support and preservation) with a single block grant for child welfare and CPS. In principle, states would have a good deal of discretion in spending this money (for example, they could transfer up to 30 percent of the child protection funds to preventive services for children and families), but in practice, if funds were limited, and demand for services increased, the net effect would probably be a reduction of preventive services such as family support and child care.[22]

The federal welfare reforms enacted in 1996 and the companion reforms enacted by the states will make narrowing less likely or, if narrowing is pursued, a minimalist scenario all but certain. Block-granting of IVE will have the same effect. Cuts in welfare and IVE might also provoke a different type of narrowing. Rather than including the toughest cases in terms of child protection, CPS might be pushed into including cases on the basis of other criteria, particularly financial necessity. At the margin, placing a homeless child might take precedence over placing a child at risk of physical or sexual abuse. Thus, the system might be narrowed, but not in the way that those concerned about child protection would recommend.

The "Narrowing Plus" Scenario versus the Minimalist Scenario

The contrast between the "narrowing plus" and the minimalist scenarios is striking. In the former, we expect that families—both those served in the new narrowed CPS and those served in the new alternative system—will receive services that better meet their needs. In the minimalist scenario, there are legitimate concerns that families might receive worse services than they do today. Those excluded from the system might get fewer services than they would otherwise receive, and the new narrowed CPS system might still be overloaded by referrals. The political mandate for the "narrowing plus" scenario is uncertain, and the current political climate casts doubts on the prospects for narrowing in general and narrowing plus in particular. There are real risks that those who advocate narrowing in the hopes of attaining an improved alternative system will end up with a minimalist scenario instead. In making the case for narrowing, then, advocates need to be aware of the risks and need to formulate a strategic plan to minimize them. The next section considers various options for narrowing, not just in terms of their feasibility and impact on service delivery, but also, and more importantly, in terms of their likelihood of bringing about the "narrowing plus" rather than the minimalist outcome.

How "Narrowing Plus" Might Be Accomplished

If agreement was reached to narrow the focus of CPS and to build an alternative service delivery system to accompany the new narrowed CPS, how might these tasks be accomplished? At what stage would families be diverted from CPS, and how would they and others apply-ing directly or referred by the community access the new family sup-port system?

Narrowing could occur at three different points in the CPS intake process: reporting, screening, and investigation. The degree of public support for narrowing and for an alternative service delivery system will depend largely on when it occurs. The more involved CPS is with assessing a family's need for services—that is, the later the point at which the narrowing occurs—the more the public will support the provision of services as being necessary to prevent the abuse or neglect of a child. Thus, a strategy of "closed referrals"—that is, investigation by CPS, followed by referral to the alternative system—would get the most public support. However, this approach would replicate one of the worst features of the current system, requiring families to run an investigative gauntlet in order to access services. For this reason, most advocates of narrowing would prefer a strategy of "open referrals"— that is, no report to CPS, and direct referral to the alternative system— so that families could directly access the services they need, allowing CPS to use its scarce resources for only the most serious cases.[23]

Given this dilemma, a mixed strategy probably makes the most sense, at least initially. For example, some resources in the alternative system could be reserved for closed referrals and some for open refer-rals. With these factors in mind, let us explore the feasibility of nar-rowing at the three intake points more closely.

Narrowing at the Point of Reporting

Operationally, narrowing at the point of reporting would be the most difficult way to implement a narrowing strategy, since it would require changing the behavior of the entire pool of potential reporters. To get reporters to refer a more narrowly defined set of cases, a CPS agency would first have to promulgate new regulations with a new definition of what constituted a reportable condition. It would then have to publicize those changes widely and, in particular, attempt to notify all the mandated reporters. After the promulgation, publicity, and notification, there would still be a lengthy adjustment period, as new reporters learned of the change in mandate and as all reporters began to understand what the new regulations meant in practice.

How would CPS handle the cases that would have been reportable under the old paradigm but no longer fit under the new narrowed definition? Probably the best option would be to use some form of consultation, either formal or informal. That is, rather than simply refusing to accept reports that no longer fit within the narrowed mandate, agencies could explain to the reporter why the report should not be made and perhaps recommend an alternative service provider to contact. This would spare families unnecessary involvement with CPS and would educate reporters about the appropriateness of referrals.

Does a case that is no longer reportable then become a CPS referral to the alternative system, and if so, does it have priority for service? If yes, this might satisfy the public's desire for accountability by certifying that the families served in the alternative system were in fact at high risk. However, giving priority to cases called in to CPS but not deemed reportable would create an incentive for reporters to continue to call these cases in to CPS even though they knew that these families did not meet the new narrowed mandate. This would set up perverse incentives that would defeat the purpose of narrowing. Giving priority to nonreportable cases would send a mixed message to reporters, who would be struggling to understand the new scope of CPS in the first place. Another disadvantage is that it would generate a substantial work burden for CPS screeners. For this reason, it seems prudent to treat cases that are not reportable to CPS as open referrals to the alternative system, that is, referrals that do not have CPS endorsement and that receive no special priority. Although these cases would lose an opportunity for CPS validation, over time the alternative system would presumably do its own certification of the need for its services.

Narrowing at the Point of Screening

As we saw in Chapter 4, there is currently a great deal of variation in the discretion that states allow their CPS staffs in deciding whether to accept a report for investigation. Some states require an investigation of every report filed, even if the reporter is not credible. Others allow screening out in principle but discourage it in practice. And many states do not screen out reports on open cases. Requiring investigations of such reports uses precious intake resources on cases already under the agency's supervision. Even if there were narrowing at the point of reporting—with tighter definitions and more education and consultation for reporters—CPS would still receive some reports that do not fit its mandate or that do not warrant investigation. There is ample room, then, for narrowing at the level of screening.

Screening is also an opportune point for providing feedback to reporters about the mission of CPS by informing reporters about the outcome of their report. Such feedback does not always occur in the current system. Providing this type of feedback would help educate reporters as to which cases were now appropriate for referral to CPS and which cases should be referred to the alternative system.

Again, the issue arises as to how screened-out cases should be treated in the alternative system. Assigning them priority would create an incentive to keep referring such families to CPS, even though they should and will be screened out. Therefore, these families, if referred to the alternative system, should not receive priority over other families who have referred themselves or been referred by others in the community without going through CPS.

Narrowing at the Point of Investigation

Even with consultation at the point of reporting and tighter guidelines at the point of screening, not all cases investigated by CPS will be substantiated. Those that are not would be prime candidates for referral to an alternative service delivery system. Another group that might be referred to an alternative system would consist of cases that have been substantiated but are not serious enough to keep open for CPS intervention.[24]

If these families are referred to the alternative system and apply for services, they should receive priority, both on the grounds that they would have the greatest need for protective/preventive services and on the grounds that referring such families would help give legitimacy to the alternative system as the preventive arm of CPS. But clearly there are dangers in this approach, too. Reporters may be tempted to refer families to CPS and to do their utmost to get them screened in and investigated in order to get the families priority in the alternative system. This outcome would unduly tax the resources of CPS and would force families to go through the CPS system just to get services. Another danger is that if the alternative system became known in the community as a place to which CPS referred families, the system's services might be stigmatized, making families hesitant to use them.

For these reasons, it makes sense to adopt a mixed or alternating intake rule for the alternative system, maintaining a balance of CPS-referred and self- or community-referred families. For example, if resources were extremely limited, 50 percent of slots might be reserved for CPS referrals and 50 percent for self-referrals or community referrals. If resources expanded or the alternative system gained credibility in its own right, then a community might shift to a majority of self- and community referrals and a minority of CPS referrals.

Unresolved Issues

In evaluating the case for narrowing, we have made progress in considering the two main scenarios for narrowing and how a "narrowing plus" scenario might be implemented. However, a number of important issues remain unresolved. Taken together, these issues make it clear that narrowing alone cannot solve the problems of CPS today.

One important concern is the degree of uncertainty about the cost implications of the types of changes discussed here. The following questions remain unanswered:

1. If a narrower definition were implemented, what percentage of the current CPS caseload would remain in CPS, and what are the likely costs associated with these cases? What percentage of the current caseload would no longer fall under the mandate of CPS, what would be the cost savings to CPS associated with losing those cases, and what would be the costs to serve those who wanted services in an alternative service delivery system?
2. How many families currently in CPS could have been served earlier if voluntary protective/preventive services had been available? What are the costs (and cost savings) associated with these types of families?
3. If voluntary protective/preventive services in the community did exist, what percentage of families they served would be

diverted from CPS intervention and what share would be families never seen by CPS?

There is also uncertainty about the level of risk associated with a narrowing strategy. Excluding some cases that are now seen by CPS increases the risk that some serious cases of abuse or neglect will be missed. Since we cannot predict risk of abuse and neglect with anything like certainty, the process of sorting cases into or out of CPS is fraught with danger. When we consider that families are not always as they first appear, and that families change over time, it becomes clear that this sorting process will have to take into account the possibility that some families will be placed in the wrong group and that someone will have to discover the error and change the grouping accordingly. Changing definitions of abuse and neglect will not ensure consistent, accurate, and safe sorting of families into those that warrant authoritative intervention and those that do not.

Moreover, simply dividing cases into two groups begs the question of how the system should respond to the range of families that will be included in each group. Families for whom authoritative intervention is warranted are not all alike; nor are families that are at risk of abuse or neglect but fail to meet the threshold for authoritative intervention. Clearly, improving the ability of CPS—with or without an alternative system—to protect the children at highest risk of serious abuse and neglect and to prevent abuse and neglect in lower risk-families will require more far-reaching changes in the basic orientation of the system and in front-line casework practice.

Given these persisting uncertainties about costs, risks, and the types of responses appropriate to families' needs, it makes sense to approach narrowing, and reform of the child protective services system generally, in an incremental fashion, so that reformers can learn as they go along, and to think about narrowing as being only part of a larger, and more complex, strategy to improve child protection.

In the chapters that follow, I outline a more complex strategy for reforming CPS, one that takes "narrowing plus" as a starting point and builds from there.

Differential Response: A New Paradigm for Child Protection

Narrowing the scope of CPS, though necessary to solve some of the problems facing the system today, may not achieve an adequate level of child protection. Such efforts run the risk of not having an alternative family support system to serve those who no longer qualify for CPS but still need services to prevent maltreatment. Moreover, even under a "narrowing plus" scenario, with alternative services in place to support families, CPS would still need to identify which families required those services and to ensure that children's safety needs were met in the support agencies as well as in CPS. Recommendations for narrowing fail to specify how cases should be handled in a new CPS and in a new family support system. The challenge remains to ensure that CPS and other agencies respond to cases appropriately—to approach families in a nonpunitive way that builds on their strengths but also remains focused on protective issues. The families remaining in a narrower CPS will vary as widely in terms of their problems, resources, and needs for services as the families served outside the agency. To respond appropriately to the diverse needs of families, all parts of the system must provide a more customized response.

The new paradigm proposed here—differential response—takes "narrowing plus" as a foundation and adds several elements to build a more comprehensive strategy for improving child protection. Three elements are key. First, recognizing the diversity of families, differential response places greater emphasis on how CPS identifies the families to be served by each part of the child protective services system and how it develops case-specific assessments and service plans, in order to deliver a customized response. Second, it does not envision one agency acting alone to ensure child protection in the most serious cases, while other agencies handle the less serious cases. Instead, the differential response paradigm calls for a community-based system, in which CPS continues to play the lead role but works with the criminal justice system and with other public and private agencies to provide preventive and protective services for the full range of children in need of protection. Third, recognizing the importance of family support in preventing child maltreatment, the differential response approach calls for informal and natural helpers, drawn from families and communities, to play a much more active role in child protection, in partnership with CPS and the other agencies in the community-based system.

The new paradigm proposed here differs sharply from the current approach to child protection. It sees child protection as the responsibility of the local community, as well as the state. Accordingly, public CPS agencies that have traditionally had sole responsibility for child protection will continue to exercise responsibility but will do so in collaboration with a broad range of community partners, including formal resources such as police, other public agencies, and private agencies, and informal sources of help such as neighborhood associations, congregations, and families themselves.[1]

In a differential response system, the relative responsibility of CPS and the community will depend on the seriousness of the particular case and the need for authoritative state intervention. For the highest-risk cases, those for which authoritative intervention is warranted to assure children's safety, CPS will exercise primary responsibility, drawing upon other community providers as needed. For example, in cases of sexual, or other criminal, assault against a child, the police will be involved as co-investigators. In cases involving substance abuse, the police may be involved, especially initially, as they often come across abuse and neglect in the course of an investigation or arrest; but other community partners, such as substance-abuse treatment programs and public health agencies, will play a more active role, sharing responsibility with CPS. In lower-risk cases, if parents are willing to participate in services on a voluntary basis, a public or private community-based service provider will take the lead role, and CPS itself will not be involved unless the circumstances of the family change to require more authoritative intervention.

These allocations of responsibilities between CPS and other community agencies are not static. An apparently low-risk case may turn out to be high-risk after all, or a family's situation may deteriorate over time. Conversely, a case initially thought to be high-risk may prove not to be so, or may improve over time. Thus, differential response places high value on the ability of workers, both in CPS and in community agencies, to assess families' needs on an ongoing basis.

This chapter sets the differential response paradigm in the context of the paradigms that have historically dominated child protective services, outlines its key features, and then uses initiatives in Missouri, Florida, and Iowa to illustrate some of those features.

Paradigms for Child Protective Services

Two main paradigms have dominated child protection in the United States.[2] In the latter part of the nineteenth century and the first two decades of the twentieth, child abuse and neglect was seen as a *social problem,* and child protection was part of a larger child-saving movement. This movement peaked during the Progressive era and regained some influence during the New Deal but became dormant for much of the 1940s and 1950s. In the 1960s, with the rise in concern about the "battered child syndrome," child maltreatment was viewed instead as an *individual problem.* Following a medical model, child abuse was situated in the psyche, character, or family background of the parent, and the appropriate response was seen to be diagnosis and treatment by a qualified professional. Since the 1960s, perceptions of child abuse have shifted somewhat. No longer is it seen as a condition or behavior falling within the realm of physicians. Rather, it is now seen as coming within the purview of social workers, psychologists, psychiatrists, and other helping professionals, but even so, the dominant model continues to be one of child maltreatment as an individual problem.

Another important dichotomy concerns the basic orientation of the system. At times, the goal of child protection has been *child rescue;* at other times, the goal has been *family support.* These competing goals are not neatly tied to one paradigm or the other. During the years when child abuse and neglect was seen as a social problem, the system alternated between attempting to rescue children and attempting to support families. Similarly, although more recently the dominant approach has been to see child maltreatment as an individual problem, the pendulum continues to swing from child rescue to family preservation and back again.[3] Nevertheless, child rescue has tended to assume greater importance when child abuse is seen as the result of parental failings, whereas family support has been more likely to dominate when child maltreatment is seen as a social problem.

Neither the social nor the individual paradigm has proved adequate to address the problem of child abuse and neglect. Nor has either the child-rescue or the family-support orientation succeeded in achieving adequate child protection. An unacceptably large number of children remain at risk for abuse and neglect. The reason for these failures is clear: neither paradigm, neither orientation, is sufficiently differentiated to address a nonunitary and multidimensional problem, and one that is not static over time. Children are placed at risk in a wide range of situations, and multiple individual and social problems are likely to coexist in a family at any given time. Furthermore, families' situations change over time; new problems may emerge or assume greater importance while others may subside.

Although social workers have long recognized the diverse and changing nature of the families referred to CPS, the tendency of the system overall has been to place families in categories and to standardize the way in which CPS responds to them. As we have seen, there has also been pressure on the system to identify one type of intervention to achieve child protection, whether child rescue or family support. These pressures are understandable. Child abuse and neglect, particularly as seen in cases that become public, raises strong feelings of horror, outrage, and grief. We demand action to make sure that the maltreatment will never happen again, and for this reason we are willing to invest a substantial degree of power and authority in the system. But we do not want to see this power used inappropriately, with parents wrongly accused and children removed from their homes, only to be maltreated in foster homes or group homes that were no safer. Such abuse of authority can inflict irreparable damage on children and on families. Therefore, as a society we also demand that the child protection system make sure that this, too, never happens again. In short, we demand nothing less than a perfect system— one characterized by neither underintervention or overintervention.

These high expectations have pushed the system to find *the* solution to child maltreatment. However, the truth of the matter is that there is no single or absolute answer to child abuse and neglect. Child maltreatment has many causes and characteristics, and families' problems are not one-dimensional, nor do they remain constant over time. For this reason, the differential response paradigm calls for a customized approach to child protection that will vary case by case and, for each family, over time. A basic tenet of this approach is that child protection is not the exclusive preserve of CPS. To meet the diverse, multiple, and changing needs of families, CPS will have to draw upon and form closer partnerships with a wider range of resources in the community, including other public agencies, private agencies, community members, and families themselves.

The Diversity and Complexity of Families Referred to CPS

The principal underlying assumption of the differential response paradigm, and the one that sets it apart from previous approaches to child protection, is its recognition of the diversity and complexity of families that come to the attention of child protective services. Families are seen as diverse in terms of the problems they present, the strengths and resources they possess, and the services they need. Families are complex in that they are likely to have multiple problems, both individual and social, that place their children at risk. Another source of complexity is that families' problems, strengths, resources, and needs change over time.

The idea that child maltreatment comes in many forms is not new, of course. It is customary for statutory definitions to distinguish between physical abuse, neglect, sexual abuse, and emotional abuse; depending on the jurisdiction, other categories (such as educational neglect or medical neglect) may be specified as well. Although the literature on child abuse and neglect has been criticized as being "as replete with myths as it is with well-validated facts,"[4] research has provided some evidence on the correlates of the various types of child maltreatment and on how various types of cases respond to particular treatments. Keeping in mind that more than one form of abuse or neglect may be present in a family at one time and that the type of maltreatment may also change over time, we nevertheless can draw some useful conclusions from the research in this area.[5]

We know, for example, that there is a higher incidence of both physical abuse and sexual abuse in families in which a man is present who is not the biological father of the children. The heightened risk posed by a nonrelated man was noted by historian Linda Gordon in case records dating from the late 1800s, and it remains the case today.[6] We also know that there is a much higher incidence of reported maltreatment—in particular, neglect—in families who are poor or low-income.[7]

We also know a good deal about the connections between mood-altering substances and child maltreatment. Alcohol has long been linked with physical violence in the home, while heroin was traditionally associated with neglect. More recently, crack cocaine has posed a dual threat to children, as mothers' usage has been linked to neglect, while usage by boyfriends of mothers has been associated with physical injury to both mothers and their children.[8]

We also know something about the types of treatment that are or are not likely to be effective in promoting child safety in different types of cases. For instance, in cases of physical abuse it is important to clearly communicate to parents norms about physical discipline of children; it is also important to relieve or provide alternate outlets for stresses that may provoke instances of abuse. In cases of sexual abuse, treatment for the victim is extremely important in aiding the child's recovery, and a combination of prosecution and treatment for the perpetrator is likely to be warranted. In cases of neglect, a combination of tangible support and social support is likely to be needed; in many instances, the parent will also need some form of treatment (such as for substance abuse or depression) if she or he is to benefit from the support being provided.

Although we do not know as much as we would like about the etiology of different types of child maltreatment and the effectiveness of different interventions, problems arise not so much from a lack of knowledge as from the occasional failure to take what we do know into account. Service plans for families all too often call for one generic form of treatment, such as a parent support group, rather than for packages of services tailored to the particular type(s) of abuse. This means that in some cases the treatment may be inappropriate to the case.

Even when treatment plans do take the type of abuse into account, they are rarely responsive to a family's unique set of problems and needs. Social workers typically have a limited range of services from which to choose, so service planning usually amounts to choosing the best item(s) from the menu of available services rather than developing unique service plans from scratch.

Rarer still are individually prescribed treatment plans that draw upon the unique resources of each family. One of the legacies of seeing child maltreatment as an individual problem is that families who come to the attention of child protective services are seen as incompetent and dysfunctional. Even extended family members and members of the family's social network are suspect, often seen as having potentially contributed to the problems the family is currently experiencing. Early research on child maltreatment suggested that a high proportion of abusive parents were themselves abused as children.[9] Seen in this light, a child's grandparents, uncles, or aunts would be unlikely to be called upon by child protective services to help improve the functioning of the child's family and prevent further abuse and neglect. Similarly, to the extent that child maltreatment is understood as a social problem, and one that is concentrated in impoverished neighborhoods, there is a tendency not to see a family's network of friends and neighbors as helpful resources. Yet in even the most dysfunctional families and most disadvantaged neighborhoods, there are likely to be some resources that can be called upon to help prevent a child from being abused or neglected, and parents, family members, and communities typically have strengths as well as weaknesses. Seeing families as heterogeneous opens up the possibility of drawing upon family and community resources. This is not a totally new idea for social workers, but it represents a new approach for the child protective services system.

Features of the Differential Response Paradigm

A Customized Response to Families

The first defining feature of the differential response paradigm is its emphasis on a customized response to families. This feature poses challenges for administrators and social workers alike. To successfully implement a differential response approach, administrators must give social workers more discretion and autonomy. Yet doing so creates risks that social workers may not meet society's demands of the child protection system. We want a high standard of protection and are willing to grant the system a good deal of authority to achieve it, but we do not want this authority abused or children or families harmed in the process.

Differential response also poses a challenge for social workers and other frontline staff. They will need to have stronger casework skills than they do at present, skills that make them adept at identifying families' needs. Moreover, they will have to be able to use those skills on an ongoing basis.

A Community-Based System of Child Protection

A second defining feature is that the differential response approach does not envision one agency acting alone to ensure child protection but rather calls for community-based systems of child protection. Such community-based systems do not exist today, but they are essential if CPS is to provide a more customized response that better meets the diverse needs of families.

The challenge here will be to give frontline staff greater access to services that cross not only agency lines but also the boundary between public and private. The barriers to collaboration are many. Efforts to build community-based systems will be hampered by fiscal and caseload pressures, bureaucratic inertia, and risk aversion. They will also be constrained by features of the existing child and family services system. Categorical funding streams encourage agencies to draw a sharp line between those they will and will not serve. The assumption that clients are better served by specialized professionals rather than generalist workers will also be a problem, as will a history of "turf" battles, rivalries, and mistrust among agencies now expected to collaborate.[10] Overcoming these barriers is essential if agencies are to work together in a community-based system. For example, frontline staff will have to be able to access substance-abuse treatment for parents in cases involving drug or alcohol use.[11] The issue involves more than having enough places available, in programs that can accommodate parents; it involves having a place available at the moment a parent is ready to take it. In a child and family services system that is fragmented and categorical, this is a problem that poses challenges for both administrators and social workers.

The pathway to reform—how to get from today's CPS to the community-based systems of the future—will undoubtedly vary community by community, and thus cannot be identified with certainty at the outset. Given the high stakes involved in child protection, this uncertainty means that efforts to build community-based systems must proceed incrementally. It also means that individuals participating in the reforms will have to be given an active role in planning and implementing the change effort. If community-based systems are to succeed in this kind of "bootstrapping" reform, those participating must have the opportunity for what political scientists call "learning by doing," so that they can make course-corrections as the reforms proceed. Moreover, those leading and supporting the reforms should also take the opportunity to learn from the participants, through a process that Charles Sabel has called "learning by monitoring." Learning by monitoring requires that state planners be open to learning from localities, and that administrators be open to learning from frontline workers as the reforms proceed.[12]

A Larger Role for Informal and Natural Helpers

Recognizing the importance of family support in preventing child maltreatment, differential response also foresees a larger role for informal or natural helpers—members of the community or families themselves—than has traditionally been the case in the American child protective services system. Previous approaches have tended to discourage reliance on informal sources of support. The differential response approach neither dismisses the potential importance of family support in preventing child abuse and neglect nor views it as a panacea. Rather, the role of family support, and the resources called upon to provide that support, would vary case by case, depending on an assessment of the family's needs and the resources available to meet those needs.

Some general guidelines and caveats should guide the use of family support in child protective services.[13] The first general guideline is that many families at risk of abuse and neglect could benefit from family support, but that the quality of support probably matters more than the quantity. Prior research has established that families that are abusing or neglecting their children are more likely to be socially isolated, in that they have less contact with their extended family and with social networks of neighbors, friends, co-workers, and so on.[14] There are, of course, exceptions to this trend. Research on families in which children died of child abuse, for example, found that many of these families had extensive networks of family and/or friends, but that these networks were not effective in preventing the abuse because their method of being supportive was to not confront the parents about their abusive behavior.[15]

A second general guideline is that the type of support should depend on the characteristics and situation of the family. Developing a supportive relationship with parents who are abusive or neglectful is not always straightforward, and it can be very demanding to maintain such relationships. Some families may have violated community norms to such an extent that it would be unrealistic to expect a community member to offer support. Others may have burned their bridges with family and friends, or may have networks that would be more stressful than supportive.[16] Still others may have personal characteristics that at least temporarily prevent their forming relationships except with more formal sources of support that are better prepared to deal with resistance and other limitations such as substance use, mental illness, or retardation.[17] Individuals vary a great deal in how they approach service providers and in the extent to which they are able to engage in a relationship with providers.[18]

Another general guideline is that the use of informal sources of support will depend on the resources available to the family. Many children at risk of abuse or neglect live in neighborhoods that are so impoverished that contacts with community members, even where available, may not be very effective at providing support that will relieve parental stress.[19] Deborah Belle's research with low-income single-mother families suggests that their networks offer less support than do the social networks of more advantaged women.[20] The reason seems to be that among the low-income single mothers, network members have fewer other resources and call upon network members to do more. For example, they ask network members to provide material assistance such as help with child care rather than supportive assistance such as advice about childrearing.

The extent to which informal helpers will confront rather than condone abusive and neglectful behaviors is particularly likely to be an issue if there are family or community norms about, say, corporal punishment or the supervision of young children that conflict with the values of the broader society, or if the informal helper sees confronting abusive behavior as interfering with her or his supportive role.[21] Trained social workers, too, have trouble balancing authority with support, but they are more likely to be aware of this tension than are informal helpers from the family or community. If informal supports are used to monitor and confront abusive and neglectful behaviors, these expectations must be made explicit both to the helper and to the parent being helped. Informal supports will often need support themselves, so that they can maintain the helping relationship in the face of this and other types of tension.[22] Informal and formal support efforts are best seen as complementary; the effectiveness of both sources of support will surely be enhanced if social workers can coordinate their efforts with those of informal helpers, and vice versa.

This feature of the new paradigm—the need to forge linkages with informal sources of support—represents a major change for both administrators and frontline staff. Difficult though it may be for CPS agencies to coordinate their efforts with those of other public and private agencies, it will be even more difficult to establish links with informal sources of support. Organized groups of natural helpers, such as tenants' associations or churches, may be disinclined to establish formal working relationships with CPS. It is likely to take diligent efforts by local CPS administrators to break down the distrust and hostility with which many community members currently view the child protective services system.

An even greater problem is that most informal sources of support are not organized into groups. Informal and natural helpers will, more often than not, have to be organized on an ad hoc basis, as they will by definition vary from case to case. Much of the burden of identifying and pulling together informal sources of support will fall to the frontline worker. This task, too, represents a tremendous change in case practice.

Moving to Differential Response

Although the new paradigm poses tremendous challenges for CPS staff and others who will be called upon to play a greater role in child protection, these challenges are not insurmountable. In several states and localities, the child protective services system is moving toward a differential response paradigm. The experience of three states—Missouri, Florida, and Iowa—illustrates the progress that can be made. Missouri is providing a differential response to families referred to CPS, distinguishing those cases that require an investigative response from those that can be approached in a less adversarial manner. Florida, which has also been providing a differential response to families referred to CPS, is taking the reform process a step further by increasing the involvement of family and community partners in the child protective services system in selected communities. Building partnerships at the community level is also central to Iowa's reform efforts.

Missouri

Missouri began its experiment with differential response reform in 1994.[23] Missouri's child protective services system—the Division of Family Services—is in many ways typical of CPS agencies nationwide. Like most states, Missouri has been the subject of lawsuits alleging that its child protective system was not operating in compliance with state and federal requirements. Like other states, it has had cases that have gone horribly wrong, including that of Michelle Gray, the child who died of malnutrition despite having been reported to Missouri CPS on numerous occasions.

In 1994 Missouri received 52,774 reports of child abuse and neglect, covering some 86,000 children. Only 36 percent of these reports came from mandated reporters (as compared to the national average of 53 percent), about an equal share (39 percent) came from nonmandated reporters, and fully 25 percent were made anonymously. Only 22 percent of the reported cases were substantiated. Although there was little difference in the substantiation rate of reports from mandated versus nonmandated reporters, the substantiation rate for reports made anonymously was markedly lower, only about 10–13 percent.

Missouri's system is state-administered, and its operations have historically been fairly centralized. All reports are made to a statewide Central Registry Unit, which forwards them to the appropriate local office for investigation. The local office is required to initiate most investigations within 24 hours and is expected to complete them within 30 days. The compliance rate with these two timelines was only 70–75 percent in 1994. These compliance levels may have been related to the fact that because of lack of funding the agency was then operating with only 70 percent of its staff positions filled; caseloads were about twice as high as recommended by national guidelines. Lack of funding and weak unions have also affected the pay of CPS staff. According to one of the social work unions, there are only three other states in which social workers are paid less. As a result, few social workers have higher degrees, and turnover is high.

In 1994 Missouri's state assembly passed legislation moving the state toward differential response. The impetus for the bill was consensus among liberals and conservatives on two key points. First, it was agreed that Missouri's CPS agency was intervening too aggressively in many families that should instead have been offered services on a voluntary basis. Second, the system was failing to intervene aggressively enough in the most serious cases, in part because the system was overwhelmed with large numbers of nonserious cases and in part because CPS was treating serious and nonserious cases alike.

Despite this consensus, advocates were wary, and they pushed to have the reforms introduced on a pilot basis. As a result, the reform bill, S.B. 595, authorized the Division of Family Services to pilot a dual-response system in five areas, with the possibility that the reforms could subsequently be extended statewide. The underlying principle of the legislation was that "families coming to the attention of the Division of Family Services have different intervention needs and require flexible responses from the division and the community in order to protect children and meet the needs of the family."[24] To meet these different needs, the legislation delineated two different types of responses from CPS. For families in which it was likely that a crime had been committed or that an alleged perpetrator or a child would have to be removed, the response would take the form of an investigation by CPS, in cooperation with law enforcement. For all other families, a new type of response—called a Family Assessment and Service Delivery response—would be made.

The primary distinction between the investigation and the assessment response is that only the investigation is mandatory. A family referred for assessment may refuse it, although at that point the family can be switched to the investigation track if the risk to the child seems serious enough to warrant an involuntary investigation. Further, a family can be switched to the investigation track at any point if new evidence is uncovered to indicate that the case is appropriate for investigation rather than assessment. The two responses differ in content as well. An investigation focuses on evidence-gathering and always includes a referral to law enforcement, although law enforcement may decline to participate. Because child safety is paramount, investigators must follow specific rules such as viewing the child within 24 hours with or without the parents' consent. An assessment, on the other hand, is designed to be a process in which parents are partners right from the start. Thus, an assessment worker does not view the child before speaking with the parents if there are other means (for example, talking with the child's teacher) of confirming that the child is all right. Only investigations can result in a perpetrator's being listed in the state's Central Registry.

Although reports continue to be made to the statewide hotline at the Central Registry, the pilot areas are responsible for deciding which response to provide on a case-by-case basis. Pilot areas were given extensive training and provided with standardized checklist forms for this purpose. Both the training and the forms emphasized that cases should be assigned to the new assessment response unless a compelling reason existed to do an investigation, and the pilot areas got the message. In the first month of the reforms, 85 percent of the cases across the five pilot areas were being referred for assessment and only 15 percent for investigation; in subsequent months, 70 to 80 percent of the cases have continued to be referred to the assessment track. Parallel coding by the Central Registry was more conservative; they would have assigned only 60–65 percent of the referrals to the assessment track had they been responsible for the decision. Nevertheless, the local coding is thought to be going well, and as the reforms proceed, local reporters are being told that they may call in reports to be assessed directly to the local office, rather than to the statewide hotline. Thus, one of the unintended consequences of the reforms may be that screening of reports will eventually shift to the local areas. This shift makes sense, since the local areas are better positioned to assess each family's situation in the context of local resources and services. It also allows local CPS staff to build relationships with reporters over time and to improve communications between reporters and CPS.[25]

From the perspective of the CPS offices involved in the pilot, the reforms have required changes in organization as well as in case practice. Typically, offices involved in the pilot have assigned a supervisor to "screen" reports (previously the statewide hotline staff did this) and to decide whether to assign them to an investigator or an assessment worker. These assignments have worked fairly smoothly. In one St. Louis office participating in the pilot, for instance, 75 percent of the first 240 cases were referred for assessments in the first three months, and only 3 of these cases subsequently had to be switched to investigations. Given the importance attached to investigative training, volunteers for the new assessment positions were drawn from the ranks of current investigators. A further organizational change is that every effort is now made to have the assessment worker continue as the family's social worker, rather than moving the case after assessment. This change stems in part from the emphasis in the assessment and service response on responding quickly, providing services right from the start, and then ending CPS involvement as quickly as possible.[26] There is no evidence that the reforms are saving money, since the assessment response is as labor- and time-intensive as the investigation response, but that was not the intended goal. The goal was to provide a more flexible and more appropriate response to families.

It is too soon to predict the long-run effects of these reforms. The data collected thus far suggest that the screening decisions are not perfect—some families referred for an assessment have to be switched back to the investigative track, and vice versa. This outcome was to be expected, however, since family needs change over time. More data are needed to determine whether the primary goals of the reforms are being met, that is, whether children are being better protected, and families are being approached in a more helpful way.

Florida

Florida has undergone a number of CPS reforms in recent years. Some have been notable successes; others have been spectacular failures.[27] The most successful, and most emulated, reform was its development of team investigations of sexual abuse cases in the early 1980s. Local teams worked together to gather the evidence needed to prosecute perpetrators while minimizing the need for multiple interviews with child victims and their families. Florida's success in this area was impressive. However, the system as a whole was thought to function poorly, and the basic operations of the Florida CPS system were totally overhauled later in the 1980s, with Greg Coler as the new chief administrator. Coler imposed more state control over the system, centralizing screening, for example. He also tried to introduce a computer system to track Florida's caseload, but this initiative was plagued by mismanagement and cost overruns. In the meantime, the caseload was continuing to grow, with a surge in reports in the late 1980s. By the early 1990s, there was impetus to reform the system yet again.

In 1994 Florida's Department of Child and Family Services (CFS) received 189,000 calls alleging child abuse and neglect, of which 113,000 (about 60 percent) were screened in. Nearly half (47 percent) of these reports came from professionals, and 37 percent came from friends, neighbors, or other sources. Anonymous reports constituted 14 percent of the total and, as in Missouri, had a much lower substantiation rate (14 percent) than those from other reporters. Overall, 40 percent of Florida's reports are substantiated, a rate that is notably higher than Missouri's but in line with the average for the United States overall.[28]

Florida, like Missouri, has a state-administered CPS system, with a great deal of centralized control. Since 1988, reports have been made to a statewide hotline, where they are screened and then referred to the local areas for a response. As indicated above, approximately 40 percent of the calls are screened out at this level. Before 1993, cases that were screened in and referred to the local areas received an investigation response, which had to follow certain detailed procedures. The investigation had to be initiated and the child seen within 24 hours, and the investigation was to be concluded in 30 days. The investigator was required to interview not only the parents but also their relatives and neighbors. At the conclusion of the investigation, if the case was substantiated, the alleged perpetrator was listed in the state's Central Registry. A Central Registry listing would disqualify the person from employment involving work with children.

Florida's dual-response reforms were introduced as part of a larger reform process. As in Missouri, the aims were both to intervene more effectively in the most serious cases and to intervene less aggressively in the less serious cases. The Florida reforms also emphasized building better working relationships with communities and community partners, as well as with parents; in this regard, the reforms built on Florida's successful experience a decade earlier in building community teams to respond to sexual abuse cases. In 1992 state legislation established smaller local districts and required them to create local advisory boards. The legislation also required the Department of Child and Family Services to come up with a new plan to increase the role of communities in child protective services and to improve the relationship between the department and the families it served. Florida's dual-response legislation was implemented in 1993.

Under the reform (which served as the prototype for Missouri's), serious cases of physical abuse or neglect and cases of sexual abuse would be investigated as they had been in the past and, if substantiated, would be reported to the Central Registry. Less serious cases would no longer be investigated but instead would receive an assessment from a new Family Services Response System. Assessment cases would not be listed in the Central Registry.

Because Florida's dual-response reform occurred in the context of a larger plan devolving authority to local areas and emphasizing community and parental involvement, it gave new discretion both to local offices and to individual social workers. Local offices were to decide which types of cases would be handled as investigations and which as assessments, and local areas, in collaboration with their local planning boards, were to decide what types of services to provide to families and children. Social workers had more flexibility in their handling of cases assigned to the assessment track; for example, they were not required to interview neighbors and relatives.

Florida's reforms took another step forward when use of the Central Registry for employment screening was discontinued in 1995. This change eliminated one of the most important reasons for drawing a sharp distinction between investigations and assessments. The 1995 legislation also strengthened the role of law enforcement in investigations, so that CPS social workers were focusing primarily on assessing children's safety and family needs even in cases receiving an investigation response. For these reasons, many in Florida felt that the time was right to move toward an assessment response for all families reported for abuse and neglect, not just for the less serious cases. As a result, a single-response investigative system that had been replaced by a dual-response investigative and assessment system evolved into a differential response assessment system. Under the new Family Service Response System, assessment workers are expected to work on a case-by-case basis to identify each family's problems, strengths, resources, and needs and to develop plans for customized services.

Florida's reforms have not been problem free. The reform efforts have encountered resistance both within and outside CPS. Within CPS, many staff are skeptical about whether this latest wave of reforms will be permanent or whether it is just another swing of the pendulum. They are also fearful that they will be blamed if a child dies under the new system.[29] Staff have also expressed concern that they are not being given sufficient support to go along with their new responsibilities. To redress some of these concerns, the CPS agency submitted a plan to the legislature, which it enacted in 1997. The proposal greatly expanded training of social work staff, with an extended period of training and evaluation before a new social worker assumed full responsibility for a caseload. It also created new job classifications tied to a new, higher pay scale and eliminated the pay differential between protective investigators (and their supervisors) and other social workers (and their supervisors), which previously tended to draw the best staff into investigations and away from assessments. Under the legislation, child and family counselors (and supervisors) were upgraded to the level of protective investigators (and supervisors). Third, the bill forged closer links between CPS and Florida's schools of social work. Key components include increasing the rate of student placements in CFS and related agencies; placing more emphasis on child protection in the social work curriculum; increasing the number of CPS staff with social work degrees by hiring more staff with social work degrees (the goal is that at least 50 percent of new staff should have a social work degree within five years) and supporting more staff in attending schools of social work; and increasing links between CFS and schools of social work faculty.

Not all the barriers to reform have been internal. It has been difficult to bring in community members as partners in child protection, particularly without new funding to buy their services. In some communities there are few resources, formal or informal, to draw upon; this is a particular problem in migrant communities, for example. In other areas, informal community resources such as churches are willing to help but are hard-pressed to do so. Many prospective community partners express fears about their liability as they become more involved in child protection. Their involvement raises hard questions about accountability. If a child is being monitored by someone other than the formal CPS agency, by agreement with CPS, and that child suffers further harm, who is held responsible? Will CPS share accountability, or will community partners be left to face the public on their own?

Despite these difficulties, there have been several instances of successful cooperation between CPS and community partners. Florida's district 12 has been piloting a team approach to serious cases of abuse and neglect, with protective investigators and police officers collocated in a local agency. When criminal abuse or neglect occurs, the team responds, with the police officer focusing on investigating the crime and the social worker focusing on assessing the child and family's need for services.

Elsewhere the collaboration has gone further, with community members assuming responsibility for protective supervision or oversight of families at risk of abuse or neglect. In Florida's district 15, nurses from the county public health department are providing the initial assessment for substance-exposed newborns. These nurses, rather than CFS workers, are developing safety plans with the families and referring families to a local service provider who specializes in working with drug-involved mothers. Families are referred to CFS only if other issues of abuse and neglect arise.

Another Florida district, which includes the city of Jacksonville, has taken the use of community resources a step further. In addition to formal community partners such as health departments and schools, Jacksonville is drawing upon informal sources of support such as families' friends and neighbors. These resources are identified by the family and the social worker on a case-by-case basis. A "community safety agreement" is then developed, detailing what the community resource person will do to support the family and under what circumstances the person will recontact CFS. Stewart Wakeling, in his 1996 case study of the reforms, describes several examples of such agreements. In one case, a local housing manager agreed to keep an eye on a family living in his building. In another, a minister's wife agreed to visit a neighboring family twice a day to make sure that the child was up and ready for school in the morning and fed and doing homework at night. Those involved in such agreements say that they "empower" community members to take a more active role in protecting children, by making this expectation explicit. Although this more active protective role can sometimes involve reporting families to CFS, families said they appreciated the support of the designated community member, and that they would rather have a community member than a CFS worker provide protective oversight.[30]

The Florida reforms have drawn national attention. Missouri modeled its efforts on Florida's original two-track reforms, and other states are now interested, too. In 1995 Iowa and North Dakota began using an assessment model; in 1996 South Carolina and Virginia began implementing multitrack response systems; and other states are currently considering such reforms. Although the evidence on the Florida reforms is not all in, the one completed evaluation found greater family satisfaction, more community partners involved in cases of abuse and neglect, and better safety outcomes for children in the districts that were implementing the new differential response model.[31] These preliminary results are promising, but the challenges of changing the role of social workers in CPS and bringing new partners into the child protection system will continue to confront Florida and other states as the reforms unfold.

Iowa

The Patch Project in Linn County, Iowa, uses a neighborhood-based interagency team to deliver child protective services, along with other child and family services.[32] Though not a legislatively mandated CPS reform like those discussed above, the Patch Project transforms the operations of the CPS system in important ways. As such, it illustrates how elements of a differential response paradigm might be implemented at the community level.

The "patch" model that Iowa is using originated in Britain in the 1970s and 1980s as an effort to better integrate service delivery to children and families and to provide services on a more local level. Patch-working, as it is called in Britain, involves assigning social workers and other staff to cover a specific "patch," or neighborhood, as members of a neighborhood-based interagency team. In some areas the team combines child protection and health workers; in others, child protection and housing workers are linked. In Britain, patch-working is seen not as primarily a child protective services reform, but as a general social services reform. In Iowa, too, patch-working is best understood in the context of other service integration reforms.

The Patch Project in Linn County, Iowa, began with a federal grant that ran from 1991 to 1994. It was then transferred to the Linn County Decategorization Project and continues under that umbrella today. The link with the Decategorization Project is not accidental. Indeed, the Patch Project is very close in spirit to the work that has been under way in Iowa for several years to "decategorize" spending for social services.[33] The goal of decategorization—and the goal of the Patch Project—is to remove barriers to service integration. In the case of decategorization, the emphasis is on moving funds from categorical accounts that are earmarked for specific programs or populations into flexible funding pools that can be used to meet a wide range of problems that children and families present. Similarly, the emphasis in the Patch Project is to move workers from specialized roles in separate agencies into flexible interagency teams that can respond to diverse, complex, and changing child and family needs. Thus, the Patch Project changes service delivery and case practice in ways that complement the funding changes made by decategorization.

Another goal of the Patch Project is to deliver services at the neighborhood level. The rationale is that basing workers in the neighborhood allows them to develop and strengthen links with community-level resources, both formal and informal, that can be drawn upon to help children and families there. It is also thought that basing workers in the neighborhood helps workers gain expertise with regard to the families in the area, particularly if those families are from racial or ethnic minority groups.

In Britain a patch team typically serves an area of some 10,000 residents. Following this model, in Linn County, Iowa, the patch chosen for the project was an inner-city neighborhood of just under 10,000 in Cedar Rapids. Compared to the rest of the city and state, the area is a diverse one: 15 percent of its residents are African-American, and other racial and ethnic minorities make up an additional 4–5 percent. It is also a poor area, with nearly half the children living in single-parent families. Reflecting these demographics, the area has a higher rate of abuse and neglect reporting than the rest of the city and state. It also has a very high rate of foster-care placement, nearly 21 per 1,000 children in 1991, three times as high as the national average rate (under 7 per 1,000) that year and over four times as high as the statewide average (less than 5 per 1,000) that year.

In 1993 Iowa received 20,886 reports of abuse and neglect involving some 30,000 children. Of these reports, 31 percent were substantiated. Thus, Iowa's substantiation rate is somewhat lower than the national average but still considerably higher than Missouri's.

The area covered by the reform project was formerly served by a downtown Cedar Rapids office of Iowa's child protective services agency, the Department of Human Services. Under the Patch Project, the department instead assigned four social workers to join a local team that also included a juvenile probation officer from the court, a housing inspector from the city, a homemaker from the county, and a worker from a local community center. After 1994 other local human service workers, such as welfare workers, were added to the team. The team is based in the neighborhood, initially in a church basement and now in its own space in a brownstone.

The four CPS social workers assigned to the team handle all the CPS cases in the neighborhood, but they handle them as team members. Other members of the team, such as the probation officer or housing inspector, work with them on an as-needed basis. If one of the CPS social workers is out of the office, another team member will step in to respond to a client's needs. As one Patch client noted, "Patch is wonderful because if I call and my worker is not there, I am immediately referred to one of the other ones, who always seems willing to answer my question. That doesn't happen anywhere else. Do you know how unusual that is?"[34] The team approach also means that CPS social workers are sometimes involved as team members with families who have not been referred to CPS. Since social workers need not wait for an official report to get involved, CPS can act more proactively in some cases.

One of the most striking results of the Patch Project thus far is the extent to which workers have developed closer working relationships not just with their colleagues on the team but also with clients. Because the team is located in the neighborhood, clients sometimes drop in, a practice that was virtually unheard of when the workers were stationed downtown. For their part, social workers report that they are spending more time in their clients' homes and are more likely to see their clients informally in the neighborhood. As anticipated, social workers also report that they are better able to draw upon informal resources in the neighborhood to help their clients.

Another striking result is the extent to which the CPS workers on the team now define family problems differently. Team members are less likely to cite child abuse and neglect as their clients' primary problem and more likely to cite problems such as poverty, inadequate housing, mental illness, unemployment, and substance abuse. It seems that in focusing more on assessing clients' needs rather than identifying abuse or neglect, social workers are more likely to identify the underlying problems that contribute to abuse and neglect. Developing this more nuanced understanding of abuse and neglect is an essential step in providing a differential response.

Implementation has not been problem free. For example, social workers who are doing more proactive work and more informal preventive work have raised issues about how to count it for caseload credit. Day-to-day supervision is also an issue, since the CPS workers on the Patch team are supposed to be supervised by staff in the downtown office even though they work full-time in the neighborhood site.

Overall, however, the Patch Project has been considered a success. It has now been incorporated into the county's decategorization project and expanded to include welfare workers, public health nurses, and staff from many other child and family services agencies. The Patch Project is also expanding to cover five additional sites in Iowa, including one rural site.

There is now national interest in the patch model. Other states, such as Oregon, Pennsylvania, and Vermont, are moving forward with patch initiatives of their own, and the American Humane Association is tracking these efforts and disseminating information about them.[35] These initiatives will provide valuable information about the effectiveness of this model in other, more diverse settings.

The differential response paradigm differs from both the individual and social-problem paradigms that have historically dominated child protection. Instead of seeing child maltreatment as a unitary phenomenon, differential response sees child abuse and neglect as encompassing various types of situations of risk to children that may derive from both individual and social problems. Moreover, the differential response approach recognizes that the problems that give rise to child maltreatment are likely to be multidimensional and to change over time. Seen in this light, it is clear that a system to promote child protection cannot have one uniform orientation (whether child rescue or family support) but rather must be prepared to use a range of treatment modalities and resources to promote its overarching goal of protecting children from abuse and neglect. Further, the range of resources is unlikely to be found within the CPS agency itself; rather, CPS will have to draw upon the resources of other public and private agencies and of family and community members. In this sense, one can usefully think of CPS as needing to use a team approach, with a child protection team constituted for each family depending on the family's own needs and resources.

Missouri, Florida, and Iowa provide three examples of how states and localities are beginning to move from the current single-problem paradigms to a differential response paradigm. Missouri has implemented a dual-response system, in which the majority of cases receive a voluntary, service-oriented assessment rather than a mandatory, investigative response. Florida also implemented a dual-response system and has since moved on to a single but more differentiated response system in which virtually all families receive an assessment and service response that is provided in collaboration with formal and informal community partners. Linn County, Iowa, borrowing the "patch" model from Britain, has pioneered the use of neighborhood-based service integration teams, to link child protective services and other child and family services workers in the community.

If one thinks of child protection as having to proceed along parallel tracks—the reform of operations within CPS and the involvement of a wider range of partners in the community—then Missouri began with the CPS track, Iowa began with the community track, and Florida began with both. As its reform efforts proceed, Missouri is also moving to make reforms on the community track, particularly in St. Louis. Iowa, which began with the community track, is also moving on the CPS track, implementing a new assessment response in five pilot sites, including Cedar Rapids. And Florida is continuing to work on both tracks. These continuing efforts are being supported and tracked by the Edna McConnell Clark Foundation, which is funding community partnerships for protecting children in all three states.[36]

Ultimately these two tracks will have to converge, so that CPS and its community partners work together as one child protection system. To gain some insight into what such an integrated child protection system would look like, and how CPS could get from here to there, we turn in the next chapter to Britain, where the "patch" model that Iowa is using was first tested. In the last decade, Britain has placed special emphasis on reforming its child protective services system.

Chapter 7

Working Together: Child Protection Reform in Britain

As Missouri, Florida, and Iowa move toward a differential response system, we can visualize what the endpoint of their reform efforts might be, and what challenges might be encountered along the way, by taking a look at child protection reform in Britain, which is similar in spirit to those under way in the United States. The British case provides a longer-term view. Major reforms in child protective services introduced under the Children Act of 1989 have been carefully monitored and offer several useful lessons about the reform process, both in terms of best practices and in terms of pitfalls to be avoided.

The Development of the British CPS System

Before 1989 the British child protective services system looked a good deal like the U.S. system, though with some important differences. The development of child protective services followed a similar path in both countries, beginning with a surge of interest in child protection in the late nineteenth century and the formation of private societies for the prevention of cruelty to children. In Britain, however, government also was involved from an early date. In 1889 Britain passed two pieces of legislation specifically related to child protection and child welfare: the Prevention of Cruelty to and Protection of Children Act, and the Poor Law (Children) Act. The Prevention of Cruelty to and Protection of Children Act established criminal penalties for parents or guardians who "wilfully ill-treated, neglected or abandoned the child in a manner likely to cause unnecessary suffering or injury to health"; the Poor Law (Children) Act set out conditions under which poor children with incompetent parents would be cared for by the guardians of the Poor Law.[1]

In Britain as in the United States, progressive reformers in the early twentieth century were concerned about child safety and health, and by midcentury attention shifted to child and family welfare more generally. In Britain, the responsibilities of the state were clearly set out in postwar legislation. Together with its companion legislation the National Assistance Act, which abolished the Poor Law, the Children Act of 1948 was a "water-shed for services to needy children."[2] The Children Act of 1948 formalized government's role in child welfare, centralizing responsibility in one national government department and establishing local area Children's Committees.

As the British welfare state was built in the years following World War II, a social safety net was developed that is at once deeper and broader than that in the United States. The importance of universal health insurance provided by the National Health Service (NHS) cannot be overestimated. A broad range of social services is delivered under the auspices of the NHS. For example, the NHS funds health visitors who provide home visits to every newborn in the country and follow-up services to those at risk. Widely regarded as the "eyes and ears of child protective services," health visitors provide supervision and monitoring for high-risk cases that otherwise might be referred to CPS. Young unwed mothers, for instance, who in the United States are often referred to CPS, in Britain are monitored by local health visitors. Similarly, many disabled parents and children receive supportive services through local disability workers; this arrangement lessens the likelihood that they will be referred to child protective services just so that they can access services.

In the 1960s there was a resurgence of interest in child abuse and neglect as a distinct condition requiring intervention by the state. As interest in child protection grew, so did the involvement of the public sector. In Britain as in the United States, this public-sector concern was formalized in new legislation in the 1970s, but the thrust of the legislation was very different. In the United States, legislative efforts focused on the passage of mandatory reporting laws. In Britain the focus was on reform of the social services delivery system. The Seebohm Committee report, issued in 1968, recommended that the separate departments covering child welfare, educational welfare, mental health, day care, and home help services be pulled together into unified social services departments; it also called for more social work professionals to be based in local areas so that they could work more closely with other service providers in the community.[3] In response to this report, local social services departments were established by legislation in 1970 and began operation in 1971.

During the 1970s responsibility for child protection increasingly shifted to the new social services departments.[4] The departments quickly developed specific policies and procedures for handling child protective as well as other social services referrals. Cases of child abuse and neglect were now identified separately from other cases and were handled differently, often by specialist social workers. As increased attention to child protection resulted in more referrals and in more of these referrals' being identified as potential cases of abuse or neglect, the child protective services cases began to dominate social services departments, crowding out other referrals in which child abuse or neglect was not an issue. As a result, the social services departments began to focus more exclusively on child protective cases.

The trend toward a narrower focus on child protection was very similar to that in the United States, but with the important difference that in Britain a clearer mandate existed for the social services departments to continue to provide social services for other children and families. In line with the Seebohm report, the social services departments were mandated to provide preventive services to those at risk, as well as services to those who had already experienced abuse, neglect, or other problems. Although families in need of preventive services were seen as a lower priority, they could not be excluded altogether.

The child protective services system is much more decentralized in Britain than in the United States. Child protective services, like all other social and educational services, are administered and delivered by local authorities.[5] These authorities, of which there are 109 in England alone, cover fairly small areas; in rural parts of the country, a local authority may span several small towns, while larger cities (such as London) are divided into several local authorities. Local authorities are bound by regulations and guidelines promulgated by national bodies such as the Department of Health and are subject to inspection by national entities such as the Social Services Inspectorate and Audit Commission, but they are not part of a national department or agency. Thus, each local authority, though bound by national legislation, regulations, and guidelines, operates its CPS system autonomously.

The British local authorities provide a useful infrastructure for the development of community-based systems of child protection. In the United States, in contrast, the local CPS divisions have less autonomy, and their jurisdictions do not always coincide with those of other agencies. For example, it is quite common for a CPS catchment area to be different from a local mental health or public health catchment area, and for all of these to be different from local school districts. These different area boundaries make coordination across agencies more difficult, since a local CPS office first has to establish which agencies are responsible for which areas and indeed often has to contend with several different offices of a given agency. Further, it means that there is no one individual or body that is expected to be accountable for the operations of all these agencies in the local community in the way that a local authority in Britain is.

Entry to child protective services in Britain begins with a report to the local authority's social services department. The dominant concern in British child protective services has been physical abuse, and in more recent years sexual abuse. As we saw in Chapter 2, however, many referrals to child protective services concern neglect, although neglect constitutes a smaller share of reports than in the United States. As in the United States, families reported for neglect are more likely to be headed by a lone parent and living on low incomes.

Although Britain does not have mandatory reporting laws, most referrals are made by professionals.[6] Schoolteachers are the most common source of referrals (23 percent), followed by health professionals (17 percent), household members and other nonprofessionals (17 percent), social services professionals (13 percent), police or probation (12 percent), and other types of reporters (12 percent); only 6 percent of reports are made anonymously. Reports are screened, and about 25 percent are screened out. Many of the screened-out reports are handled by the social services department as voluntary family support cases; others may be referred to another agency for services or may receive no response at all. The reports that are screened in as protective services cases are investigated by a social worker, who visits the family and contacts others who might have knowledge bearing upon the case. Although parents are very fearful of losing their children during the investigation, in fact only 4 percent of children reported to CPS are removed from their families by court order as a result of CPS involvement.[7]

An important element of the British system is the child protection conference, which is held at the conclusion of the investigation for about 25 percent of cases originally reported to CPS. The purpose of the conference is to assess the level of risk to the child, develop a plan to protect the child, and decide whether to list a child on the area child protection register. The area child protection register, unlike central registries in the United States, is not meant to be a listing of all children who have been abused or neglected (nor is it meant to be a list of perpetrators). Rather, the register is intended to be a list of children who have been abused or neglected *and* who are in need of continued interagency services to prevent further abuse or neglect. Functionally, however, the register is fairly close to a complete list of all children who have been victims of serious abuse or neglect, since most of this group will need services from more than one agency.

In 1995, just under two-thirds (63 percent) of cases for whom a child protection conference was held were listed on the register. Nationally, an average of 32 children per 10,000 were listed on a child protection register in 1995, but this rate varies a great deal by local authority district. The London borough of Islington had the highest rate of children on the register in 1995 (85 per 10,000), while the suburban London area Kingston Upon Thames had a rate nearly ten times lower (9 per 10,000).[8] This variation across areas has been fairly constant over time: areas that are more likely to register children today have also been more likely to register children in the past. Jane Gibbons and her colleagues surveyed the registration practices of local authorities in 1991 and identified operational differences that help explain some of the variation. For instance, some areas list children who have died as a result of abuse or neglect, while others do not. Sociodemographic factors also account for some of the variation in listing rates. Cases are more likely to be listed on the register in areas with high unemployment rates, high rates of public housing tenancy, and high rates of unwed motherhood. Cases are also more likely to be listed in areas where services are reported to be in short supply.[9] These latter findings suggest that areas with a high demand for services and/or with a short supply of services may be using the register as a "passport" to services, in much the way that CPS involvement is sometimes used as a gateway to services in the United States.[10]

The Impetus for Reform

Child maltreatment, and the CPS system's response to it, have been the subjects of increasing attention and concern in Britain since the 1970s. Public awareness of children in need of protection, and dissatisfaction with CPS, have been heightened by a series of cases in which children died or suffered severe maltreatment and in which official inquiries found that the child protective services system was at least partially to blame. Between 1973 and 1994 there were 43 public inquiries into cases in which a child died or was severely maltreated.[11] Although in some instances the deaths or other injuries were deemed to have been unavoidable, in a majority of cases the ensuing investigation determined that CPS had failed to protect children adequately even when it had been warned that a child was at risk. CPS, however, was not the only agency judged at fault. Although CPS is clearly viewed as the agency with lead responsibility for child protection, in Britain other agencies are seen as sharing in this responsibility. Accordingly, the inquiries examined the actions of other agencies and individuals in the community, and in many instances they found them wanting as well. In particular, those reviewing the cases condemned the lack of interagency coordination and communication among professionals coming into contact with children at risk of abuse or neglect. The inquiries called for changes not only within CPS but also across other involved agencies.

In response to these inquiries, local authorities formalized their procedures for dealing with reports of child abuse and neglect. Child protection registers and child protection conferences were adopted in 1974 following the recommendation of the inquiry convened to look into the death of a child named Maria Colwell. Registers were designed to ensure that local authorities identified children in need of protection and paid special attention to them; conferences were designed to involve other agencies in this process.

Another consequence of the greater public attention to child protection, and of the numerous inquiries that faulted social workers for failing to intervene aggressively enough to protect children at risk, was that the CPS agencies adopted a more interventionist stance with families reported for abuse or neglect. Individuals and agencies in the community, too, reacted to the climate of the times by reporting more families to CPS and by advocating that CPS intervene more aggressively with those families. Thus, at the same time that CPS intervention was becoming more formalized, the threshold for that intervention was lowered. As a result, more families were brought into the system and conveyed deeper into it.

By the mid to late 1980s, however, the tide had turned; there were increasing concerns that the system was intervening in the lives of too many children and families, and not always to good effect. There were several well-publicized instances of child protective services removing children from their families without good cause, damaging the children and the families in the process. Several scandals involved unfounded allegations of sexual abuse and unwarranted removals of children. The last straw for many was the removal of 121 children from their families in a town called Cleveland in northeast England from February through July 1987, on grounds of suspected sexual abuse following diagnosis by two pediatricians. By the following year, all but 23 of the children had been returned home. This episode aroused strong feelings. One member of Parliament wrote a book alleging a conspiracy on the part of local social services and health personnel.[12] Other observers likened it to the witch-hunts that swept Salem, Massachusetts, in 1792.[13]

The official inquiry into the Cleveland case, conducted by Lord Justice Elizabeth Butler-Sloss, concluded that social workers had acted too hastily. Thus, rather than being criticized for insufficiently protecting children, CPS was now being criticized for intervening in too authoritarian a manner. In this respect, the Cleveland inquiry report was different from the 40 or so that had preceded it, but like the earlier reports it emphasized the importance of interagency cooperation. Butler-Sloss pointedly stated that "no single agency . . . has the preeminent responsibility in the assessment of child abuse generally and child sexual abuse specifically."[14] She called upon agencies to work together. She also called upon CPS agencies to work together with parents; for example, she recommended that parents be included in the child protection conferences.

Cleveland, unfortunately, was not an isolated incident. Reports of sexual abuse continued escalating into the 1990s, as did CPS agencies' sometimes overly aggressive responses and the public backlash against them. In an infamous case that occurred in February 1991 (before the new Children Act came into effect), social workers investigating allegations of sexual abuse removed nine children from their homes in the Orkney Islands, off the coast of Scotland, and flew the children to foster homes on the Scottish mainland.[15] Although the children were returned six weeks later, it was widely believed that the damage done to the children, their families, and their small island community was irreparable. Moreover, the removal of the children was deemed by many to have been unwarranted in the first place. The inquiry, for the most part, validated these concerns, finding that the social workers had "acted too hastily in determining to remove the children and failed to take time to pause and think before embarking on precipitate action."[16]

Although public attention was increasingly focused on child sexual abuse cases, the majority of cases continued to involve physical abuse and neglect, and there was dissatisfaction about the handling of these as well. Children who had been reported for abuse or neglect were in many instances not faring well, as evidenced by a series of cases in which children were left at home and suffered further maltreatment; but there were instances of apparent overintervention as well. In some cases, children were maltreated after being removed from their parents, as a result of being placed in dangerous foster homes or institutional settings. There was also research that pointed to the risk that children placed in care, even if they escaped abuse or neglect, would all too often simply drift in a state of emotional limbo, neither returning to their own homes nor entering new permanent homes. Placements tended to be poorly planned, and once children were placed, social workers' attention turned to other children at more immediate risk.[17]

A common theme in the government inquiry reports and other reviews leading up to the reforms was that many children seen by child protective services had multiple and complex needs, and yet services for them, when they existed, were fragmented and uncoordinated. There were also shortages of services to support children in their own homes. In the face of these shortages, priority for support services was given to children identified by child protective services, with the result that these services became inaccessible to the non-CPS population. This situation led to some cases' being referred to CPS in order to gain access to services. At the same time, services that had previously been seen as providing family support came to be seen as services for abusive and neglectful families; as a result, many of the services became stigmatized and parents were less willing to use them. The services themselves changed as well, as their mission shifted. For example, many of the local child care centers converted themselves into centers for families referred by protective services. Although these family centers often served an extremely useful role, the child care places that had previously been available to the community were lost. Moreover, the new family centers often lacked the capacity to serve families on a voluntary basis, so only a narrow range of families in the community benefited from them.[18]

Not surprisingly, then, there was a perception that the provision of preventive services, which might have helped stop situations of family stress from escalating to abuse and neglect, was inadequate. In child protection, as in other areas, one can usefully identify three categories of preventive service that might be provided to prevent abuse or neglect. Primary preventive services are those offered universally. In Britain, this category would include the home visits to newborns funded by the NHS and the child care provided by local authorities or local schools or local family centers if these services were universally available. Secondary preventive services are those offered to families identified as at elevated risk of abuse or neglect but who have not actually abused or neglected their children. In Britain, this category might include child care or family centers for young parents, lone parents, or those living in disadvantaged areas. Tertiary preventive services are offered only to those who have already abused or neglected their children and who are at risk of doing so again. In Britain, this category would include a range of services, including child care or family centers, so long as the criterion for receiving the service was substantiated abuse or neglect.

From these examples it can be seen that the distinction among the various levels of prevention is not so much in the type of service but rather in the criteria for entry. Child care, or a family center, could be part of a universal primary prevention program or a secondary prevention program for at-risk groups. The reason for limiting a service such as child care or family centers to child protective services cases is not that it is appropriate only for them; rather, it is a way of rationing scarce resources. Concern about this type of rationing, and the scarcity of primary and secondary preventive services, provided an important impetus for the 1989 reforms.

The Children Act of 1989

The Children Act of 1989 had two principal goals. First, it aimed to improve the response to children in need of protection, providing better protection to children without subjecting their families to unwarranted and unhelpful intervention. Second, it aimed to improve the response to children in need of preventive services, a group referred to in the Act simply as children in need.

For children in need of protection, the Children Act sought to achieve a better balance between child protection and family privacy. The Introduction to the Act explained:

> The Act seeks to protect children both from the harm which can arise from failures or abuse within the family and from the harm which can be caused by unwarranted intervention in their family life. There is a tension between those objectives which the Act seeks to regulate so as to optimise the overall protection provided for children in general.[19]

Thus, the law spells out provisions for the protection of children as well as provisions for "protection from protection." The law emphasizes that state intervention is warranted only when a positive decision is made that intervention will promote the child's well-being and will be in the child's best interests; finding that a child has been abused or neglected is not sufficient.[20]

To protect families further from unwarranted intervention, the law narrows the criteria for listing children on the child protection register. Effective in 1991, the law prohibited the use of "grave concern" as a criterion for listing children on the register. This was a dramatic change for the British CPS system; before 1991 grave concern had been the reason given for fully half of all listings. Beginning in 1991, child protection conferences had to find either that a child had in fact already been abused or neglected, or that in the judgement of professionals, the child was at elevated risk of abuse or neglect.

The effect of this change can be seen in the registration data shown in Table 7.1. The table shows that registration rates were trending upward from 1988, the first year that national data were collected, until 1991, at which point the registration rates abruptly turned

Table 7.1 Children registered in England, 1988–1995

Year	Numbers listed			No. per 10,000		
	All	Boys	Girls	All	Boys	Girls
1988	39,200	—	—	36	—	—
1989	41,200	19,700	21,400	38	35	40
1990	43,600	21,100	22,500	40	38	43
1991	45,300	22,200	23,100	42	40	44
1992	38,600	18,800	19,700	35	34	37
1993	32,500	16,000	16,400	30	29	31
1994	34,900	17,400	17,400	32	31	32
1995	34,954	17,600	17,200	32	31	32

Sources: 1988: Jane Gibbons, Sue Conroy, and Caroline Bell, *Operating the British Child Protection System: A Study of Child Protection Practices in English Local Authorities* (London: Her Majesty's Stationery Office, 1995), chap. 2; 1989–1995: Department of Health, *Children and Young People on Child Protection Registers* (London, 1996), table 1.19, p. 33.

around.[21] There is a sharp fall from 1991 to 1992 and another from 1992 to 1993. The timing of the fall reflects the fact that grave concern was not eliminated as a category until October 1991 and that this change may not have been implemented in a timely manner by all authorities.[22]

The Children Act of 1989 also spelled out for the first time the responsibility of local authorities with regard to children in need of preventive services. It established a new category, child in need, which it defined as follows:

A child is in need if:
(a) he is unlikely to achieve or maintain, or have the opportunity of achieving or maintaining, a reasonable standard of health or development without the provision for him of services by a local authority under this Part [of the Act];
(b) his health or development is likely to be significantly impaired, or further impaired, without the provision for him of such services; or
(c) he is disabled.[23]

The law also imposed several new requirements on the local authorities with regard to children in need and the provision of preventive services. First, it required local authorities to take steps to identify children in need. Second, it established "the general duty of each local authority to provide a range and level of services which are appropriate to the needs of children in their area who are in need so as to: (a) safeguard and promote the welfare of such children; and (b) so far as is consistent with that aim, promote their upbringing by their families."[24] Third, it established a requirement for local authorities to provide primary and secondary preventive services, "to prevent children in the area from suffering neglect or ill-treatment."[25] Fourth, it required the local authorities to provide two specific preventive services. Local authorities were required to provide family centers for any children in their area "as they consider appropriate"; they were also required to provide day care for children in need and were authorized to provide day care for any other children.[26]

For both groups of children—those in need of protective services and those in need of preventive services—the Act placed greater emphasis on "working together." An important goal in this regard was to improve outcomes for children by promoting closer collaboration between parents and CPS. The measures to increase parental rights and responsibilities were intended not just to safeguard families from overintervention, but also to help CPS work more productively with parents to promote better outcomes for children. British reformers reasoned that since most children referred to child protective services would remain with their parents, effective intervention would have to involve the parents to be successful in the long run.

British research on child maltreatment has highlighted the extent to which parents reported for various types of abuse or neglect tend to share a parenting style that is "low on warmth, and high on criticism."[27] Moreover, this parenting style seems to be associated with long-term problems for children. Many children experience isolated instances of maltreatment or periods of inadequate care, but serious harm is more likely to arise when these problems are lasting and cumulative. Thus, engaging the parents and providing support services for them would have to be an important component of reforms to build a more effective child protection system.

A related goal of the Children Act reforms was to promote teamwork among professionals from various agencies and various parts of the system as well as nonprofessionals and other community members. Researchers had noted a curious pattern with regard to collaboration between CPS and other parties.[28] At the start of a case, someone other than CPS was always involved in making the initial report, and it was quite common for individuals outside CPS to be involved in the initial stages of the investigation. However, as the case proceeded, involvement of individuals outside CPS became less and less common, and over time CPS was increasingly likely to be operating on its own, even though the family might still need and be receiving services from other agencies. The progression would be reversed only if the case was reported again, at which point the cycle would begin anew. Clearly, building better links with individuals outside CPS, and maintaining those links over time, would have to be an essential element of the CPS reforms.

These two goals—promoting partnerships with parents and teamwork with professionals and others in the community—received a great deal of attention. It is noteworthy that the government's official guidelines to the Children Act, as well as the reports on its implementation, are titled "Working Together."

What lessons can be drawn from the British experience of working together subsequent to the Children Act of 1989? What are the implications for reformers in other countries? Three observations are particularly striking.

First, there is now a good deal of evidence from Britain that outcomes for children are better when parents and CPS work together. However, such collaboration is difficult to achieve. One of the primary vehicles for ensuring that parents and CPS work together is the child protection conference, which is convened at the conclusion of the investigation to assess the level of risk to the child, to decide whether the child's name should be listed on the register, and to develop a protection plan. According to the Working Together guidelines, parents are supposed to be invited to participate in the conference, a dramatic change in practice; before passage of the Children Act parents were virtually never included in these conferences. This change was slow to come about. In a study conducted shortly after the Children Act went into effect, June Thoburn found that even in local authorities that said they valued parental participation, nearly a third of parents were not attending these conferences.[29] More recently, this record has improved, and parents are now routinely attending their children's conferences, although, as we shall see, parents' experiences are not uniformly positive.

With regard to collaborating with other agencies, recent research by Christine Hallett suggests that both clear procedures and a specific mechanism for working together can be very helpful in promoting interagency coordination. In the cases she examined, Hallett found that local workers appreciated clear procedures spelling out how to coordinate their efforts with others involved in CPS cases. She also found that the child protection conferences were generally thought to be extremely helpful in promoting cooperation across agencies. Hallett also identified several barriers to successful coordination, most importantly, resource shortages and resource allocation schemes that tended to reinforce agencies' tendencies to keep resources for their own clients.[30] Hallett and other observers have also noted that more work is needed with particular professionals such as general practitioner physicians to encourage them to give higher priority to participating in child protection conferences.[31]

"Patch-working" has proved to be another useful technique for building closer links between professionals from different agencies, and between professionals and families. In patch-work, CPS social workers are part of a local team that includes workers from many agencies. Together the team focuses on one particular neighborhood, or "patch." Patch-working is valued because it builds relationships both among professionals and between these workers and families in the area. The emphasis on local work can be seen as far back as the Seebohm report in 1968 and the establishment of local social services departments in 1971. It was also an important element of the review undertaken by a National Institute for Social Work committee in 1982. One of the members of that committee strongly endorsed patch-working as a way to draw upon more informal resources, although another member expressed reservations that it would simply be used to justify cuts in formal services.[32] Experience since then indicates that there are trade-offs involved in patch-working, and it is not seen as the right solution for all areas. A recent Audit Commission report recommended patch-working in areas of high and concentrated need to enable the local patch team to build links with community members and with community-based providers; the same report recommended a more traditional service delivery structure in areas of lower or less concentrated need.[33]

These conclusions are interesting for child protection reformers in the United States, where the procedures and mechanisms that have been found to be so helpful in Britain are generally lacking. For example, the reports of parents and social workers alike indicate that requiring a case conference makes a significant difference in getting social workers and parents to work together. The patch-working model, too, is proving useful in pilot projects in areas such as Cedar Rapids, Iowa.

What problems did the British reforms encounter? One of the greatest challenges was to involve parents in a way that was respectful and promoted partnership. Conversations with parents who have participated in child protection conferences suggest that although they welcome the opportunity to be present at the meeting, they often find it intimidating and do not participate as fully as they would like. Of particular concern to parents is that they are typically asked to leave the room for part of the meeting: "I came in there, discovered an enormous room full of people I didn't know from Adam, was introduced to them and then asked to clear off into a little room in the middle of nowhere! . . . And I thought, 'What is that? What's the point of inviting you to a meeting?'"[34]

Another problem with the implementation of the Children Act was that a large number of lower-risk families continued to be referred to CPS and to receive an investigative response. Although the Children Act set up what can be seen as a parallel track (under section 17 of the law), not many cases initially referred on the investigative track (under section 47) moved there. Yet there are clearly cases on the investigative track that do not need a full-blown investigation and could be served in a more family-friendly way. Only 15 percent of the cases initially referred to CPS, and only about one-third of the cases investigated, are listed on the child protection register. Many observers have concluded from these statistics that a large share of the cases currently being investigated by child protective services could be served in a less adversarial way.[35]

Another continuing problem is that families who are not referred under the guise of child protection do not always receive much in the way of social services or support. Nor do families referred for protection but found not to be in need of it. Local areas have continued to give priority to children in need of protection and do not see how they will be able to act otherwise unless new resources are allocated or unless the number of children in need of protective services declines. Inspections of eight local authorities over the period 1993–

1995 found that cases of children in need are seen as low priority unless they meet the definition of abuse or neglect; not surprisingly, then, referring agencies continue to believe that it is necessary to refer a child as in need of protection in order to get services for the child.[36] Thus, many children in need are still not being served, and services to prevent abuse and neglect are still in short supply.[37]

The concerns being voiced in Britain echo the concerns of reformers in the United States. But the difference is that Britain, as result of its earlier reforms and its more fully developed welfare state, has at least some of the infrastructure that might help solve these problems. It also has something of a head start—and some momentum on the road to reform—having begun the process in 1989. The British reformers are now taking another step forward in the reform process, moving beyond the Children Act.

Beyond the Children Act

In June 1995 the Department of Health reported the results of 20 research studies tracking the status of children in need of protection, and the operations of child protective services, in the four years since the implementation of the Children Act in 1991.[38] The same publication issued new guidelines for local social services departments to enable them to fulfill their mandate under the Children Act.

The overall message of the new guidelines is that since the vast majority of cases reported for abuse and neglect are not ultimately judged serious enough to list on the child protection register, child protective services should use a "lighter touch," approaching those families in a less authoritarian and more sensitive manner. The research also raised the questions of why these families were being treated as cases of abuse and neglect when in fact they were not, and why children were not being provided services when they met the definition of children in need set out in the Children Act and were being nominated as such by someone in the community or by their own families.

Moving beyond the Children Act and implementing the new guidelines poses challenges for local administrators and for social workers. For administrators, a major challenge is to figure out what share of their child protection caseloads might be handled instead as children in need of preventive services, to identify the services they might require, and to shift resources accordingly. This cannot be done by child protective services on its own. Rather, it requires a concerted effort across local agencies, because the most radical changes will involve children in need and services for them. Britain's Audit Commission, in its 1994 report on coordinating community child health and social services for children in need, has laid out one vision of how a reformed system for children in need of preventive services might come about.[39] The Audit Commission recommends that each local authority, in conjunction with voluntary agencies and with input from consumers, develop a children's strategy plan, detailing the roles of health, education, and social services in meeting the needs of children in the local area. Such a plan would include provisions for specific services, such as family centers and family support services. It would also include a plan for diversion of some families from targeted social services for children in need of protection to more universally available services for children in need. To make this plan a reality, each area would have to redirect resources from the existing protective services to fund new or expanded preventive services. And indeed, some areas are doing this. One manager I spoke with in a London local authority, for example, explained that in his area, family support cases made up about a third of his social workers' caseloads, with other children in need served on a voluntary basis by specialist workers providing services to homeless families, disabled children, and so on. Nevertheless, the demand for services to children in need continues to exceed this area's capacity, and so the area's interagency child care committee is discussing ways to broaden services to families with children in need.[40]

The other challenge for both administrators and social workers is to introduce a lighter touch into casework practice. Evidence from local authorities that are proceeding along this path suggests that social workers find the opportunity to provide a differential response to families rewarding but also very difficult. As one social worker said, "You have to make decisions and do your assessment, whereas before you could hide behind the procedures."[41]

The new approach offers more opportunity for flexibility and discretion but also feels more risky: "The security of the old route was reassuring. Although I agree that having more flexibility is a good thing, I'd like permission for it to be spelled out. If anything goes wrong, I think they are going to point the finger at me and my manager."[42] Interestingly, then, social workers and administrators do not want to see the process become too informal and discretionary, because the responsibility and resultant accountability would then become too great for an individual social worker and manager to bear. This tension has pushed local authorities in the direction of establishing new protocols and new procedures, spelling out which cases should be treated with a lighter touch and how these cases should be handled. With these new protocols, cases that previously would have been referred to the police are now being handled by CPS, and cases that would have been handled by social services departments as protective are now being handled as family support cases.[43]

At the same time, CPS administrators are trying to intensify the focus on assessing families' needs, as well as the risk of abuse or neglect. Training for CPS workers is now emphasizing not only how to identify whether a child has been abused or neglected, but also how to identify what services a child and family need. This training is starting to have an effect on practice. A local manager used the following case as an example of the shift in practice. A woman called the office saying that she was at the end of her tether and had just hit her nine-year-old child with a broomstick. Although the child had been injured, and the case passed the threshold to be screened in for a protective investigation, the duty worker and manager decided to treat the case as a voluntary family support case, because that was the type of intervention they thought this family needed.[44]

Another innovation, as local authorities move beyond the Children Act, is the use of "network meetings." A network meeting pulls together the various parties involved in a case, including the parents, local authority staff, and agency staff, to discuss the child's situation and to develop a plan for services. In this respect, the meeting is like a child protection conference, but with an important difference in focus. The purpose of a child protection conference is to confirm whether a child has been abused or neglected and to decide whether to list the child on the local register. At a child protection conference, the discussion of the child's needs and a plan to meet those needs is usually of secondary importance; in fact one study found that child protection conferences spent on average less than 10 minutes at the end of the meeting discussing the plan of services for the child.[45] In a network meeting, in contrast, the child's needs, and a customized plan for services to meet those needs, are the primary focus. And the perspective of the network meeting is explicitly collaborative; the emphasis is on identifying what each member of the team, including the parents, will do to help provide the services that the family needs.

According to social work staff in one London local authority, the response of parents to these network meetings has been positive:

> There are a lot more network type meetings now. These are low-key meetings with all parties involved with the family, including the family themselves, discussing what the issues are and drawing up some kind of agreement as to who is going to support the family and how. The advantage is that parents do attend, they respond to that low-key approach, they appear to be more willing to participate in a discussion of that kind, and they appear to feel more part of the decision-making process, not being told this is what is going to happen.[46]

Compared to the child protection conference, the network meeting represents a step forward in creating a forum in which parents can participate on a more equal footing.

A further step in this direction has been the introduction of "family group conferences." The family group conference, which originated in New Zealand in the late 1980s, is a forum in which family members, identified by the child and parent, come together and take primary responsibility for making a plan to protect the child. This model has been piloted in several British local authorities and is under consideration by several more. Family group conferences convened under the British model consist of four stages.[47] In stage one, the case is referred to an independent coordinator (not a CPS worker), and the family and coordinator agree who should be invited to the meeting. In stage two, the coordinator convenes the meeting and asks the professionals to tell the family about their concerns about the child. The professionals then leave the meeting so that the family can plan in private. In stage three, the family members meet with the coordinator to develop a plan to protect the child, including a backup plan in case the original plan fails. In stage four, the professionals rejoin the meeting, and the parties try to come to agreement about the plan and about what resources will be provided by the parties to the plan. If the family's plan will adequately protect the child, the plan is accepted and the meeting is adjourned. If the plan is not adequate, and an adequate plan cannot be agreed, then the case may move to a more formal proceeding, such as a child protection conference or a court hearing.

It is apparent from this brief description how different these meetings are from the traditional child protection conferences in Britain, and from typical case conferences or case review meetings in the United States. In the family group conferences, families play the lead role, and it is the CPS workers and other professionals who are asked to leave the room for part of the meeting. Although the evidence is not yet in, proponents of this model argue that it represents an important change in the way that CPS workers and parents approach one another, and one that will help build partnerships between them. Family group conferences may also help strengthen and empower families, increasing their capacity to protect their children in the long run. Another benefit noted by children who have participated in family group conferences is that these meetings sometimes provide the impetus to bring in a family member who has been absent for a time (a father or an in-law, for instance) and to re-engage this person in the child's life. This, too, can provide lasting benefits for children.

Britain's latest reforms are similar in spirit to those being undertaken in parts of the United States. British social workers' description of parents' reaction to the lighter touch is reminiscent of what social workers in Florida and Missouri say about their new assessment response. The intent is to see parents as partners in their children's protection rather than as adversaries, unless the severity of the abuse or neglect makes that impossible. Another point of commonality is the focus on assessing children's and families' needs and strengths, in addition to investigating the risk of abuse or neglect.

However, the context in which reform is occurring is very different. Britain has a greater infrastructure of community-based services, including some provided by local social services departments, health departments, and other providers. Britain also has a more fully developed set of procedures for coordinating those services on an area and case-by-case level. As a result, British reformers have been able to adapt their child protection conference into a new forum—the network meeting—to coordinate service delivery for families of children in need of preventive services, and this experience in turn seems to have made local areas more open to the idea of trying family group conferences, in which family members play not only an active but a leading role. In the same way, area planners in Britain, in seeking to improve service delivery for children in need, already had a forum in which to develop their children's strategy plans. Such an infrastructure is lacking in most parts of the United States, as are mechanisms that could be used or adapted to coordinate services across agencies.

Britain is clearly moving toward what many reformers in the United States think of as the endpoint of CPS reform. This is the point where the two tracks of reform—improving services for children in need of protection and building new preventive services for children in need—converge so that individuals and agencies in the system work together to provide better protection for children. Crucial to this outcome is the need to change frontline practice, the way CPS workers and workers in community agencies approach families, other agencies, and informal sources of support.

Chapter 8

Changing Frontline Practice

The preceding chapters have outlined a new paradigm for child protective services and illustrated some of its features in reforms under way in the United States and in Britain. What are the implications of this new paradigm for the social workers who staff the front lines of the child protective services agencies that have traditionally had responsibility for child protection, and for workers in the community-based agencies that will now be part of communities' response to children in need of protection? What can states, counties, and localities do to bring about the needed changes in practice? This chapter addresses these questions.

Implications of the New Paradigm

The differential response paradigm for child protective services differs sharply from the current approach to child protection. It calls for public CPS agencies to develop partnerships with a broad range of community agencies, such as police, schools, and other public and private agencies, as well as informal sources of help such as neighborhood associations, congregations, and families themselves.

In a differential response system, the extent of CPS as opposed to community responsibility for a particular case will depend on the seriousness of the case and the need for authoritative state intervention. For the highest-risk cases, those for which authoritative intervention is warranted to assure children's safety from serious harm due to abuse or neglect, CPS will exercise primary responsibility, but in partnership with other community providers as appropriate. In lower-risk cases, if parents are willing to participate in services on a voluntary basis, a community-based service provider, from a public or private agency other than CPS, will take the lead role, again drawing on other community partners as appropriate. These assignments will need to be reviewed constantly by social workers in CPS and their community partners. A case that at first appears to be low-risk may turn out to be high-risk after all, or the family's situation may deteriorate over time. Conversely, a case that is initially thought to be high-risk may turn out not to be or may improve over time.

The new paradigm for child protection has five major implications for frontline practice in CPS and in community partner agencies.

1. CPS workers will have to be prepared to handle cases that are more serious and more resistant on average than those in the current mix.
2. Because cases served by the community-based partner agencies will be at greater risk of child abuse and neglect than the typical families served by those agencies today, community agencies will have to play a more active role in confronting issues of abuse or neglect.
3. Both CPS and the community partner agencies will have to provide a more customized response to families.
4. In both sets of agencies, workers will have to screen and assess cases on an ongoing basis and in partnership with family and community members.
5. CPS and other agency staff will have to work in closer partnership with each other, other service providers, community resources, and families themselves.

A Greater Share of High-Risk and Resistant Cases in CPS

A primary goal of the new paradigm for child protection is to ensure that CPS handles only the most serious cases, those most in need of authoritative state intervention. This means that CPS workers' caseloads will be composed of a greater share of difficult cases than today, and a much greater share than a decade ago. These cases are more difficult in at least three respects.

First, the material living conditions of the children and families are worse, and inevitably disheartening to social workers. Often the situations are also frightening; social workers going into dangerous neighborhoods and dealing with parents who have the potential for violence may well fear for their own safety. Social workers also worry about their potential liability when they are unable to provide adequate oversight and services to high-risk families. Many CPS workers cite the changed caseload as a major cause of low morale and high turnover. In the words of one Michigan supervisor, "What we are asking workers to do is maintain high caseloads on high risk families . . . workers are getting more and more frightened . . . we are not going to be able to keep quality PS [protective services] workers."[1]

A second way in which these cases are tougher is that the families are in general more resistant, so that the work of engaging parents in identifying and solving problems is more challenging. This resistance takes numerous forms: active resistance (such as hostility to the social worker), passive behaviors (such as withdrawing or keeping silent), flight (such as canceling appointments or not answering the door when the social worker comes to visit), and avoidance (such as denying that the problem exists, lying, or changing the subject).[2] Even very resistant families can be reached by good casework practice—practice that is focused on working to reach agreement with the client about the nature of the problem and the goals of the intervention; but such work takes time and patience, as well as a high level of skill.[3]

Third, the families in these cases are more likely to have multiple problems that require a range of services beyond a CPS worker's direct control; the worker can document a need for services but cannot access them. The resulting frustration is a recurrent theme in conversations with social workers and supervisors. One social worker in Missouri recited a list of services that her clients needed but that she could not get for them, and then concluded, "here I am but I'm not able to help you, but I've invaded your presence, I've invaded your home, separated your family, and there is nothing here for you."[4] The extent to which social workers can or cannot control the resources needed for the job also affects the level of stress they experience and the effectiveness of their service delivery.[5]

The proposed CPS reforms will result in even more dramatic changes in the caseload and will require even more far-reaching changes in practice. For example, with the softest half of the caseload shifted out of the system, the current proportion of cases involving criminal abuse or neglect may double, to as many as one in five. Such a change will mean more cases involving serious injuries to children and recalcitrant parents. It will also require social workers to spend more of their time working with police and prosecutors. This will entail a culture change for social workers, who are accustomed to seeing themselves as helping professionals allied with the health and education professions, rather than with the criminal justice system.

In terms of the types of issues families present, it is likely that a higher proportion of cases remaining in CPS will be drug-involved, so social workers will need to have more interaction with substance-abuse treatment programs and will have to become more expert in this area themselves. Similarly, there will be a larger share of domestic violence cases—cases in which there is abuse of an adult spouse or partner as well as abuse or neglect of a child—and workers will have to become more knowledgeable in this area as well.

The reforms may also provoke something of an identity crisis for social workers as they struggle to define their roles as helping professionals in an agency that is specifically designed to exercise state authority vis-à-vis parents.[6] The importance of authority in child protective services casework practice has been acknowledged by scholars and practitioners for at least fifty years.[7] In 1946, when casework theorist Henrietta Gordon set out to describe child protective services, the authoritative and involuntary nature of the intervention was the defining theme. Gordon's description neatly captures the distinctive characteristics of child protective services:

First, service must be initiated by the agency; since the application or the referral is a complaint of neglect or abuse, the individual who needs the help is not asking for it.

Second, the individual to whom help is being offered is not free to decide that he does not want the services of the agency.

Third, the agency cannot withdraw the service only because the parent has refused or is unable to take help.

Fourth, should the parent or guardian be unable to improve the condition while the agency sees it as one that endangers the children, the agency must bring the matter to the attention of the court with recommendations for proper care.[8]

Modern-day social workers might disagree with Gordon on the first point, as some individuals do come forward on their own to request help, but otherwise the description applies as well today as it did in Gordon's time. However great the emphasis on working with parents and developing mutually agreed-upon plans for services, the bottom line in child protective services is that intervention is mandatory so long as the issues of abuse or neglect have not been resolved.[9]

Although the problem of the appropriate use of authority in child protective services has proved intractable in the past, it is not necessarily insurmountable. Indeed, it may prove easier to define social worker roles when the role of CPS itself is defined more narrowly and more clearly. Today too many CPS workers use the breadth of the CPS mission to avoid making direct statements to parents about the allegations of child abuse and neglect and the mandatory nature of the intervention, instead falling back on vague offers of services to help the family. This evasiveness is not helpful to the family, but it is common when workers are uncomfortable with the use of authority.[10] When CPS intervenes only in cases in which authoritative intervention is warranted, social work practice will have to change accordingly. For example, at initial contact it will have to be standard practice to give parents a clear explanation of the reasons for CPS involvement and an explicit statement of their rights and responsibilities.

So far we have considered mainly the formal authority vested in CPS by society. However, social theorists have long distinguished two types of authority: formal or constituted or social authority, which derives from one's office or role in society; and informal or inherent or psychological authority, which is earned by an individual by virtue of his or her wisdom, knowledge, leadership, or other attributes.[11] CPS workers not only need to learn how to handle their formal authority appropriately; they also face the challenge of translating that formal authority into informal authority.[12] The best way to overcome resistance in involuntary clients, including abusive and neglectful parents, is to engage them in an agreement as to the nature of the problem and the goal of the intervention. Although CPS social workers ultimately have the power to make major decisions about children's lives—because of their constituted authority—they will have failed if they have to resort to using this power. Social workers cannot be in the home 24 hours a day; to be effective in the long run, they must exert influence so that parents themselves provide better care and protection for their children. To accomplish this, social workers need informal authority, which can be developed only by building relationships with parents that are characterized by openness, mutual respect, and trust.

A More Active Role for Community Agencies in Confronting Child Abuse and Neglect

The implications for frontline practitioners in community agencies that will now be partners in child protection may be even more far-reaching than for those in CPS. In a differential response system, community-based agencies will be responsible for protective oversight of some cases of child abuse and neglect that under the old system would have been supervised by CPS. As a result, community-based providers will have to be more able and willing to address issues of abuse and neglect with their clients. Many do not now see this as part of their professional role; rather, they see their mission as providing support to families and children. Even when they do have the skills to identify child maltreatment, they are often reluctant to confront it.

Massachusetts' experience with contracting out child protective cases is instructive.[13] The Massachusetts CPS agency, the Department of Social Services (DSS), historically assigned a very small share of its protective cases to private nonprofit agencies. In 1989 DSS increased the share it contracted out to about 15 percent of its protective caseload. At the same time, it sought to standardize the services provided by the 63 community-based "partnership" agencies with which it was contracting for CPS investigations, assessments, and case management. DSS instructed the agencies to handle these cases in accordance with the state's regulations, policies, and procedures, and DSS provided training on this material for staff from the agencies. In principle, DSS provided oversight on the cases managed by the partnership agencies, as it did on cases managed in-house. However, the sheer number of agencies made oversight more difficult. The Boston regional office, for example, was responsible for monitoring 5 DSS area offices, which carried the majority of the cases, and 20 partnership agencies, each of which carried only a small share of the region's cases. From the perspective of the regional office, providing oversight for the private agencies was more trouble than it was worth. The new program was problematic from the agencies' perspective as well, since it required them to take on an authoritative role that many saw as in-compatible with their mission. Yet the agencies felt that they had to participate, since otherwise they would lose funding from the state.

The partnership program, then, met with resistance on both sides, and many were relieved when the state legislature drastically cut back the contracting in 1991. Reasoning that child protective services could be delivered more efficiently and with greater accountability in-house, the legislature limited contracting out to two categories of cases: cases involving conflicts of interest, and cases involving populations that the state agency had historically had difficulty serving (this category in-cluded special-needs children as well as children from some ethnic minority groups). As a result, the share of the caseload contracted out fell to about 3 percent, and the number of agencies with such contracts fell to 18.

In 1994 a child was very badly injured in a case managed by one of the remaining agencies with a protective contract. The investigation by DSS, which resulted in termination of the agency's contract, points to several problems that may arise when community agencies are asked to play a more active role in child protection. The investigation re-vealed that in spite of the training and orientation they had received, the agency's staff felt ill prepared to handle these protective cases; moreover, they were not comfortable with the protective mandate and apparently had accepted it only so that they would not lose their state funding. One gets the sense that their hearts just weren't in it. One also gets the impression that the agency's frontline staff just didn't have enough experience—and know-how—to tell when a case of abuse or neglect was escalating into a life-threatening situation. The investiga-tion also confirmed that frontline practice in the agency was poor; workers were failing to make home visits, court appearances, and other contacts essential to monitor and promote children's safety. The agency did not provide adequate supervision and monitoring of its workers. Nor did the agency have enough oversight and assistance from DSS.

The Massachusetts experience with using community-based agen-cies for child protective services work suggests that community-based providers will need to engage in this work voluntarily, and also that they will need fairly extensive training and support. Tighter manage-ment and oversight are needed as well. Partnership agencies should be monitored as closely as CPS agencies. The Massachusetts case indicates that a large part of the problem was that the partnership agencies were outside the CPS management structure. Whereas local CPS office directors were held accountable for key performance indicators at monthly management meetings, the partnership agency directors were not. Bringing partnership agency staff into the existing management and accountability system would make a difference.

The families who are diverted from CPS or who apply for services voluntarily will need a wider range of preventive services than are available today. Therefore, community-based providers must know which services are effective in preventing child abuse and neglect and how best to deliver them. Family support programs, such as family centers and social network programs, offer a patently sensible and sometimes successful approach.[14] However, using family support programs to prevent child abuse and neglect has turned out to be more complicated than it first appeared. As one director of a community-based program explained, family support agencies and CPS have trouble even agreeing on what preventing child abuse and neglect means:

> . . . what CPS defines through their legal mandate as child abuse and neglect is not the very same definition that people generally in family support use. When you ask them, do they do programs to prevent child abuse, almost exclusively everyone will say yes, we do programs to prevent child abuse. When you really get to the question of the real issues of mandated monitoring, scrutinizing authority, then there is a real pulling away, backing up and saying, no, no, no, we don't do those things.[15]

It is not at all straightforward to reconcile the original mission of these programs—to provide universal, nonstigmatized, and voluntary services to struggling families—with a heightened focus on issues of child abuse and neglect. This tension, which was also apparent in the Massachusetts contracting case, suggests that it will not be easy for community-based agencies to develop and deliver preventive programs for families identified as at risk of abuse and neglect.

A More Customized Response to Families

The most challenging implication of the new paradigm for frontline practice derives from its emphasis on a more customized response to families. Both CPS and the community-based agencies will have to offer a range of responses, many of which will involve other partners from public and private agencies. To provide this customized response, social workers in CPS and in its partner agencies will need more skills in assessment, service planning, service provision, and client engagement than they possess today.

The differential response model will also demand more autonomy and discretion on the part of frontline staff. In order to provide customized services, social workers—whether in CPS or in a community-based agency—will have to be free to work out with each family, on a case-by-case basis, what type of assistance the family needs to reduce the risk of abuse or neglect. Even the process of investigation or assessment will be different, since the information gathered and the sources contacted will be determined by the worker and family, case by case, rather than spelled out by the standardized procedures used today.

This will be a welcome change for most social workers and their agencies, but a difficult one. Most social workers want more autonomy and flexibility, but they also know that there is only so much they can do with caseloads as high as they are currently. Social workers also fear that they will not be given the resources to do the job and then will be blamed when something goes wrong.

CPS social workers are currently a very diverse group, with widely varying levels of training and ability. Some of those currently employed in CPS and in community agencies would not want to exercise more responsibility and discretion or would not be qualified to do so. Mechanisms must be put in place to allow these workers to opt out or to be selected out. The rest will have to receive more preservice training, more orientation when they start on the job, and more professional development and supervision on an ongoing basis. They will also have to be assigned smaller caseloads. Building relationships with parents—and with others in the community—takes time, and current CPS caseloads, of 30 or 40 or more families in many jurisdictions, simply do not allow enough time per family for the type of casework envisioned here.

Ongoing Screening and Assessment in Partnership with Family and Community Members

To provide more customized services without losing sight of children's safety, social workers in both CPS and the partner community agencies will need to be more skilled at screening and assessment, to see these as ongoing processes rather than as onetime steps in the life of a case, and to be prepared to undertake these processes in collaboration with family and community members. This will be a challenge for workers in CPS. CPS agencies have put a great deal of effort into developing an array of risk-assessment tools,[16] but only recently has attention been paid to designing family assessments that focus on child and family needs and strengths as well as child safety.[17] Such assessments require clinical skills that must be taught to the full range of social workers who have responsibility for cases and then supported through ongoing supervision and professional development.

For frontline staff in community agencies, the type of screening and assessment demanded will be an almost entirely new area of responsibility. Staff in community agencies do have some familiarity with the current definitions of abuse and neglect and frequently make decisions about reporting cases to CPS, but these decisions are not necessarily accurate, and the criteria for entry into CPS in a differential response system will be different from the current definitions. The new paradigm will require decisions about when it is appropriate to serve a family without involving CPS and when it is appropriate to report a family to CPS.

Both in CPS and in community agencies, the new paradigm will require frontline workers continually to reassess the families with whom they are working. This will be a fundamental change in casework practice. Social workers handling child protective services cases weigh large amounts of often conflicting evidence and make weighty decisions in the face of uncertainty. To do so, social workers, like other human beings, use several common techniques of reasoning; these techniques help us make sense of the world, but they are also subject to error.[18] One of the most problematic techniques is the tendency to rely on first impressions and to discount evidence that flies in the face of those impressions.[19] This problem can be seen in cases in which an initial decision to keep a child at home is never overturned despite repeated reports of further harm. From the social worker's perspective, one can see how the new evidence was discounted, since it conflicted with the decision that he or she had made about the situation; but in hindsight, when a child is harmed, it is hard to understand how the social worker could have been blind to those new reports. Moreover, social workers tend to operate using a "rule of optimism," believing that through their efforts they can salvage dysfunctional family situations.[20]

A very powerful antidote to these human errors in reasoning is "double vision," that is, the ability to keep in mind alternative viewpoints about a family.[21] Another remedy is for social workers to see their assessments as tentative and to review them on an ongoing basis, by a process that Donald Schon has called "reflective inquiry in the practice situation."[22] Reflective inquiry enables social workers to update their decisionmaking in the light of new experience and information, rather than persisting with first impressions that may no longer be correct. Ideally, supervision provides a framework for reflective inquiry and double vision, but in practice, with supervisors overseeing 100 or more cases, supervisory sessions all too often focus on the minimally necessary paperwork, procedural requirements, and the like. The assessments and reassessments called for under the new paradigm will require reflective inquiry, while the emphasis on constantly reconsidering whether a case belongs in CPS or in the community track will encourage social workers and their supervisors, in both CPS and community agencies, to practice the sort of double vision that is required if families are to be reassessed on an ongoing basis.

Closer Partnerships between CPS, Community Agencies, Other Community Members, and Families

A key implication of the new paradigm is that social workers—whether from CPS or from a community agency—will be collaborating more closely with other formal and informal helpers involved with the family. Frontline workers will no longer be operating in isolation, as they all too often are today; rather, they will be part of a community-based team that shares responsibility for assessing a family's needs and for mobilizing services from an array of agencies and individuals to meet those needs.

One of the greatest challenges for social workers in CPS and in partner agencies will be to learn to work in closer partnership with families. Such partnerships are possible—and outcomes for children and families are better—when frontline workers build trusting relationships with parents based on mutual respect, honesty, reliability, and a bottom-line concern for the safety of the children.[23] Such relationships are critical in overcoming parental resistance, so that parents and social workers can work together to make progress in solving the problems that led to the child protective concerns in the first place. They are also important in the longer run. Most children referred to

CPS will receive services for only a short time and will remain with their family for the remainder of their childhood. If children are to be better protected in the long run from abuse or neglect at the hands of their parents, influencing the decisions parents make about their children and their actions toward them is essential.

Lessons from Earlier Initiatives to Change Frontline Practice

Initiatives in CPS

Two previous initiatives—one a response to federal legislation, the other a response to changes in the caseload—offer some lessons about how to change frontline practice in child protective services. The first is the implementation of permanency planning, which was required by the Child Welfare and Adoption Assistance Act of 1980 (P.L. 96-272). The second is the development of a team approach for cases of child sexual abuse, which was prompted by the sudden increase in sexual abuse referrals in the early 1980s.

The goal of the permanency planning legislation was to achieve long-term planning for children coming into contact with the child protective services and child welfare systems. The law established a set of requirements intended to prevent unnecessary placements and, for those children for whom placement was necessary, to ensure swift movement toward permanency. Chief among these were reasonable efforts to prevent placements, case plans for children in placement, and periodic case reviews for children in placement, including a dispositional review no later than 18 months after placement. Parental participation in case planning and case review was required, and the law also introduced mechanisms for external reviews by citizen panels or judges. These requirements demanded several major changes in casework practice. To accomplish these, states incorporated the new requirements into their policies and procedures, revised their case-record systems and management information systems, conducted training sessions on the principles of permanency planning, and set up mechanisms for court or citizen review of foster-care cases.

Although the permanency planning legislation had less impact than its authors would have liked, it had an effect on frontline practice in CPS (and in child welfare more generally). These changes in practice, in turn, seem to have had some effect on outcomes for children. National statistics indicate that the growth of the foster-care caseload slowed in the years immediately following the passage of P.L. 96-272.[24]

The second reform initiative, the development of a team approach for sexual abuse cases, emerged in response to changes in the caseload. In the early 1980s, as sexual abuse referrals rose dramatically, CPS agencies realized that these cases, unlike most other CPS cases, needed a criminal investigation, as well as a social services investigation, because these cases involved criminal acts that might be the subject of future prosecution. CPS workers could not conduct such criminal investigations, but neither could the police or district attorney's investigators conduct an assessment of the child's and family's need for services.

Initially CPS agencies handled the new sexual abuse cases as they had always handled the few criminal cases that came to their attention: CPS and the criminal justice authorities conducted their own, independent investigations. This approach proved to be a hardship for families, as it involved subjecting children to multiple interviews and examinations. There were also concerns that the first investigators on the scene were not responding appropriately to the full range of what these families needed, since these cases typically required both action to remove and prosecute the alleged perpetrator and action to identify and respond to the needs of the child victim.

As a result, CPS and local criminal justice investigators developed a new response to sexual abuse cases. Together they developed clear procedures for coordinating their investigations, with the goal of minimizing the trauma for children and families while attending to the full range of needs presented by each case. Many communities adopted a team approach, in which CPS and criminal justice investigators met the family and conducted the interviews together. The use of teams was at first bitterly resisted. Social workers feared that it would lead to the criminalization of child abuse, while criminal justice staff worried that adding social workers would impede their investigations. To overcome this resistance, CPS and criminal justice agencies did not just issue new policies and procedures. They also used "cross-training" to support the new collaborative approach. In cross-training, a curriculum was developed with input from both child protective services and criminal justice, and staff from both agencies were trained together. Cross-training ensured that staff received the same information and had a chance to discuss it together. It also helped build bonds across agencies, as staff had a chance to get to know each other informally at these training sessions.

Initiatives in Child and Family Services

In their review of innovative state strategies to develop more comprehensive and family-centered service delivery systems, Charles Bruner and Dick Flintrop found several instances of frontline practice models that are both more flexible and more comprehensive in meeting the range of families' needs.[25] For instance, many states, building on the early Homebuilders program in Washington state, have now implemented family preservation programs using a casework practice model that emphasizes flexible, intensive, and comprehensive services for families at risk of abuse or neglect.

Bruner and Flintrop's review suggests several elements that are essential if social workers are to exercise more discretion and provide more coordinated services for families. First, social workers must have an appropriate level of training and professionalism. Second, there must be organizational and supervisory support for social workers to exercise discretion. Third, it is important that agencies provide adequate salaries and other supports, in order to reduce staff turnover. Fourth, caseloads for both workers and supervisors must be realistic. Fifth, social workers should have access to flexible funds and to other community resources.

Earlier reforms also indicate that states that want to change frontline practice may have to make other systemic changes. Funding changes are particularly important. Iowa, for example, has been a leader in the "decategorization" of social services funding, allowing social workers to use funds more flexibly to meet families' needs.[26] Maryland and other states have moved aggressively to keep children out of expensive institutional placements, freeing funds for customized services to support families.[27]

Another systemic change that can support changes in frontline practice is to give frontline workers more control over funds. This approach was adopted by North Dakota and Maryland as part of a comprehensive child welfare reform initiative funded by the Annie E. Casey Foundation. In North Dakota's Families First program, social workers were given control over flexible funds for the families in their caseload; up to $200 of these funds per family could be used at the social worker's discretion for food, rent or utility deposits, alcohol treatment, and the like, with up to $1,000 per family in additional flexible funding available if approved by a local board.[28] Workers in Maryland's Families First program had access to similar flexible funds, and workers and families in that program said that these funds often made all the difference between being able to keep children at home or having to remove them.[29]

How States and Localities Can Help

Several current CPS reform efforts offer lessons about what states, counties, and localities can do to help CPS and community partner agencies meet the five key challenges identified above.

A Greater Share of High-Risk and Resistant Cases in CPS

Faced with a caseload composed entirely of families for whom authoritative intervention is warranted, social workers will have to gain skill in exercising authority and confronting parents about their abusive and neglectful behaviors. Training in these areas, for frontline staff and their supervisors, should emphasize the use of authoritative intervention, which continues to be problematic for social workers.[30] More careful screening of prospective employees will also be essential. CPS agencies will have to ensure that social workers taking this responsibility are able and willing to do so. Closer supervision will also be necessary to ensure that frontline workers exercise their authority in a responsible manner.

Setting realistic caseload limits for both social workers and supervisors is a key element in improving the capacity of frontline staff to protect children at high risk of abuse or neglect. If frontline workers will no longer be going by the book and performing standardized investigations but rather making independent judgements case by case, they must have the time to gather and review all the pertinent information and to build relationships with families. Even if a state cannot allocate new funding to hire additional social workers, it can review existing caseloads to ensure that cases are equitably distributed and that only those needing services are kept open. States such as Illinois, Massachusetts, and New York have had some success in using such reviews.

States and localities can also make sure that staff are qualified to do the job and that they know what they are doing. Florida is attempting to raise the level of staff qualifications and to provide stronger preservice training, ongoing training, and professional development for social workers and supervisors. Florida is also trying to reduce turnover by providing more attractive salaries and other supports. Reducing turnover is important because the components of effective casework practice—doing comprehensive assessments, developing service plans with families, and engaging families in resolving problems—are to a large extent skills that must be learned through practice. CPS agencies that want to improve casework practice will have to do a better job of retaining seasoned social workers, who can be called upon to handle the tougher cases and to provide support and guidance to new workers.

New York City's 1996 reform plan attempts to address several of these issues.[31] The city's child protective services system was historically very troubled. CPS was not clear in its expectations about child protection, and many staff were not up to the job. For example, the CPS agency for many years had a 90-day time frame for investigators to complete an investigation and either close the case or transfer it to another social worker for ongoing services. Following the death of Lisa Steinberg in 1987, the time frame was reduced to 60 days, but the agency never enforced the rule. Indeed, the system provided an incentive for investigators to hang on to cases indefinitely, since this would keep their caseloads high and protect them from being assigned new cases. As a result, some workers were carrying very high caseloads but with many inactive cases, while others had lower caseloads but with all active cases. Meanwhile, in part because caseloads were so high on paper, many cases that needed services could not be served at all.

Nor were workers—at any level—held accountable for errors. A diagnostic report prepared as part of the 1996 reforms concluded: "Because disciplinary action against child welfare employees has been so rare, workers and supervisors have come to believe that there will be no adverse consequences for shoddy work. Conscientious caseworkers resent those who are not, and supervisors often feel helpless to enforce even minimal rules."[32] This lack of accountability placed children at risk, by allowing incompetent workers to continue on the job. It also affected the performance of the competent workers by undermining their morale and their credibility with families and other service providers.

It was not until 1996, after Nicholas Scoppetta took over the agency in the wake of Elisa Izquierdo's death, that a worker and supervisor were disciplined for errors leading to the death of a child. Disciplining these workers was a key component of Scoppetta's strategy for refocusing the attention of the agency on its core protective mission and letting staff know that they would be held accountable if they failed to provide adequate protection to children. Scoppetta also enforced the 60-day investigation time frame, insisting that workers either close or transfer any case that they had held for longer than 60 days. As a result, average caseloads dropped from 26 per investigator in February 1996 to 22 just five months later, and caseloads have fallen even further since.[33]

The New York City reform plan also spelled out a number of steps to improve the quality of the agency's investigative staff. The CPS agency now recruits at schools of social work and is taking steps to create a new job title to attract and retain staff with master's degrees in social work. It is screening new recruits more carefully and rejecting those who cannot pass a test of proficiency in the English language. The New York City agency is also strengthening its preservice training. Before the 1996 reforms, new staff received 20 days of preservice training; the curriculum focused mainly on paperwork, with no training on frontline practice. With the 1996 reforms, preservice training has been extended to 25 days and is supplemented by ongoing training for 10 months.[34] Workers now receive specific training on frontline practice skills and on domestic violence, substance abuse, and mental illness. At the end of preservice training, workers must pass a test on this material before they are assigned any cases.

The New York City case also illustrates the role that administrative reforms can play in improving an agency's capacity to hire and retain competent staff. As part of the 1996 reforms, CPS was split off from the other human services agencies and is now a separate entity, the Administration for Children's Services (ACS). The purpose of the separation was to refocus the agency on its protective mission and to make the commissioner directly accountable to the mayor for child protection, thus keeping it more prominent in city government.

One of the other benefits of the split is that the civil-service positions in ACS are now distinct from other human services positions in the city. Prior to the split, if one wanted a human services job in New York City—for example, as a probation officer—the best point of entry was through the child protective services agency, which tended to have more openings because of its high turnover. Once in the agency, a social worker could then apply for other human services jobs as a transfer candidate, taking priority over those applying from outside the system. Thus, many individuals joined the CPS agency only to gain transfer rights to move to a more desirable agency. At the supervisory level, the flow often worked in the opposite direction, but again with ill effects. One could pass the civil service exam and be placed on the supervisory list, and then by virtue of seniority be awarded a supervisory position in CPS, without ever having worked in CPS and without having any substantive knowledge of child abuse or neglect. Nor would the new supervisors necessarily stay in CPS long enough to learn about child protection, since they, too, could subsequently exercise transfer rights and move to supervisory positions in a more desirable agency. Now that the agency is separate, workers are no longer able to transfer out. Nor are supervisors without any background in child protection able to come in from other agencies, and all new supervisors now have to attend a week of training before assuming their duties.

The intent of New York City's administrative reforms is that those who are working in CPS will have selected that work, and have been selected for it, with the clear understanding and expectation that their job is to protect children from abuse or neglect. The challenges of improving the qualifications of staff and holding staff accountable for children's safety, for a system as historically troubled as New York City's, are monumental, and New York City's CPS agency still has a long way to go; but these efforts show at least the potential value of administrative reforms.

Another challenge, as the cases remaining in CPS become tougher, is for CPS workers to be better equipped to handle cases involving criminal activity, alcohol, drugs, or domestic violence. Training within CPS can be very helpful, but cross-training is essential as well, so that CPS, criminal justice, substance abuse, and domestic violence professionals are working from a shared set of principles and a common knowledge base about the definitions of abuse and neglect, the criminal statutes, and the recommended course of treatment and prognosis for parents who are alcohol- or drug-involved and for cases of domestic violence and cases involving criminal acts. Cross-training at the local level can be extremely helpful in building working relationships among professionals who will be expected to collaborate as part of their community's system for child protection. In designing such training, CPS administrators can draw on the lessons learned in developing a coordinated, cross-agency response to sexual abuse in the 1980s. They can also draw on materials developed for cross-training on substance abuse and domestic violence.[35]

A More Active Role for Community Agencies in Confronting Child Abuse and Neglect

There is no single model to draw upon for changing practice in a community agency to focus more sharply on child protective issues. One option is for CPS to offer intensive seminars for community agency staff on the types of cases seen in the child protective services system, the issues they raise, and how experienced CPS workers handle them. This training model has been used successfully with police officers taking on new responsibilities for identifying and responding to children at risk; officers who received the training said it gave them a better appreciation of their responsibilities.[36]

Cross-training is another good option. Community agency social workers can gain a great deal from participating in some CPS preservice and ongoing training. San Diego's Partners for Success program, for example, brings together staff from all the child-serving agencies in the community—CPS, police, teachers, financial assistance workers, and public health nurses—for two and a half days of cross-disciplinary training on child protection. Participants say that after the training they are more knowledgeable about child abuse and neglect and related issues such as domestic violence and substance abuse. They also learn from the training experience how they might work together on these issues in the future, and why it is important that they do so.[37]

Team-working—partnering a worker from a community agency with a frontline worker from CPS—is another way to enhance the skills and knowledge of staff in community-based partnership agencies. Team-working can also change attitudes that might stand in the way of collaboration. For example, police participating in a CPS-police partnership program in Chicago reported that "they were impressed by the complex mandates that DCFS investigators must meet; by their professionalism and commitment in doing a difficult job; by their skill in dealing with children and families; by the core of knowledge that investigators had; and by their willingness to routinely face high-risk or hostile situations alone, without back-up."[38] This kind of enhanced respect and understanding is a prerequisite to closer collaboration between CPS and community agencies who will now be assuming more responsibility for child protection.

In assuming more responsibility for child safety, community agencies will have to offer a broader array of programs aimed at preventing maltreatment. Some of the lessons from family support programs and home-visiting programs may prove helpful.[39] However, because these programs will have to be tailored to local needs and capacities, frontline staff must be prepared to learn as they go along, and administrators must be prepared to learn by monitoring them.[40]

A More Customized Response to Families

To provide a more customized response to families, frontline workers will have to be more skilled in engaging parents and in changing parents' attitudes and behaviors. This is not something that frontline workers currently know how to do. According to Paul Vincent, who oversaw fundamental reforms in casework practice in child protective services in Alabama, "workers don't know how to engage families, they are too reliant on social controls and imposing solutions on families."[41] Susan Kelly, who is leading the effort to change casework practice in Michigan, concurs, noting that "frontline workers have tremendous power, but that power has been relatively ineffective in changing parents' behavior toward their children."[42] Across the nation, CPS agencies that are trying to improve frontline practice are increasingly turning to models of casework practice that engage and empower families, and are investing substantial resources to implement these models.

The first step in bringing about this type of change in casework practice is to change the way agencies train their staff.[43] Currently, most preservice and in-service training in CPS focuses on departmental policies and procedures, abuse and neglect, child development, and family problems such as substance abuse or mental illness. Little if any time is devoted to training on frontline casework practice. If the goal is to reform practice, CPS agencies will have to provide much more training on casework practice. Agencies will need new training curricula that use role-playing and coaching to teach basic skills such as how to engage families, display genuineness and respect, attend to what clients are saying, listen reflectively, and refocus attention on the problems at hand. Florida is trying to make this kind of change with its revised training curriculum on family-focused intervention; Michigan is using a new curriculum that emphasizes empowering families to do a better job of protecting their own children. Illinois is moving in this direction with a new curriculum that focuses on teaching staff how to do relationship-based social work with intact families.

Changes in practice cannot be made overnight. In Illinois, for example, the retraining effort involves pulling every worker and supervisor out of the field, on a staggered basis, for six weeks of training in the new approach to casework. Nor can social workers' attitudes and practice be changed in a vacuum. The other staff with whom social workers interact—at a minimum, the supervisors and local office managers—must be trained too. If not, the message of the training will not be reinforced, or may even be undermined, when social workers return to the office. Getting supervisors on board is especially important, because they have the most interaction with, and influence over, frontline social workers. In its casework practice reforms, Alabama adopted the strategy of never training a worker without training her or his supervisor.[44] Illinois is using this strategy as well, while Michigan is taking this approach one step further by training its supervisory staff first.

Service delivery reforms can also support a more customized response. To provide frontline social workers with easier access to resources held by other agencies, administrators will have to develop service delivery models, interagency agreements, and working relationships that facilitate more coordinated service delivery. In doing so, administrators can draw upon lessons from the child welfare and service integration initiatives discussed above.[45] They can also draw on the lessons from experiments with "patch-working" and other geographically based case-assignment systems. Many CPS reformers view the move to patch-working as an essential element in building a differential response system, because working consistently in one community over time provides an opportunity for staff to understand better the families they are working with in the context of their communities' particular needs and resources.

There are two different models that can be used to link staff to a specific neighborhood or patch. In the out-stationing model, used in the Patch Project in Cedar Rapids, Iowa, CPS staff and community partners are based in the neighborhood. This model increases the visibility of the staff in the neighborhood and also increases their contacts with clients and collaterals. Out-stationing makes supervision more difficult, however, unless enough workers are outposted to warrant having a supervisor there as well. Another problem with out-stationing is that it may be difficult to calibrate workloads by geographic area, since reports may fluctuate over time and since the average number of reports in an area may not match easily with an exact number of workers. The experience of Cedar Rapids suggests that these problems are less serious than might be anticipated, but they must be thought through and addressed.

The alternative model, being used in Chicago's reforms, is for workers to be located in a central office but to be assigned caseloads on the basis of geographic area.[46] This model offers many advantages over out-stationing from the CPS agency's perspective. Since workers are centrally located, the geographic case-assignment model poses fewer management and supervision problems. It also allows for more staffing flexibility, since a centrally located worker, even if principally assigned cases from one neighborhood, can more readily be assigned overflow cases from another neighborhood than a worker who is located far from the central office. Depending on the city, however, it may be inefficient to base workers, and support systems such as telephones and computers, at a central office when their caseload is located in another community some distance away.

These examples suggest that there is no one right model for linking CPS workers to specific communities. The choice will depend on the geography of a given area, the distribution of its CPS caseload, and the CPS agency's ability to work out supervision and office arrangements.

Ongoing Screening and Assessment in Partnership with Family and Community Members

In a differential response system, frontline workers in both CPS and community agencies will need better skills in screening and assessment and will be called upon to use these skills on an ongoing basis, in partnership with family and community members. The challenges for CPS are particularly daunting: to move from an assessment of risk to a more comprehensive assessment of child safety and child and family needs; to shift from the use of a screening or assessment tool at one point in time to the application of a skill on an ongoing basis so that assessments can be updated as family needs change and as new information about those needs becomes available; to see assessment not as something done to a family but rather as a process undertaken with family and community members; and to broaden the segment of the workforce expected to have screening and assessment skills from screeners and intake workers to all frontline workers.

Meeting these challenges will require a major training initiative, supported by continuing professional development and quality supervision. Agencies will be able to draw to some extent upon the existing knowledge base about risk assessment and, more importantly, family assessment.[47] Material on assessment in child protective services being developed by the Child Welfare League of America could be particularly helpful.[48] The CWLA material is being specifically designed for use by CPS and community agency practitioners; thus, it is well suited for cross-training and for use by workers who will be part of cross-agency teams. Another strength of the CWLA material is that it emphasizes identifying family and community strengths and building partnerships with family and community members; this focus on the family and community and the emphasis on strengths mark a dramatic change from the way most assessments are conducted currently.

Frontline staff in community agencies will need training in these areas as well. Cross-training will prevent staff in CPS and community agencies from working at cross-purposes and giving conflicting messages to families and others in the community. It will also help build cooperative working relationships across agencies.

Closer Partnerships between CPS, Community Agencies, Other Community Members, and Families

To support frontline workers in identifying family and community strengths and needs, and working in partnership with other agencies, and with family and community members, at every step of the way, reformers can draw upon lessons from earlier social services reforms, as we saw above.[49] They can also draw upon lessons from current initiatives.

A critical partnership for CPS agencies will involve joint or coordinated investigations with police, district attorneys, and other criminal justice staff. These partnerships are working well in many areas as a result of states' experience with building such teams to respond to sexual abuse cases in the 1980s, but there is still room for improvement.

Chicago's recent experiment with CPS-police partnerships highlights some ways in which links between CPS and the criminal justice system could be strengthened. Chicago, which like many other jurisdictions pairs CPS and police investigators in cases of criminal child abuse, decided to experiment with extending these joint investigations to cases that involved noncriminal but nevertheless very serious child abuse or neglect. The results suggested that although partnering on all such cases would not be practicable or affordable, given current levels of resources, it would be worthwhile to conduct joint investigations on some of these high-risk but noncriminal cases. The Chicago experience also suggests areas in which CPS could benefit from police training, and vice versa. Those participating in the joint investigations felt that CPS investigators had much to learn from the police about interviewing techniques and investigation procedures. CPS investigators tend to do "face-value investigations," taking the information that families provide at face value without verifying critical items such as the identity and location of children.[50] Participants also felt that police can learn from their CPS counterparts in interviewing young children and identifying community-based resources for child protection.

Another reason to build closer links between CPS and criminal justice is the potential for improved sharing of information. In responding to emergency referrals, particularly at night, CPS often needs to access criminal records, to see if there might be criminal activity in the child's home and also to determine whether relatives might be suitable placement resources. However, such access is not routinely available. Chicago is now locating computer terminals hooked up to the criminal justice management information system in CPS offices, so that CPS staff will have easier access to criminal record data.

One unexpected benefit of Chicago's experiment using CPS-police teams on high-risk but noncriminal cases was that police and CPS investigators who responded as a team said they were less likely to remove children than if they had responded alone. Officers and investigators cited three reasons for this:

- They received greater cooperation as a team from parents and involved persons.
- Police felt they had better access to resources that provided alternatives to custody.
- They were able to assess situations and make decisions as a team.

There was more confidence in the decisions, and participants felt
less inclined to take drastic action because they were unsure
about the best course of action.[51]

The team approach can be extended to include other community
agencies such as schools or health departments as partners in joint
investigations or assessments. It might also be possible to involve informal partners, such as ministers or extended family members, in
investigations or assessments of cases for which these resources can be
identified at the time of the initial report.

A particularly interesting innovation in building closer partnerships
with families is the family group conference, which was introduced in
New Zealand in 1989 and is now being used in several areas in the
United States, Canada, and Britain.[52] The family group conference is
predicated on the assumption that the family, broadly defined, has
primary responsibility for deciding how best to protect its children.
The family conference is intended to facilitate that process by bringing
together the family, the CPS social worker, and others involved with
the child (such as teachers, doctors, therapists, and police) to agree on
a plan to protect the children.

The family group conference is different from the case conference
typically used in child protective services in that parents have a seat at
the table. It is also different in that professionals, including the CPS
worker, are meant to take a back seat; in fact professionals may be
asked to leave the room during part of the conference so that family
members can decide on their own about how best to protect the child.
Except in unusual circumstances, the CPS social worker follows the
family's lead and works with the family, and the involved professionals, to pull together the services the family and the conference participants have identified as necessary to protect the child.

Adapting this model, the CPS agency in Cleveland, Ohio, is now
convening family group conferences for children entering placement.
These conferences bring together the parents and other relatives, the
foster parents (who may or may not be relatives), and others involved
with the child, such as teachers, counselors, doctors, and clergy, to
identify the child's needs and to develop a plan for meeting those needs
while the child is in foster care. These conferences are an important
innovation in two respects. First, it is unprecedented for parents and
foster parents to be brought together at the time of placement or at

any other time. Yet one can imagine what a difference it makes to the parent to have the opportunity to meet the foster parents and discuss with them the parent's preferences regarding the child's schooling, religion, diet, and so forth. Second, it is very unusual for a case conference to be held at the time of placement. Typically there is a flurry of collateral contacts with other service providers before a child is placed, but the contacts concern the problems leading up to placement, not the plan for services subsequent to placement. Under the permanency planning reforms of 1980, social workers are supposed to develop a plan to meet children's educational, health, and other needs while in placement, but since most placements are made on an emergency basis, such planning rarely occurs in more than a cursory way. The family group conferences provide a forum for this type of plan to be developed, with input from the parents and others involved with the child.

The changes that will be required of frontline workers in CPS and community agencies are substantial, but so are the potential rewards, for workers and the children and families they serve. Frontline workers will have more responsibility but also more authority and control, while children and families should get clearer information and a more helpful array of services. Most important, children should be better protected as the system as a whole intervenes more effectively in cases of serious abuse and neglect while working more helpfully with lower-risk families.

The changes in practice explored here cannot occur in isolation. Implementing the new paradigm for child protection will require a concerted effort by CPS agencies and their community partners to move forward on several dimensions. What will it take to move from the current system, which all too often provides a one-size-fits-all authoritative response that fails to protect children or help many of the children referred to it, to one that, by providing a more differentiated response, will more effectively and consistently protect children and meet their needs? We turn to that question in the next chapter.

Chapter 9

Reforming Child Protection

In recent years, public confidence in the child protective services system has steadily eroded as children like Lisa Steinberg and Elisa Izquierdo—victims of horrendous abuse and neglect whom the system failed to protect—have come to view. Cases such as these have led to calls for a new and better system of child protection.

The public is right to be concerned about the current state of child protection, but many perceptions about children in need of protection, and about the system designed to provide that protection, are inaccurate. Contrary to popular perception, the typical child reported to CPS is a victim of neglect, not of physical or sexual abuse, and only a small share of the children reported are subsequently removed from their homes. Indeed, most children reported to CPS receive no intervention beyond an initial screening or investigation; more alarmingly, many children at risk of abuse or neglect are reported more than once with little apparent result.

The public perception is correct in one regard: the child protective services system in the United States does not do a good enough job of protecting the children reported to it. Although in some cases CPS intervenes swiftly and effectively, in others the system goes badly wrong. In too many high-risk cases, repeated warnings are ignored or misread, and children are left to suffer at the hands of cruel or incompetent parents. And in too many low-risk cases, struggling families receive only a heavy-handed investigation, but no real services to help them become better caregivers for their children.

Nor does the U.S. system look much better in comparative perspective. More children are reported to CPS in the United States than in comparable countries such as Canada, Britain, and Australia, and more of these cases are kept open for monitoring on an ongoing basis; but this extra reporting and oversight do not necessarily produce better protection. In fact they may even be counterproductive, since the sheer volume of cases interferes with the system's ability to provide adequate protection to the families referred to it. The evidence from Canada, Britain, and Australia, together with the evidence from the United States, confirms the impression that the current model of child protective services is badly flawed.

The Current Child Protective Services System

Child welfare professionals share the public's critical view of the operations of the CPS system, and this concern has been mounting. In 1990 the U.S. Advisory Board on Child Abuse and Neglect declared that "child abuse and neglect in the United States now represents a national emergency."[1] In the past decade several organizations have issued major reports recommending that CPS be overhauled.[2] And at the end of a comprehensive three-year review in 1997 the Harvard Executive Session on Child Protective Services likewise concluded that a new approach to protecting children was needed.[3]

The deliberations of these diverse groups have identified five overarching problems with CPS as it operates in the United States today: overinclusion, capacity, underinclusion, service delivery, and orientation.

The Front End of the System

The problems of the current system are particularly acute at the "front end," that is, in the reporting, screening, and investigation phases. Many observers attribute the overinclusion and capacity problems at the front end to the mandatory reporting laws that are in place throughout the United States, and in some provinces of Canada and Australia. Closer analysis reveals, however, that mandatory reporting laws cannot fully account for these problems, since the number of reports continued to escalate long after the reporting laws were established. Variation in mandatory reporting laws may help explain differences in levels of reports across jurisdictions, but it is harder to make a case that these laws explain changes in reporting within jurisdictions over time, since most of the laws have not changed much over time. Nor do mandatory reporting laws help explain the low substantiation rates observed in the United States, since it is the mandated reports that have the highest substantiation rates. National data for 1977, 1985, and 1995 (shown in Table 4.5) indicate that the substantiation rate for reports made by professionals has consistently been about 15 percentage points higher than the rate for reports made by nonprofessionals. This pattern was confirmed in the Boston case-record study; as we saw in Chapter 2, about half of the reports made by mandated reporters were substantiated, compared to less than one-third of reports made by nonmandated reporters, and an appalling one-tenth of reports made anonymously.

The evidence is mixed on whether substantiation rates are higher in countries that do not have mandatory reporting laws: England has a somewhat higher substantiation rate than the United States, but Ontario, Canada, apparently does not.

The problems at the front end of the system—and the solutions—lie elsewhere. Instead of eliminating mandatory reporting laws, states and localities should be focusing on incremental reforms that address specific problems in their reporting, screening, and investigations of abuse and neglect. Foremost among these reforms are:

- Improving the accuracy of reporting by changing or clarifying the definitions, adjusting the incentives for reporters, and exploring the possibility of discretionary reporting for some mandated reporters

- Improving the effectiveness of screening by expanding the extent and scope of screening and by moving screening to the local areas

- Improving the quality of investigations by increasing the thoroughness of investigators' work with families and collaterals, changing practice to provide a more helpful intervention for families, and enhancing communications between investigators and reporters

Several states and localities are working to implement such incremental reforms, as we shall see later in this chapter.

Narrowing as a Strategy to Reform CPS

Another frequently heard criticism of CPS is that the reporting laws are too broad. This has led many observers to call for narrowing the definitions of abuse and neglect as the first step toward reforming CPS. Indeed, narrowing is at the heart of virtually every proposal to reform CPS in the past 20 years.[4] Narrowing is considered essential because the system is swamped by cases of relatively less serious maltreatment and so cannot give sufficient attention to any of the cases—even the most serious ones—being referred. In this view, it is not so much the mandatory nature of the reporting laws as the broadness of their definitions that results in too many referrals to CPS. Another factor increasing the tendency to refer low-risk cases to CPS is that as other parts of the child and family service system have contracted, CPS has become the only entry point to services in many jurisdictions.[5]

However, simply narrowing the criteria for entry into the formal CPS system will not substantially improve the protection of children. One problem is that such a strategy does not address the issue of who, if anyone, will respond to families excluded from that system. Most narrowing proposals simply assume that a new child and family services system will spring up to serve those families. Sources of political support and funding for such a system are seldom addressed. Nor is it stated how this new system will operate, which families it will serve, and how it will coordinate its efforts with the formal child protective services system. These are critical omissions, in the face of evidence that contractions in the child and family service system prompted much of the overreliance on CPS in the first place.

Today, when we are witnessing a historic retreat from a public commitment to aid needy families, there is no reason to believe that a new publicly supported system will spring up to meet the needs of families and children whose cases are deemed not serious enough to warrant full-blown CPS intervention. Moreover, any strategy that raises the threshold for entry into CPS also raises the likelihood that CPS will miss serious cases that should receive authoritative intervention.

A second problem is that narrowing proposals take for granted that separating out the most serious cases of abuse or neglect, and providing an unambiguously investigative response to them rather than a response that blends investigation and helping roles, will automatically improve the protection of children in high-risk cases. While there is no doubt that narrowing the mandate of CPS would sharpen the focus on child safety within CPS and could therefore lead to improved child protection on high-risk cases, it is by no means clear that by itself it would produce a system that effectively and reliably assures children's safety. Even in the narrow range of high-risk cases that would remain in CPS, families would have differing needs and strengths. A one-size-fits-all investigative model would no better meet their needs, and build on their strengths, than it does for the high- and low-risk families seen in CPS today. A simple narrowing strategy also begs the question of how many cases would remain in CPS and what level of resources they would require.

A New Paradigm for Child Protection

The new paradigm proposed here is a differential response system in which CPS, in partnership with other formal and informal resources in each community, responds to families on a case-by-case basis, using authoritative or voluntary intervention as appropriate. The differential response system would cover the full range of families seen in CPS today. It would address the needs of both the small share of high-risk families that require authoritative intervention and the larger share of lower-risk families that could be safely engaged on a voluntary basis. Indeed, the new system could potentially serve a wider range of families than are served today, because it would have the capacity to offer services to some families earlier, before their situation deteriorates into full-blown abuse or neglect.

A narrowing approach assumes that there is one correct investigative response for all high-risk situations of abuse or neglect. The differential response paradigm distinguishes between high-risk cases that warrant authoritative intervention and lower-risk cases that can be approached on a voluntary basis, but it also sets the expectation that CPS and the other components of the child protection system will respond to each child and family on a case-by-case basis. Because the differential response system recognizes the need to draw on a wide range of resources, it emphasizes collaborative partnerships among the CPS agency, families, community agencies, and other formal and informal resources to provide a coordinated response to protect children and meet their needs.

In the new paradigm, the CPS agency provides a customized response, depending on each family's needs and strengths, and shares responsibility for child protection with a wide range of partners in the community, including criminal justice, other public agencies, private agencies, individuals, and families. The provision of a differentiated response is key. Since child maltreatment is not a unitary phenomenon, and families' problems are complex and can change over time, the standard one-size-fits-all CPS response ill serves most families. To better protect children and meet their needs, CPS and its partners must provide a response that is tailored to each family's problems, strengths, resources, and needs as determined by an ongoing process of assessment and reassessment, conducted in partnership with families.

The reliance on community partners is a crucial feature of the paradigm. Currently, CPS is all too often the gatekeeper for child and family services. This encourages the reporting of too many low-risk families to CPS, which then closes their cases after a cursory screening or investigation. In a differential response system, other partners in the community will have an explicit, agreed-upon role to play in protecting children. On high-risk cases, CPS will retain primary responsibility for assuring children's safety but will team with community partners on a case-by-case basis. On lower-risk cases, non-CPS partners will have primary responsibility for working with the family and will provide services on a voluntary basis. Across all cases, families and informal resources will play a more active role, in partnership with CPS and other community agencies.

The case examples in Chapter 6 illustrate how Florida, Iowa, and Missouri are moving toward systems that provide a more differentiated response. Both Florida and Missouri have piloted differential response at the front end, providing an authoritative, investigative response to high-risk cases and a less authoritative, more assessment-oriented response to lower-risk cases. On the basis of their success so far, Florida and Missouri are now providing an assessment-oriented response to the majority of their cases. Iowa, too, is now piloting an assessment response in Cedar Rapids and several other communities.

Florida, Iowa, and Missouri are also making progress in building community-based partnerships, which involve formal and informal partners in providing services alongside, or in some cases instead of, CPS. These partnerships could be especially helpful in cases in which children need services although their families have not technically crossed the line into abuse or neglect. In one of the cases in the Boston study, for example, CPS closed the case of a young mother who was unable to cope with her difficult toddler, because the case had not crossed the line into abuse or neglect, although there was some risk that it might and the mother clearly wanted help with her child.[6] In closing this case, the CPS worker relied on a community-based agency to step in and help the family, but without any explicit agreement that this agency would do so. Under the Florida model, instead of simply asking the agency to help, CPS would draw up a safety plan with the family and the agency, spelling out what they were expected to do to help protect the child and spelling out the circumstances under which the case might be reopened at CPS. If the safety plan worked as anticipated, the family would be more likely to receive the services it needed, and less likely to fall through the cracks.

Careful evaluations of such state experiments are essential if other jurisdictions are to move forward to a differential response system for child protection. It is hard to think of a public endeavor that has higher stakes than child protection. If an error is made, a child's life could be at stake, and this fact makes innovation very difficult. The experience of Missouri, Florida, and Iowa can provide useful information for other states that want to proceed with differential response reforms but are rightly hesitant to do so without hard evidence that they can better assure children's safety.

The early results from Missouri, Florida, and Iowa are encouraging.[7] In Missouri, area staff have been able to do as good a job as centrally located screeners in separating high-risk and low-risk cases. On the basis of area staff's screening decisions, about 70 percent of the protective service referrals are now being handled with the new assessment response. Only rarely has a case initially assigned to the assessment track had to be reassigned to the investigative track because it turned out to be more serious than it first appeared; and when such reassignments have been necessary, they have gone smoothly.

In Florida, where the reforms are further along, a preliminary evaluation completed in December 1996 by researchers at the University of South Florida concluded that districts implementing the new differential response model were achieving the following results:

- An increase in family satisfaction with services
- An increase in the ability of Protective Investigators to provide assistance to families
- A reduction in the number of children experiencing family disruption
- A decrease in the length of staff time for investigations
- An increase in the number of community partners

- Improved outcomes in the safety of children
- Reconceptualized child protective services
- Sustained and systemic changes in service delivery[8]

The results to date from Iowa are positive as well. An evaluation completed in 1995 by a team at the University of Iowa found that social workers who were out-stationed and assigned to community-based teams in the Patch Project developed closer working partnerships with colleagues in the community. They also developed closer relationships with families, with clients dropping in at the office more often and social workers visiting clients' homes more often. CPS workers in the pilot project are defining family problems differently. Rather than seeing their clients' problems in general terms of abuse or neglect, they are more likely to identify problems in specific areas such as poverty, inadequate housing, mental illness, unemployment, and substance abuse. Making these differential diagnoses is an essential step in providing a differential response.

Although these efforts are still in their early stages, they are being viewed with a great deal of interest. In 1995 Iowa and North Dakota adopted the assessment model that was piloted in Missouri and Florida. The following year, South Carolina and Virginia introduced differential response reforms modeled on the initiatives in Missouri, Florida, and Iowa; and in 1997 five more states (Arizona, Delaware, Nevada, Texas, and Washington) did so. At the same time, New York, Illinois, and other states are incorporating selected elements of differential response into their child protective services reforms.

The British Example

Experience in Britain is also providing useful information. Following a review indicating that many families referred to CPS did not need an authoritative, investigative response, the British Department of Health is now recommending that social workers approach lower-risk families with a "lighter touch." Social workers are also experimenting with ways to work more collaboratively with families and other resources in the community. Two of the most interesting innovations are the "network meeting"—at which CPS social workers and other service providers meet with the family to assess the family's strengths and needs and to develop a plan of action—and the "family group conference"—at which family members take the lead role in developing a plan to protect their children and then present that plan to their CPS worker and other involved professionals.

Another lesson from the British case is how to deal with children who need services but who have not been abused or neglected. This is a pressing problem for the American system, too. Cases that are screened out or unsubstantiated because they do not involve abuse or neglect per se nevertheless often involve children who need help. For example, one of the cases in the Boston study involved a 13-year-old girl who was doing drugs and running wild, but whose case was screened out by CPS because there was no evidence that a parent was abusive or neglectful. The child was clearly in trouble and might have responded positively to services provided by CPS or a community agency on a voluntary basis. Given the probability that the girl's behavior would result in a high-risk teen pregnancy, it seems tragically short-sighted for CPS not to have provided assistance; yet most American states have no system in place that would do so.[9]

Britain's progress in defining "children in need of services" could be particularly useful for the United States. The Children Act of 1989 precisely spells out what is meant by "children in need of services," and this precision has proved very helpful in subsequent efforts to assess the extent to which the needs of those children are being addressed. The British reforms also point to some difficulties. As in the United States, when resources are scarce, there is a push to prioritize among cases and to provide services only to cases involving abuse or neglect. Britain moved forward in this regard by establishing a legislative requirement that local areas also provide services to specific categories of children in need of preventive services. Because legislation alone has proved insufficient to change local authorities' practices, Britain is now experimenting with strengthening local boards that would identify children in need and allocate resources to them. Several states have begun experimenting with such local planning boards, as part of child protective services reforms or as part of broader child and family services reform efforts.

Changing Frontline Practice

Changing frontline practice is the single most important element of a reform agenda. It is also the single most difficult element, since it involves changing the attitudes, skills, and behaviors of social workers, and their supervisors and managers, throughout the system. Five specific changes must be made to move from current practice to the kind of practice required in the new paradigm: (1) CPS will have to be prepared to handle a greater share of high-risk and resistant cases; (2) community agencies will need to pay more attention to, and be better prepared to respond to, issues of child abuse and neglect; (3) CPS and community partners must provide a customized response; (4) CPS and community partners will have to be able to conduct screening and assessments on an ongoing basis, and in collaboration with families; (5) CPS and community partners will have to work in closer partnership with each other, other service providers, community resources, and families themselves.

These challenges are daunting but not insurmountable. Prior reforms in child protective services, and in child and family services more generally, offer hope that systemic change is possible, as well as some ideas about how to bring it about. Current reform efforts in several states and localities offer useful lessons about what it takes to change frontline practice. These initiatives are finding that most social workers welcome the added responsibility and autonomy that come with a more enriched model of frontline practice. However, not all social workers can handle the increased discretion, and those who cannot should be assigned other work. Another lesson from state initiatives is that changing frontline practice will require training models that teach new methods of practice as part of preservice training for new staff, and in-service training for existing staff.

Moving toward a More Fully Differentiated System

A differential response system of child protection will, by definition, provide a range of responses to children and families. In a more fully differentiated system, CPS, in partnership with police and others in the community, will respond swiftly and authoritatively to the most serious cases of abuse or neglect. In less serious cases, non-CPS partners will work with families, extended families, and natural helping networks on a voluntary basis. For cases of moderate risk, some of whom may require authoritative intervention at some point, CPS and its community partners will work together with families and community resources to protect children. In all cases, the response of CPS and its community partners will be tailored to the needs and strengths of each child and family.

What steps can states or localities take to support a system that provides a differential response to children in need of protection? Reform must proceed along two tracks: improving the capacity of the formal CPS system to respond more effectively to children in need of protection, and building the capacity of community partners to play a more active role in child protection. Both paths lead to the same endpoint: a more fully differentiated response system in which the formal CPS agency shares responsibility with a range of community partners and the response is customized to fit the seriousness of the abuse or neglect and the child's and family's needs and strengths.[10]

Each area will have to follow its own path to reform. Just as there is no one response that is right for all families referred to CPS, there is no one approach to reforming child protection that will be right for all CPS agencies and communities. In this kind of "bootstrapping reform," each community will have to develop its own strategy to meet the needs, and draw on the strengths, of its unique set of families and resources.[11]

There are several other reasons that each jurisdiction will have to follow its own path. The first is path dependence. The steps that an agency takes toward reform will depend to a large extent on where it starts the reform process, and this starting point in turn reflects the steps that the agency has taken in the past. Second, in making innovations in the face of uncertainty, agencies and communities cannot know all the answers in advance. Practitioners must learn by doing, and state planners must learn by monitoring. Third, in a domain as fraught with risk as child protection, a community's reform strategy must proceed with special care, evolving through incremental steps.[12]

Improving the Effectiveness of the CPS System's Response

Any reform effort must be concerned first and foremost with children's safety. CPS currently does an inadequate job of protecting children. There are several incremental steps that CPS agencies can take to improve their performance, especially in the most serious cases of abuse or neglect. The logical starting points are screening and investigation.

Improving the Quality of Screening

One of the simplest screening reforms is to move the screening function from centralized, statewide units to specialized units in local offices, so that the staff making screening decisions can work more closely with other CPS staff, reporters, and other individuals in the community. Depending on the size of the local offices, local screening might be assigned to one or more social workers in each office, as in Massachusetts, or to local intake supervisors, as in Missouri's pilot reforms. Staff who formerly performed screening at the central office can be reassigned to local offices or assigned other functions at the central office. If the potential quality of local screening is uncertain, screening can be moved to the local offices incrementally, as in Missouri, with staff from both the centralized unit and the local office reviewing incoming reports as an interim step to test the feasibility and reliability of local screening.

A second screening reform is to establish a differential response at the point of screening, by sorting cases into two or more groups on the basis of the seriousness of the abuse or neglect and the level of the risk to the child. This kind of sorting occurs already in some states, such as Illinois; other states would have to develop criteria spelling out which cases need an investigative response and which could receive an assessment response. One useful step in developing criteria is to convene a working group with representatives from the CPS agency and potential partner agencies to review a sample of cases referred to CPS. Reviewing actual cases can be helpful in fleshing out criteria and is also a useful way of inventorying the current caseload. Once criteria are developed, they can be integrated into screening forms, such as the checklist forms used in Missouri's reform initiative, and training can be provided accordingly.

There are risks associated with implementing a differential response at the point of screening, but there are also ways to minimize those risks. The experience of Missouri and Florida demonstrates that a differential response at screening can be introduced incrementally, by using pilot projects or parallel screening. It is also important to clearly establish mechanisms for moving cases from one track to the other if the initial decision to treat a case as high-risk or low-risk needs to be overturned.

Improving the Quality of Investigations

Improving the quality of investigations will be a challenge in many jurisdictions. The first step is to recruit, select, and train individuals who are able to confront parents about abuse and neglect and able to assess children's safety. Conducting investigations is demanding work and requires maturity, good judgment, and sensitivity, in addition to specific skills in interviewing and evidence-gathering. It also requires that administrators and supervisors communicate expectations clearly and provide support. Even the best-qualified and trained individuals will not be able to provide adequate protection to all the children assigned to them if investigators are unclear about their role, are juggling multiple roles, or are carrying too many cases. Conversely, even a well-designed system, in which roles are clear and caseloads are manageable, will not provide adequate protection to children if the workers are not up to the task.

As part of its recent reforms, New York City has taken several measures to improve the quality of its investigative staff. It now recruits at schools of social work and is creating a new job title to attract and retain staff with master's degrees in social work. It is screening new recruits more carefully and providing new investigators with more extensive training on risk factors such as substance abuse, domestic violence, and mental illness. As discussed in Chapter 8, the city has also split off child protective services into a separate agency to refocus the agency on its protective mission. This move should improve its capacity to hire and retain staff who are dedicated to the agency's mission and to exclude job applicants with little interest in child protection. Nearly two years into the reforms, in the fall of 1997, the agency had made progress but still had a long way to go: a court review panel found casework practice inadequate, and a little girl named Sabrina Green died in circumstances eerily reminiscent of those in which Elisa Izquierdo died two years earlier. Whether the reforms will prove more effective in the longer run remains an open question.

A second way to improve the quality of investigations is to make greater use of community partners. For example, in the most serious cases—those that involve potentially criminal abuse or neglect—police, district attorneys, and other criminal justice staff have an important role to play in teaming with CPS investigators. Such partnerships are well established and robust in many areas as a result of states' experience with building such teams on sexual abuse cases in the 1980s; but there is still room for improvement. As we saw in Chapter 8, Chicago's recent experiment, which extended police and CPS partnerships to cases that involved noncriminal but nevertheless very serious abuse or neglect, identified several areas in which CPS could benefit from police training, and vice versa. For example, CPS investigators have much to learn from the police about interviewing techniques and investigation procedures, while police can learn from their CPS counterparts about interviewing young children and identifying community-based resources for child protection. The Chicago experiment also led to improved sharing of information.

One unexpected benefit of Chicago's experiment was that police and CPS investigators who responded as a team said they were less likely to remove children than if they had responded alone, because the team received greater cooperation, knew more about resources, and was less prone to take drastic action. This outcome suggests that CPS reformers could extend such models of partnership to other community resources in joint investigations. Potential partners for joint investigations include public health nurses, for cases of substance-exposed or other high-risk newborns; truant officers or school adjustment counselors, for cases of truancy or educational neglect; mental health counselors, for cases in which children's behavior places themselves or other family members at risk; battered women's advocates, for cases in which there are both domestic violence and child maltreatment; substance abuse counselors, for cases in which a parent's substance abuse places a child at risk; family support workers, for cases in which a young mother is isolated and needs support; and income support, employment, or housing workers, for cases in which the presenting problem is lack of adequate financial resources or adequate housing. Other teams might involve informal partners, such as ministers or extended family members, in investigations if these resources can be identified at the time of the initial report.

Teaming with other community partners on selected investigations not only helps provide an effective response; it is also an essential step toward building a system in which community-based partners will play a more active role. If CPS is to identify cases in which a community partner might usefully contribute to a child's protection—by joining forces with CPS or by providing oversight in place of CPS—it is important for both CPS and the potential partners to learn what these cases look like and what type of response the partners can offer. Partnering on selected cases also provides an opportunity to establish a track record so that CPS knows which partners can handle which kinds of cases safely.

Improving Assessment and Service Delivery through Greater Use of Community Partners

The role of partners is not limited to the front end of the system. Improving the quality of assessment, service planning, and service provision will also require greater use of partnerships with families, informal helpers, and other public and private agencies in the community. Partnerships can be built through the social worker's regular contacts with family members and collateral contacts with other service providers, and can also be strengthened through the use of forums like the British child protection conferences, network meetings, and family group conferences.

Child protection case conferences, in use in Britain since 1974, are intended to ensure that children at the highest risk of abuse or neglect are identified and listed on the area's child protection register and are brought to the attention of professionals from other agencies as well as CPS. A primary purpose of the conferences is to enable CPS workers and other professionals to jointly develop a plan for the children. Parents are now included in these case conferences.

Many local areas in Britain are now voluntarily extending this model to their less serious cases, for which a conference would not ordinarily be convened. For these cases, social workers are convening "network meetings," at which parents, CPS workers, and other professionals talk about the children's needs and how best to meet those needs. Social workers report that these meetings have been extremely helpful in developing better working relationships with parents and in developing plans to work together.

The family group conference model, introduced in New Zealand in 1989 and since adopted in many areas in Britain and Canada, takes family participation one step further. The family group conference brings together the family, the CPS social worker, and others involved with the child (such as teachers, doctors, therapists, and police). Parents and family members have a seat, and a prominent one, at the table.

Jurisdictions such as Cleveland, Ohio, and New York City are now using family group conferences for children entering placement. These conferences can also be used to prevent placement; the British experience suggests that in some cases a family group conference may enable a family at risk of placement to develop a plan to keep their child safely at home instead.

Increasing the Role of Community Partners in Child Protection

Identifying and Involving Community Partners

The first step in promoting a more active role by other agencies and individuals in the community is to identify potential partners and the types of cases for which they might be able and willing to play a more active role, whether by joining with CPS to provide protective oversight and services or by providing protective oversight and services on their own. This process can begin with efforts to involve community resources as partners on current CPS cases. As CPS and these collaborators learn which types of cases can be handled safely by which community partners, the groundwork is laid for shifting responsibility to these partners for these specific cases. Making the change gradually, and by mutual agreement, will enable CPS and its partners to work out the details of the partnership, such as who specifically in the community agency will handle the CPS cases and who in CPS will be responsible for training and monitoring the community providers.

Another advantage of partnering community staff with CPS staff is that they can learn from each other. If community partners are to become more involved in protecting children from abuse or neglect, they will have to become more aware of child safety issues, and more willing to confront families about abuse and neglect, than they have been in the past. Similarly, if CPS staff are to make greater use of community resources, they will need to learn more about what those resources are, what their strengths and limitations are, and what they have to offer to children in need of protection. Introducing community-based staff as partners in child protection is an excellent way to bring about this type of learning. It can also be a way to change attitudes that might impede effective collaboration. In the CPS-police partnership experiment in Chicago, for instance, even though CPS and the police were already working together on some cases, the police reported that the experience changed their attitudes toward CPS workers.

Many areas are experimenting with using CPS-community teams as a first step toward moving responsibility for some cases to community partners. For example, Florida first experimented with teaming public health nurses and CPS workers in cases of substance-exposed newborns before moving to a model in which public health nurses now make the first response on some cases instead of CPS.[13] Illinois, too, has moved in this direction. In all cases of substance-exposed newborns, CPS in Illinois now makes its initial response in conjunction with substance-abuse treatment counselors and public health nurses. Lower-risk cases (approximately 20 percent of the referrals involving substance-exposed newborns) are closed by CPS and assigned to either public health nurses or substance-abuse treatment workers for ongoing case management and supervision. Intermediate and high-risk cases (the remaining 80 percent of referrals) remain open with CPS but receive services from a team with members from all three agencies. The reform aims at providing these substance-exposed newborns and their families with more appropriate services.[14]

Community partners are now playing a more active role in a variety of cases. In Jacksonville, Florida, screeners are referring a broad range of low-risk cases to community-based providers as part of that city's First Call diversion program for cases that do not meet the threshold to be screened in as reports of abuse or neglect. In another innovative model, being piloted in St. Louis, Missouri, day-care centers are responding to reports of abuse or neglect involving children enrolled in their center, unless the report alleges criminal or other very serious maltreatment.[15]

The role of community partners should not be limited to cases referred to CPS. Stanching the flow of referrals to CPS and responding more proactively to children in need of preventive services will require non-CPS agencies to play a much more active role with families who have not yet been referred to CPS. CPS will always have to give priority to protective cases, but CPS, and the community as a whole, must provide some support to community partners for preventive services as well.

Some of the most promising programs in the area of prevention are the early home-visiting programs for high-risk newborns. Universal home visiting for newborns has long been part of the preventive service system in countries such as Britain, and universal home visiting was recommended for the United States by the U.S. Advisory Board on

Child Abuse and Neglect.[16] Given limited resources, however, a targeted program might make more sense in the United States.[17]

Evidence from a range of studies suggests that targeted home-visiting programs for high-risk newborns can work, but it also suggests that such programs are costly. Having professionally trained staff, who receive adequate support and supervision, seems to be critical for success. Building such programs, then, will require an initial investment, including perhaps some resources from CPS. In the long run, however, the programs should save money, if fewer parents go on to abuse or neglect their children, and if fewer cases are referred to CPS.[18]

Building Partnerships at the State or City Level

In thinking about identifying and involving partners in child protection, it is useful to make a distinction between those partnerships that can be arranged on a statewide or citywide basis, those that must be arranged community by community, and those that can be arranged only case by case. Most of the examples that come to mind involve partnerships that CPS can negotiate at the state or city level with other large public agencies, such as law enforcement or public health. Although negotiating these partnerships still involves overcoming numerous bureaucratic, political, and financial hurdles, the fact that these arrangements can be negotiated statewide or citywide makes it much simpler to reach agreement with large public agencies than it would be to reach similar agreements with partners at the community or case level.

Once agreement has been reached between CPS and other state or city agencies, cross-training is a useful way to build working partnerships on issues of mutual concern such as abuse and neglect, substance abuse, or domestic violence. Cross-training was successful in building CPS-police teams to respond to sexual abuse cases in the 1980s, and it has been used more recently to build partnerships to respond to cases involving substance abuse and domestic violence. In San Diego's Partners for Success program, for example, staff from all the child-serving agencies in the community—CPS, police, teachers, financial assistance workers, and public health nurses—received two and a half days of cross-disciplinary training on child protection. The outcome was staff who were more knowledgeable about child abuse and neglect, domestic violence, and substance abuse, and who were more open to working together on these issues in future.[19]

Building Partnerships at the Community Level

CPS agencies have used a variety of strategies, such as interagency teams and planning groups, to build partnerships at the community level. Such efforts, however, have traditionally focused more on public agencies than on private agencies. And all too often, grassroots providers—those who are most likely to live and work in the communities they serve—have been left out of the process altogether.

The establishment of "networks" of providers can help build more inclusive partnerships at the community level. Los Angeles has pioneered the use of community networks in child protection, by awarding contracts to community-based networks of providers rather than to large individual provider agencies. Los Angeles has also established a preference for providers who live and work in the communities they serve. This has made a big difference in increasing the participation of smaller, grassroots providers.[20] The Los Angeles model is a radical change from the purchase of service and contracting systems currently in place in most jurisdictions. However, current reform efforts in New York, Illinois, and Michigan demonstrate that it is feasible to move to a local network model. These examples also demonstrate the extent to which efforts to build new networks can draw on existing resources.

In establishing its new neighborhood networks, New York City is converting existing contracts for preventive services, in-home services, and substitute care, rather than starting from scratch. New York is also drawing on existing resources in communities, particularly on agencies with a proven track record in serving families at risk of abuse or neglect. Brooklyn's Sunset Park program, for instance, is nationally recognized for its success in working with high-risk families.[21] New York is also able to draw upon neighborhood boards that were already in place, on a pilot basis, in several New York City communities, through the Action for Children Together (ACT) program. These boards provide a useful model for planners from the city, and provider agencies, to envision what a local network might look like.[22] Illinois, too, is building on existing local area network boards in place as a result of earlier initiatives to bring children home from out-of-state placements and to prevent unnecessary placements. Illinois will now use these existing local area networks in two additional ways. One, the networks will partner with CPS on cases in which they have particular expertise or services to offer (for example, in cases of domestic violence, substance abuse, or mental illness). Two, the networks will assume responsibility for some lower-risk cases that are referred to CPS but are judged not to need authoritative CPS intervention.[23] Michigan will also be using local resources to provide services for families that are referred to CPS but do not require full-blown CPS intervention. Michigan is allocating new prevention dollars to family councils in each county, with the condition that these councils provide services to cases that are screened out or unsubstantiated by CPS.[24]

The New York, Illinois, and Michigan examples offer useful models for other areas that have similar local networks or boards in place, at least on a pilot basis, as a result of earlier social services reforms or service integration initiatives.[25] Rather than having to start from scratch, areas that are reforming child protective services can build on these earlier efforts.

Another element of a strategy to build community partnerships is assigning CPS staff to specific communities so that they can be closer to their partners there. Assigning staff to a specific local area or "patch" is also helpful in advancing another goal of reform, providing customized treatment for children and families rather a one-size-fits-all response. Working consistently in one neighborhood or community provides an opportunity for individual staff to better understand the families they are working with in context of their communities' needs and resources. As we saw in Chapter 6, Cedar Rapids, Iowa, pioneered patch-working in child protective services in the United States, and other areas are now experimenting with it.[26] In Cedar Rapids, CPS staff and community partners are based in a local neighborhood office. This model increases the visibility of the staff in the community and increases their contacts with clients and collaterals, but it makes supervision more difficult unless enough workers are outposted to warrant having a supervisor there as well.

An alternative strategy to link CPS workers with communities is geographically based case assignments. In Chicago's reform project, for instance, workers are located in a central office but are assigned caseloads based on geographic area.[27] This model poses fewer management and supervision problems and allows for more staffing flexibility, but it may create efficiency problems by basing workers at a distance from the communities where their caseloads are. This model may also be less effective than patch-working at building links between CPS workers and the community.

How can a state or locality decide whether to out-station or to assign caseloads by geographic area? Convening a local working group, with representatives from CPS and from the local community, to consider the pros and cons of various models given the area's geography and caseload might be a useful approach to identifying which model makes sense for a given community.

Building Partnerships at the Case Level

Building partnerships at the case level will involve the most far-reaching changes for frontline workers in CPS. CPS has traditionally tended to approach parents as adversaries, not as partners in child protection. Despite a good deal of rhetoric in child protective services about involving families in assessment and service planning, most social workers have been trained to see assessment and service planning as something that they do to and for their cases, not with them. Nor do most CPS workers consistently think about how they might draw upon a family's own resources, whether extended family or other informal sources of help, to help children in intact families. The use of kin and other informal sources is now well established as an alternative to foster care for children, but few CPS agencies have taken the next step and looked at kin and other informal sources of help as resources to help prevent placement and to keep children safe in their own homes.

Building partnerships at the case level will demand fundamental changes in casework practice. CPS workers have been trained and oriented to tell parents what to do, rather than to work with parents collaboratively. However, the reality is that the vast majority of children referred to CPS will not be placed in foster care, and most will be open for supervision with CPS or another agency for only a short while. Thus, if CPS is to break the cycle of abuse and neglect and bring about lasting changes in protection for children, it will have to do so in most cases by changing parents' attitudes and behaviors. This is not something that workers currently know how to do. Thus, CPS agencies increasingly are working to develop models of casework practice that engage and empower families, and are investing substantial resources to implement these models.

The first step in bringing about this change in casework practice is to change the way agencies train their staff. Currently, most preservice and in-service training in CPS focuses on conveying information about departmental policies and procedures as well as some background information about abuse and neglect, child development, and family problems such as substance abuse or mental illness. To reform practice, CPS agencies will have to provide much more training on casework practice and, in that training, to place more emphasis on how to engage parents, extended families, and informal helpers, and how to work with them as partners. Florida, Michigan, and Illinois are all moving in this direction with their new casework-practice training initiatives for social workers. In Illinois, for example, every worker and supervisor is receiving six weeks of training in the new approach to casework. The fact that agency managers are willing to commit this level of staff time and resources to the training initiative suggests how effective they think this new approach will be, and also how different it is from the type of practice that is in place today.

Changing social workers' and supervisors' attitudes and case practice, and working to build closer partnerships with parents, will not make every home safe for children. Clearly, some families will not be able to provide adequate care and protection for their children, no matter how effective their social worker is at engaging them, and in those cases CPS will have to act aggressively to remove the children and provide a safe and nurturing alternative home. And even in the cases in which families can engage effectively with social workers and can make progress toward protecting their children, CPS and its community partners will have to remain vigilant in monitoring the safety of children and will have to be prepared to respond more authoritatively if necessary.

A second step toward building partnerships at the case level is for agencies to change their policies and procedures to include parents, other family members, and informal resources as partners. Although changes in policy and procedures do not always result in changes in practice, sometimes even small changes can be very effective. For example, in implementing the Adoption Assistance and Child Welfare Act of 1980, CPS agencies learned that the surest way to get social workers to share service plans with clients was to require a client's signature on every service plan. Similarly, to reinforce the idea that the parent's perspective should be taken into account in the social worker's assessment, Cedar Rapids, Iowa, now requires that parents be given a copy of the assessment.

Florida's implementation of community safety agreements provides another example of how changing policies and procedures can bring about changes in practice. In communities implementing the new agreements, Florida has spelled out the procedures by which CPS may close a case if a family can reach an agreement with one or more individuals in the community to help them in providing adequate care for their children. Social workers, families, and informal helpers have found that having these agreements and procedures has led them to make arrangements for children's safety that they would otherwise never have considered.[28]

The Endpoint of the Reforms

The endpoint of the reforms—the point at which the two tracks of reforming CPS and bringing in community partners come together—is a more fully differentiated system of child protection, one that provides a range of responses to meet the needs of children and families in the community. In a more fully differentiated system, CPS, in partnership with police and others in the community, will respond swiftly and authoritatively to protect children and prosecute perpetrators in the most serious cases of abuse or neglect. At the other end of the continuum, in low-risk cases, non-CPS partners will have the capacity to work with families, extended families, and natural helpers on a voluntary basis to ensure that children receive adequate care. For the vast middle range of families referred to CPS, some of whom may require authoritative intervention at least some of the time, CPS and its community partners will work together to provide protection for the children, taking into account each child's and family's unique set of problems, strengths, resources, and needs.

We can see elements of such a system in the community-based teams in Cedar Rapids, Iowa, where CPS workers partner with others in the community to deliver customized responses to families referred to CPS and to other families in need of services; in the assessment response in pilot areas in Missouri, where CPS workers approach families in a less adversarial manner; and in the assessment and service response in reform communities in Florida, where CPS works with formal and informal partners to provide a response that is better tailored to families' needs. We can also see the precursors of a fully differentiated system in local authorities in Britain, where community by community planners are struggling to develop models for working together to serve children in need of preventive services as well as children in need of protection.

Each community's system will look slightly different, reflecting its own mix of needs and resources, and also its own historical progression. At the endpoint of reform, however, all fully differentiated systems of child protection will have the following features in common. CPS will retain primary, but not sole, responsibility for the most serious cases of abuse or neglect, because other community partners, both formal and informal, will also play a role. For the less serious cases, non-CPS partners may exercise primary responsibility, but they too will draw upon other partners, formal and informal, on a case-by-case basis. Services will be provided by a team, rather than by a CPS social worker and other workers acting independently, and they will be provided on a voluntary basis unless the severity of abuse or neglect makes authoritative intervention necessary.

Will the community partners be more accountable for addressing issues of abuse and neglect than they have been in the past? And, with social workers at CPS and community agencies exercising more discretion, will their work also be monitored more closely? If so, who will be responsible for this increased monitoring and supervision?

For at least the foreseeable future, the formal CPS agency will have to retain ultimate responsibility for child protection, and thus will have to carry out the increased monitoring and supervision both of its own staff and of the community partner agencies. In many areas, mechanisms for accountability are already in place, but they are typically underutilized. Management information systems, particularly with the recent Statewide Automated Child Welfare Information Systems expansions, provide the opportunity to track outcomes for children by worker, office, or agency, but they have rarely been used in this way.[29] Many agencies also have systems in place to review selected case records for quality of casework, but again, this mechanism tends to be underutilized. Nor do CPS agencies make as much use as they could of client surveys to track outcomes such as client satisfaction, child safety, and child well-being.

Monitoring cases more closely, whether through management information systems, case-record reviews, or client surveys, will be costly, but there is no alternative if CPS is to track outcomes and hold individual workers and agencies accountable for them. In some instances, it may be possible to reassign existing managerial or monitoring staff for this purpose; in others, it may be necessary to hire additional staff. However, tracking outcomes, and holding staff and agencies accountable for them, cannot be viewed as a luxury. It is an essential element of reform.

Could the reform process proceed even further? The answer is undoubtedly yes. Once a fully differentiated system was in place, an entity other than CPS might assume responsibility for monitoring both CPS and its community partners. For example, an umbrella agency might operate the various programs.[30] Or a community-based governance entity might set the community's agenda for child protection and monitor the performance of the various components of the system in achieving that agenda.[31]

However, my view is that a community can achieve a more fully differentiated system for child protection without merging operations or governance, and that the disadvantages of a merger or shift in governance outweigh the advantages. There is a danger that CPS's focus on child safety would be diluted if it were joined to a broader children's services agency. There is also a danger that CPS's accountability for child protection would be diminished if responsibility for children's safety were shifted to another community entity.

Although there is much that is wrong with CPS today, the public child protective services agencies also have many strengths that can be drawn upon in building a better system of child protection. For all the system's shortcomings, we should not lose sight of the fact that CPS does succeed in many cases in providing services that help protect children. Moreover, given the high stakes involved, the risks entailed in abolishing the current CPS agencies and trying to replace them with something new would be unacceptably high. Ultimately, I believe, we must focus our efforts on reforms that take the current system as a starting point and that aim to improve that system's ability to protect children. To that end, I see community partners helping CPS, but not replacing it.

The child protective services system has struggled for much of the time since the first societies for the prevention of cruelty to children were established over a century ago. In recent years, the crisis has escalated. Unless the system is reformed, and radically, it is doubtful that CPS will be able to withstand the pressures that will face it in the coming years, in the wake of welfare reforms, social services cutbacks, and other fiscal pressures in the United States and other industrialized nations. However, given these pressures, it is not realistic to propose reforms that will cost a great deal more money. The most prudent course is to identify ways to shift resources and to use resources more effectively, rather than calling for an infusion of new funds into CPS. That is why the reforms proposed here are incremental and involve shifting resources, rather than relying on new funding for CPS or child and family services more generally.

To the extent that the child protective services system is our mechanism for protecting children from abuse or neglect, we have no choice but to care about it, and to try to make it better. We cannot simply throw up our hands and leave the task to struggling individual families, untrained and unsupervised private agencies, or others. The reason that CPS becomes involved is that these other first-line defenses for children have broken down. For good or ill, CPS is the main line of defense for the three million cases reported to it each year.

Accepting the essential role of CPS in protecting children, however, does not mean accepting CPS as it operates today. We cannot continue operating the child protective services system as is, because it does not do a good enough job of protecting the children referred to it. To achieve an adequate level of child protection, we must move forward, and quickly, on two parallel tracks of reform. First, we must take steps to improve the effectiveness of CPS in responding to children in need of protection. Second, we must take steps to build the capacity of other partners in the community to join with CPS in providing a more effective response to children in need of protection. These steps will lay the groundwork for the future of child protection: a more fully differentiated child protective services system in which CPS and its community partners provide a customized response to each child in need of protection, intervening more aggressively and authoritatively on the high risk cases, more helpfully and comprehensively with the lower-risk cases, and earlier and more proactively with the cases in need of prevention. Such a system is a long way from what is in place anywhere today, but that does not mean it is not attainable. Indeed, the steps that CPS agencies and communities could take to move forward to such a system are fairly clear. Nor does building the new system necessarily entail spending more money. Rather, it means shifting some funds, and spending other funds more efficiently.

The reforms called for here are radical, but the problems of the child protective services system require radical solutions. Millions of children are at risk of abuse or neglect each year, and the current system is woefully ill equipped to meet their needs. A full measure of protection is the birthright of every child, and we must strive to make this a reality. A better system of child protection is not beyond our resources or our knowledge. Getting there will take hard work, community by community, but our children deserve no less.

Notes . Index

Notes

1. Child Abuse and Neglect Today

1. "Abandoned to Her Fate," *Time,* December 11, 1995.
2. Elisa's death and the agency's initial attempt to hide behind confidentiality laws also led to new state legislation in New York opening up agency records in instances in which a child known to the authorities died. This legislation is widely known as "Elisa's law."
3. James Rainey, "A Child Dies, and Legal System Is Blamed," *Los Angeles Times,* April 28, 1995, p. A1.
4. Susan Kuczka, "Judge Pins Blame on Keystone Moms, Not Poverty," *Chicago Tribune,* October 28, 1994, p. 1. See also Patrick Murphy, *Wasted: The Plight of America's Unwanted Children* (Chicago: Ivan R. Dee, 1997), pp. 99–100.
5. Patricia Schene, "Chronic Neglect in St. Louis City," report prepared for the Missouri Department of Social Services, Division of Family Services, St. Louis, 1996.
6. Over the period 1994–1996, on average 45 percent of child fatalities involved neglect; Ching-Tung Wang and Deborah Daro, *Current Trends in Child Abuse Reporting and Fatalities: The Results of the 1996 Annual Fifty-State Survey* (Chicago: National Committee to Prevent Child Abuse, 1997).
7. One study of child fatalities in Washington state, for instance, found that of the 61 children who had been reported to and substantiated by CPS and later died, the greatest number (25, or 41 percent of the total) had been reported for neglect, while only 33 percent had been reported for abuse, and 15 percent for sexual abuse (11 percent had been reported for more than one type of maltreatment); Eugene Sabotta and Robert Davis, "Fatality after Report to a Child Abuse Registry in Washington State, 1973–1986," *Child Abuse and Neglect* 16 (1992), 627–635.

8. Andrew Vachss, "Crying to Be Heard," *Parade Magazine,* November 3, 1996.

9. In 1996 professionals made over half of all reports, and educators 16 percent; U.S. Department of Health and Human Services, National Center on Child Abuse and Neglect (NCCAN), *Child Maltreatment 1996: Reports from the States to the National Child Abuse and Neglect Data System* (Washington, D.C.: U.S. Government Printing Office, 1998).

10. For more detailed discussion of the stages of CPS intervention, see Peter Pecora, James Whittaker, and Anthony Maluccio, *The Child Welfare Challenge: Policy, Practice, and Research* (New York: Aldine de Gruyter, 1992), chap. 8.

11. Some jurisdictions allow other types of disposition at the end of the investigation. In 1996 13 states had a three-tier system, in which reports could be substantiated, indicated, or unsubstantiated; 5 states had a separate category for reports judged to have been intentionally false; and 20 states had a category for cases closed without a finding. NCCAN, *Child Maltreatment 1996,* p. 3-5.

12. There were 3,126,000 reports in 1996, a rate of 47 reports per 1,000 children, according to Wang and Daro, *Trends in Reporting, 1996,* table 1. Figures from NCCAN, *Child Maltreatment 1996,* are comparable but slightly lower (3,006,752 reports in 1996, a rate of 43.5 per 1,000 children). Note that a child may be reported more than once during a year, and that a report may represent more than one child. Thus, the number of reports provides only an approximate indication of the number of children reported. Another way to track how many children are in need of protection is to use incidence data, since not all children who are abused or neglected are reported to child protective services. Three national incidence studies in the United States have asked professionals in a range of community-based settings how many cases of abuse and neglect they have observed. These studies are discussed in Chapter 4.

13. Neil Gilbert, "Conclusion: A Comparative Perspective," in *Combatting Child Abuse: International Perspectives and Trends,* ed. Gilbert (New York: Oxford University Press, 1997), table 2. The rate for Canada is for the province of Ontario. Reporting rates in some of the continental European countries were even lower; in the Netherlands, for example, the rate was about 5 per 1,000, and in Belgium 3 per 1,000.

14. This rate is calculated from data in Jane Gibbons, Sue Conroy, and Caroline Bell, *Operating the Child Protection System: A Study of Child Protection Practices in English Local Authorities* (London: Her Majesty's Stationery Office, 1995).

15. NCCAN, *Child Maltreatment 1996.*

16. For a thoughtful discussion of this issue, see Mark Courtney, Richard Barth, Jill Duerr Berrick, Devon Brooks, Barbara Needell, and Linda Park, "Race and Child Welfare Services: Past Research and Future Directions," *Child Welfare* 75 (1996), 99–137.

17. Using data from the second national incidence study, Joseph Cappelleri, John Eckenrode, and Jane Powers found that African-American children are more likely to be identified as physically abused, and less likely to be identified as sexually abused, than Caucasian children; "The Epidemiology of Child Abuse: Findings from the Second National Incidence and Prevalence Study of Child Abuse and Neglect," *American Journal of Public Health* 83 (1993), 1622–24. Using the same data, Elizabeth Jones and Karen McCurdy found that African-American children are more likely to be reported for neglect, and less likely to be reported for sexual abuse, than Caucasian children; "The Links between Types of Maltreatment and Demographic Characteristics of Children," *Child Abuse and Neglect* 16 (1992), 201–215. James Spearly and Michael Lauderdale found that Texas counties with higher proportions of African-Americans had higher rates of reported maltreatment overall, and higher rates of reported physical abuse and neglect; "Community Characteristics and Ethnicity in the Prediction of Child Maltreatment Rates," *Child Abuse and Neglect* 7 (1983), 91–105.

18. Although Jones and McCurdy found that black children were more likely to be reported for neglect and white children for sexual abuse, this was the only racial difference they found, and their results indicate that poverty and family structure were more important than race in explaining reports of neglect; "Links between Types of Maltreatment."

19. See, e.g., ibid.; Robert Hampton and Eli Newberger, "Child Abuse Incidence and Reporting by Hospitals: Significance of Severity, Class, and Race," *American Journal of Public Health* 75 (1985), 56–60; and Gail Zellman, "The Impact of Case Characteristics on Child Abuse Reporting Decisions," *Child Abuse and Neglect* 16 (1992), 57–74.

20. See, e.g., Sheila Ards, "Estimating Local Child Abuse," *Evaluation Review* 13 (1989), 484–515; Claudia Coulton, Jill Korbin, Marilyn Su, and Julian Chow, "Community Level Factors and Child Maltreatment Rates," *Child Development* 66 (1995), 1262–76; Brett Drake and Shanta Pandey, "Understanding the Relationship between Neighborhood Poverty and Specific Types of Child Maltreatment," *Child Abuse and Neglect* 20 (1996), 1003–18; James Garbarino, "A Preliminary Study of Some Ecological Correlates of Child Abuse: The Impact of Socioeconomic Stress on Mothers," *Child Development* 47 (1976), 178–185; James Garbarino and Deborah Sherman, "High-Risk Neighborhoods and High-Risk Families: The Human Ecology of Child Maltreatment," *Child Development* 51 (1980), 188–198; James Garbarino and Kathleen Kostelny, "Child Maltreatment as a Community Problem," *Child Abuse and Neglect* 16 (1992), 455–464; Spearly and Lauderdale, "Community Characteristics and Ethnicity in Prediction"; and Lawrence Steinberg, Ralph Catalano, and David Dooley, "Economic Antecedents of Child Abuse and Neglect," *Child Development* 52 (1981), 975–985. My tabulations of unpublished data from New York City's CPS agency confirm the links between reporting rates and neighborhood poverty. The highest reporting rate (41 reports per 1,000 children) is seen in the Bronx, the bor-

ough with the highest poverty rate (37 percent); the lowest rate (25 reports per 1,000) is seen in the two boroughs with the lowest poverty rates, Staten Island (13.4 percent in poverty) and Queens (16.7 percent).

21. Deborah Belle, ed., *Lives in Stress* (Beverly Hills: Sage, 1984); Garbarino, "Ecological Correlates of Child Abuse"; Garbarino and Sherman, "High-Risk Neighborhoods and High-Risk Families"; Richard Gelles, "Poverty and Violence toward Children," *American Behavioral Scientist* 35 (1992), 258–274; Vonnie McLoyd, "The Impact of Economic Hardship on Black Families and Children: Psychological Distress, Parenting, and Socioemotional Development," *Child Development* 61 (1990), 311–346; and Susan Zuravin, "The Ecology of Child Abuse and Neglect: Review of the Literature and Presentation of Data," *Victims and Violence* 4 (1989), 101–120.

22. For evidence on this point, see Gelles, "Poverty and Violence toward Children"; Penelope Trickett, Lawrence Aber, Vicki Carlson, and Dante Cicchetti, "Relationship of Socioeconomic Status to the Etiology and Developmental Sequelae of Physical Child Abuse," *Developmental Psychology* 27 (1991), 148–158; and Joan Vondra, "The Community Context of Child Abuse and Neglect," *Marriage and Family Review* 15 (1990), 19–39.

23. Andrea Sedlak and Diane Broadhurst, *Third National Incidence Study of Child Abuse and Neglect: Final Report* (Washington, D.C.: U.S. Department of Health and Human Services, National Center on Child Abuse and Neglect, 1996). See also Isabel Wolock and Bernard Horowitz, "Child Maltreatment and Material Deprivation among AFDC-Recipient Families," *Social Service Review* 53 (1979), 175–194, who found that AFDC families reported to CPS, as compared to other AFDC families, were the "poorest of the poor" (p. 175).

24. Sedlak and Broadhurst, *Third National Incidence Study.*

25. Sheila Kamerman and Alfred Kahn, for example, make the point that as other parts of the social service system have been cut back, CPS has increasingly been seen as the gateway to services for families with children. See Sheila Kamerman and Alfred Kahn, "If CPS Is Driving Child Welfare—Where Do We Go from Here?" *Public Welfare* 48 (Winter 1990), 9–13, 46.

26. Ira Chasnoff, Harvey Landress, and Mark Barrett, "The Prevalence of Illicit Drug or Alcohol Use during Pregnancy and Discrepancies in Mandatory Reporting in Pinellas County, Florida," *New England Journal of Medicine* 322 (1990), 1202–06.

27. Over the period 1990–1996, on average 40 percent of reports were substantiated or indicated (see Chapter 4 for details). In 1993, for example, 38 percent of reports were either substantiated or indicated, 53 percent were unsubstantiated, and 9 percent had some other disposition. See NCCAN, *Child Maltreatment 1993*, p. 3-5.

28. The two state-level studies are Barbara Meddin and Ingrid Hansen, "The Services Provided during a Child Abuse and/or Neglect Case Investigation and the Barriers That Exist to Service Provision," *Child Abuse and Neglect* 9 (1985), 175–182; and B. Salovitz and D. Keys, "Is Child Protective Service

Still a Service?" *Protecting Children* 5, no. 2 (1988), 17–23. In the Boston sample discussed later in this chapter, the service provision rate for substantiated cases is much higher: 92 percent of substantiated cases are kept open for services.

29. NCCAN, *Child Maltreatment 1993*, p. 2-11. This figure is consistent with the average of 72 percent reported for 19 states in David Wiese and Deborah Daro, *Current Trends in Child Abuse Reporting and Fatalities: The Results of the Annual 1994 Fifty-State Survey* (Chicago: National Committee to Prevent Child Abuse, 1995).

30. Wiese and Daro, *Current Trends in Reporting, 1994*, p. 11.

31. Edmund Mech, "Out-of-Home Placement Rates," *Social Service Review* 57 (1983), 660.

32. Data for 1980 are from ibid.

33. Data for 1980 are from ibid. Data for 1986 are from M. C. Plantz, R. Hubbell, B. J. Barrett, and Antonia Dobrec, "Indian Child Welfare: A Status Report," *Children Today* 18 (1989), 24–29.

34. Fred Wulczyn, Chapin Hall Center for Children at the University of Chicago, personal communication, 1996.

35. Duncan Lindsey, *The Welfare of Children* (New York: Oxford University Press, 1994), p. 155. See also idem, "Factors Affecting the Foster Care Placement Decision: An Analysis of National Survey Data," *American Journal of Orthopsychiatry* 61 (1991), 272–281.

36. The Boston case-record study was conducted by Jane Waldfogel and Julie Boatright Wilson, with support from the Malcolm Wiener Center for Social Policy at the Kennedy School of Government at Harvard University. For further details on the study, see Waldfogel and Wilson, "A Longitudinal Study of Children Reported to Child Protective Services" (Manuscript in progress, Columbia University School of Social Work).

37. Massachusetts DSS statistics: Massachusetts Department of Social Services (DSS), *DSS Quarterly Report, First Quarter FY '94, for the Period Ending September 1993* (Boston, 1994); national screening rate: Wiese and Daro, *Trends in Reporting, 1994;* national substantiation rate: NCCAN, "National Child Abuse and Neglect Data System Summary Data Component Data Tables, 1990–1994" (Washington, D.C., 1996), p. 1994 SDC-4.

38. For data on children in big cities, see Congressional Research Service, *Selected Brief Facts about Poverty and Welfare among Urban Families with Children* (Washington, D.C., 1992). See also Alfred Kahn and Sheila Kamerman, eds., *Children and Their Families in Big Cities: Strategies for Service Reform* (New York: Cross-National Studies Research Program, Columbia University School of Social Work, 1996).

39. Julie Boatright Wilson, "Mattapan: A Community in Transition" (Paper prepared for the Executive Session on Child Protective Services, Kennedy School of Government, 1994).

40. Ibid.

41. This is an unduplicated count. When a family was reported more than once during the month (as happened in several cases), we included only the most recent report.

42. This cycling is not unique to Boston. Dean Knudsen, "Duplicate Reports of Child Maltreatment: A Research Note," *Child Abuse and Neglect* 13 (1989), 41–43, examined the more than 8,000 reports made in one Indiana county in the period 1965–1984 and found that 40 percent or more of the reports received each year concerned children who were already known to CPS. See also Ruth Laurence Karski, *Protecting Maltreated Children* (New York: Oxford University Press, forthcoming), who found that over 50 percent of screened-out cases, and over 60 percent of screened-in cases, were already known to CPS in the California county she studied.

43. See Massachusetts Society for the Prevention of Cruelty to Children (MSPCC), *Massachusetts Society for the Prevention of Cruelty to Children, First Ten Annual Reports, 1881–1890* (New York: Garland, 1987). See also Linda Gordon, *Heroes of Their Own Lives: The Politics and History of Family Violence* (New York: Penguin, 1988). Gordon draws upon records from the MSPCC and two other Boston agencies.

44. The sample is taken from MSPCC, *First Ten Annual Reports*.

45. Gordon, *Heroes of Their Own Lives*, pp. 70–71.

46. Ibid., p. 310. During the late 1800s, there were few African-Americans living in Boston (in these years, they made up less than 2 percent of the city's population), but they, like immigrants, were soon disproportionately represented in the child protective services caseload. By 1920, when blacks made up only 2.2 percent of Boston's population, they represented 5.5 percent of the child protective services caseload.

47. Ibid., pp. 148, 308. From 1880 to 1909, 42 percent of reported families were poor, and another 44 percent had subsistence-level incomes.

48. Ibid., p. 148.

49. See, e.g., *MSPCC First Annual Report, 1881*, p. 23, and *MSPCC Sixth Annual Report, 1886*, p. 18, in MSPCC, *First Ten Annual Reports*.

50. Gordon, *Heroes of Their Own Lives*, pp. 93 and 96–97.

51. Ibid., p. 207.

52. Ibid.

53. Ibid., p. 38.

54. Ibid., p. 49.

55. *MSPCC Sixth Annual Report, 1886*, pp. 18–19, in MSPCC, *First Ten Annual Reports*.

2. A Comparative Perspective

1. Gosta Esping-Anderson, *Three Worlds of Welfare Capitalism* (Princeton: Princeton University Press, 1990). See also Sheila Kamerman and Alfred Kahn, *Family Change and Family Policies in Great Britain, Canada, New Zealand, and the United States* (Oxford: Oxford University Press, 1998).

2. American Humane Association, *Twenty Years after CAPTA: A Portrait of the Child Protective Services System* (Denver, 1994); Howard Doueck and Murray Levine, "Editors' Introduction," *Law and Policy* 14 (1992), 123–128.

3. Henry Kempe, Frederic Silverman, Brandt Steele, William Droegemueller, and Henry Silver, "The Battered Child Syndrome," *Journal of the American Medical Association* 181 (1962), 17–24.

4. For a chronology of legislation and other initiatives related to child protection in Britain, see Peter Reder, Sylvia Duncan, and Moira Gray, *Beyond Blame: The Child Abuse Tragedies Revisited* (London: Routledge, 1993). For a history of Australian initiatives, see David Thorpe, *Evaluating Child Protection* (Philadelphia: Open University Press, 1994). For a review of the Canadian initiatives, see Karen Swift, "Canada: Trends and Issues in Child Welfare," in *Combatting Child Abuse: International Perspectives and Trends*, ed. Neil Gilbert (New York: Oxford University Press, 1997).

5. Following Swift, "Canada: Trends and Issues," I refer to these agencies as "semipublic" because they perform a governmental function and rely on government funds for their operation.

6. Peter Boss, *On the Side of the Child: An Australian Perspective on Child Abuse* (Melbourne: Fontana, 1980), p. 91.

7. Nico Trocme, Debra McPhee, Kwok Kwan Tam, and Tom Hay, *Ontario Incidence Study of Reported Child Abuse and Neglect: Final Report* (Toronto: Institute for the Prevention of Child Abuse, 1994).

8. Trocme and his collaborators are now conducting follow-up research on the cases in their sample.

9. Thorpe, *Evaluating Child Protection*.

10. Jane Gibbons, Sue Conroy, and Caroline Bell, *Operating the Child Protection System: A Study of Child Protection Practices in English Local Authorities* (London: Her Majesty's Stationery Office, 1995).

11. Thorpe, *Evaluating Child Protection*.

12. Across the 11 states that reported on this question, on average 35 percent of substantiated cases involved substance abuse; David Wiese and Deborah Daro, *Current Trends in Child Abuse Reporting and Fatalities: The Results of the 1994 Annual Fifty-State Survey* (Chicago: National Committee to Prevent Child Abuse, 1995).

13. Trocme et al., *Ontario Incidence Study*.

14. The share of cases involving single-parent families in the Boston sample is not much different from the share of such families in the neighborhood from which the sample was drawn. This result suggests that what accounts for the higher representation of single-parent families in CPS is not a greater likelihood for such families to be reported within neighborhoods; rather, it is the fact that these families live in neighborhoods where families with children, whether one- or two-parent, are more likely to be reported. This conjecture cannot be tested with the Boston sample, since it covers only one area, but it merits further research.

15. Cited in Trocme et al., *Ontario Incidence Study*, p. 86.

16. According to Lee Rainwater and Tim Smeeding, "Doing Poorly: The Real Income of American Children in Comparative Perspective," Working Paper No. 127, Luxembourg Income Study (Walferdange, Luxembourg, 1996), 13 percent of Australian children lived in single-parent families in 1990. According to the Australian Bureau of Statistics, this share had risen to 18 percent by 1994 (Jane Millar, personal communication, 1997). According to the British General Household Survey, 20 percent of British children lived in single-parent families in 1995 (Jane Millar, personal communication, 1997).

17. The Ontario study missed a large number of Native Canadian children because the three Children's Aid Societies that cover Native areas were not included in the study. Trocme and his collaborators estimate that had they included these offices, reporting rates for Native children would have been about six times higher than the rates for other children in the province. Trocme et al., *Ontario Incidence Study,* p. 91.

18. Another indicator of the disadvantaged economic status of families referred to CPS in Ontario is that at least 17 percent are living in public housing, compared to only 2.5 percent of families living in the province (Trocme et al., *Ontario Incidence Study,* p. 97). There may also be a link between precarious housing or homelessness and referral to child protective services. In the English sample, one in 12 families referred to CPS were in temporary housing (Gibbons, Conroy, and Bell, *Operating the Child Protection System,* table 4ii); in the Boston sample, one in 20 families reported to CPS were homeless.

19. Although it is tempting to treat Ontario's "suspected" category as analogous to the "indicated" category in use in several U.S. states, the two terms are not used in the same way. Thus, some "suspected" cases would be considered substantiated or indicated if U.S. terminology were used, but some would not.

20. Although comparable data are not available from England, Gibbons, Conroy, and Bell, *Operating the Child Protection System,* table 6iii, report that cases were less likely to be screened in if there was not a man in the house and if the referral concerned neglect; reports of neglect were also less likely to be substantiated and to proceed to a conference.

21. See American Association for the Protection of Children, *Highlights of Official Child Abuse and Neglect Reporting—1986* (Denver: American Humane Association, 1987), and earlier reports; U.S. Department of Health and Human Services, National Center on Child Abuse and Neglect, *Child Maltreatment 1996: Reports from the States to the National Child Abuse and Neglect Data System* (Washington, D.C.: U.S. Government Printing Office, 1998), and earlier reports.

22. Canada: Trocme et al., *Ontario Incidence Study,* table 7.1; Australia and Wales: calculated from data in Thorpe, *Evaluating Child Protection,* tables 4.5, 4.6.

23. A follow-up of the Ontario sample is under way; a follow-up of the Boston sample has already been completed.

24. Gibbons, Conroy, and Bell, *Operating the Child Protection System,* chap. 10.

25. This outcome is confirmed in case examples randomly selected by Gibbons and her colleagues to illustrate cases that were substantiated but not conferenced. The following two examples involve physical abuse and neglect, respectively.

"A seven year old boy living in overcrowded, poor conditions with mother and her cohabitee (a man with criminal convictions who had assaulted her) and two younger siblings was referred by teacher because of a bruised eye he claimed was caused by a punch from mother. There had been many previous investigations and all the children had previously been on the register. An older child had been seriously injured and placed for adoption. The referred child had a learning disability. SW [social worker] visited but accepted mother's explanation of an accident, even though the paediatrician advised that the nature of the injury was not consistent with the explanation. The police insisted on a strategy meeting where social services decided to take no further action." Gibbons, Conroy, and Bell, *Operating the Child Protection System*, p. 59.

"A one year old boy and seven year old sibling living with mother and boyfriend in a squat were referred by the hospital after mother had been admitted with a knife wound inflicted by the boyfriend. There was concern about the safety of the children left with this violent man who had stated he would not look after them. However, it was decided that this was a housing not a child protection issue. The case was referred to the health visitor while a student social worker tried to look into the housing problems." Ibid., p. 62.

26. The British child protection registers operate differently from the typical U.S. central registry, which would be expected to record the name and perpetrator in every case of serious child abuse or neglect, regardless of whether the child still needed services from CPS or other agencies.

27. Gibbons, Conroy, and Bell, *Operating the Child Protection System*, chap. 10.

28. Michael Wald and his colleagues followed two samples of abused and neglected children over a two-year period: one group consisted of children who had been placed in foster care; the other was made up of children who also had been abused or neglected but who remained at home because they lived in a county that was implementing a new program to prevent placement. The researchers then compared these children to each other and to a control group of children who had not been abused or neglected. Half of the at-home children were abused or neglected again during the study, and nearly all were exposed to family conflict. Further, although the foster children were faring somewhat better, both the foster children and the at-home children had higher levels of emotional and behavioral problems and difficulties at home, with peers, and in school, than the control group. See Michael Wald, J. M. Carlsmith, and P. H. Leiderman, with Carole Smith and Rita deSales French, *Protecting Abused and Neglected Children* (Stanford: Stanford University Press, 1988).

29. Jill Duerr Berrick, Barbara Needell, Richard Barth, and Melissa Jonson-Reid,

The Tender Years: Toward Developmentally Sensitive Child Welfare Services for Very Young Children (New York: Oxford University Press, 1998).

30. One of the earliest studies, C. W. Morse, O. J. Z. Sahler, and S. B. Friedman, "A Three-Year Follow-Up Study of Abused and Neglected Children," *American Journal of Diseases of Children* 120 (1970), 439–446, found a 33 percent re-abuse rate. In another early study, Anne Cohn reviewed cases from 11 different programs and found that their "severe re-incidence" rates averaged 30 percent (with a range from 13 percent to 51 percent); she also found that recurrence was thought to be more likely in cases of neglect and cases involving substance abuse. See Anne Cohn, "Effective Treatment of Child Abuse and Neglect," *Social Work* 24 (1979), 513–519. Roy Herrenkohl, Ellen Herrenkohl, Brenda Egolf, and M. Seech, "The Repetition of Child Abuse: How Frequently Does It Occur?" *Child Abuse and Neglect* 3 (1979), 67–72, followed 328 families who had been reported to child protective services and found repeated maltreatment in 53 percent of these families. T. E. Taw, "The Issue of Re-Injury: An Agency Experience," ibid., pp. 591–600, found a repeat maltreatment rate of 56 percent. W. Johnson and J. L'Esperance, "Predicting the Recurrence of Child Abuse," *Social Work Research and Abstracts* 20, no. 2 (1984), 21–26, followed a sample of physical abuse cases and found that 46 percent had a repeat report within two years. Frederick Rivara, "Physical Abuse in Children under Two: A Study of Therapeutic Outcomes," *Child Abuse and Neglect* 9 (1985), 81–87, found that 30 percent of the children in his small sample (71 families) were re-abused. Naomi Ferleger, David Glenwick, Richard Gaines, and Arthur Green, "Identifying Correlates of Reabuse in Maltreating Parents," *Child Abuse and Neglect* 12 (1988), 41–49, followed a small sample (45 families) and found that 40 percent re-abused their children. Dean Knudsen, *Child Services: Discretion, Decisions, Dilemmas* (Springfield, Ill.: Charles C. Thomas, 1988), found that at least 50 percent of reported children were reported a second time over a 10-year period. Michael Murphy, Sandra Bishop, Michael Jellinek, Sister Dorothy Quinn, and Judge Francis Poitrast, "What Happens after the Care and Protection Petition? Re-Abuse in a Court Sample," *Child Abuse and Neglect* 16 (1992), 485–493, followed cases that had been brought to court and then dismissed and found that 29 percent were substantiated again in the following two to three years; in 10 percent of the sample, the maltreatment was serious enough that the case was brought back to court on another care and protection petition. Some studies have found much lower recurrence rates, but these studies too have typically found higher rates for neglect cases and cases involving substance abuse. For instance, Arthur Green, Ernest Power, Barbara Steinbrook, and Richard Gaines, "Factors Associated with Successful and Unsuccessful Intervention with Child Abuse Families," *Child Abuse and Neglect* 5 (1981), 45–52, found repeat maltreatment in only 16 percent of their small sample (79 families). Richard Barth, Mark Courtney, Jill Duerr Berrick, and Vicky Albert, *From Child Abuse to Permanency Plan-*

ning: Child Welfare Services, Pathways, and Placements (New York: Aldine de Gruyter, 1994), found that 13 percent of the children in their sample were re-referred in a nine-month period; re-referral rates were highest for the children who had originally been reported for neglect. George Fryer and Thomas Miyoshi, "A Survival Analysis of the Revictimization of Children: The Case of Colorado," *Child Abuse and Neglect* 18 (1994), 1063–71, found that about 9 percent of their sample had been re-reported and substantiated at least once within four years after the initial report; the repeat maltreatment rate was highest—over 13 percent—for those children whose original maltreatment was physical neglect. Howard Levy, John Markovic, Urmila Chaudhry, Sharon Ahart, and Heriberto Torres, "Reabuse Rates in a Sample of Children Followed for 5 Years after Discharge from a Child Abuse Inpatient Assessment Program," *Child Abuse and Neglect* 19 (1995), 1363–77, found that 16.8 percent of their sample was substantiated again for child maltreatment, with neglect being the most frequent type of repeat maltreatment. Isabel Wolock and Stephen Magura, "Parental Substance Abuse as a Predictor of Child Maltreatment Re-Reports," *Child Abuse and Neglect* 20 (1996), 1183–93, found that more than half of substance-abusing families had a second report compared to only one-quarter of other families. See also Eugene Sabotta and Robert Davis, "Fatality after Report to a Child Abuse Registry in Washington State, 1973–1986," *Child Abuse and Neglect* 16 (1992), 627–635, who find that children reported and substantiated for physical abuse or neglect have significantly higher fatality rates than other children.

31. Thorpe, *Evaluating Child Protection,* chap. 11. Only one of these cases involved physical abuse, and only one involved sexual abuse. The remainder were cases of neglect, with the vast majority (77.5 percent) involving drug or alcohol abuse by a parent. In this latter group of cases the risk of repeat maltreatment seemed to be the most difficult for social workers to assess correctly, but fortunately the rate of serious injury was fairly low.

32. The follow-up was conducted 6 months after the child protection conference and 9–12 months after the initial report.

33. Gibbons, Conroy, and Bell, *Operating the Child Protection System,* chap. 10.

34. Ibid.

35. The follow-up was conducted in May 1997, nearly three years after the original sample was gathered in June and July 1994, and included a check of DSS's management information system for the status of each family included in the original sample. Of the 124 families in the original sample, 11 could not be tracked, either because of incomplete identifiers or because they had moved out of state; thus, the follow-up sample consists of 113 families. For further details on the follow-up study, see Jane Waldfogel and Julie Boatright Wilson, "A Longitudinal Study of Children Reported to Child Protective Services" (Manuscript in progress, Columbia University School of Social Work).

36. This pattern, with the risk of repeat maltreatment highest in the first year or

two, has been found in other studies. See, e.g., Howard Levy, John Markovic, Urmila Chaudhry, Sharon Ahart, and Heriberto Torres, "Reabuse Rates in a Sample of Children Followed for 5 Years after Discharge from a Child Abuse Inpatient Assessment Program," *Child Abuse and Neglect* 19 (1995), 1363–77, who found that the risk of repeat maltreatment was highest in the first year or two after the initial incident.

37. David Jones reports a similar range of estimates of recurrence rates (from a low of 16 percent to a high of 60 percent) in "The Untreatable Family," *Child Abuse and Neglect* 11 (1987), 409–420. See also Diane De Panfilis and Susan Zuravin, "Roles, Patterns, and Frequency of Child Maltreatment Recurrences among Families Known to CPS," *Child Maltreatment* 3 (1998), 27–42.

38. See note 30 above.

39. Rachel Swarns, "Experts Denounce Children's Agency," *New York Times,* October 22, 1997, p. 1.

40. Linda Spears, Child Welfare League of America, personal communication, November 1997. Spears notes that the intake system in Massachusetts is particularly strong compared with others in the United States because of two unusual features: a 10-day investigation model, which lends itself to high-quality investigations; and a formal assessment period after the investigation, which ensures that a second worker takes a close look at families being kept open for services. The Massachusetts CPS agency is also fortunate to be able to draw upon a relatively well-developed set of community resources to which families can be referred.

41. Trocme et al., *Ontario Incidence Study.*

42. As noted earlier, Canada has a three-tier system. Only the substantiated cases are included in the calculations. Including the suspected cases would raise the overall rate per 1,000 children from 6 to 12, and the number of neglect cases from 2 to 4, but would not change the basic finding.

43. Rainwater and Smeeding, "Doing Poorly," table A-2.

44. Case 12 (see Chapter 1), for instance, was reported and substantiated for neglect three more times in the three years that followed the substantiation of the original neglect report in June 1994. Case 4 (see Chapter 1), a physical abuse case, was also the subject of multiple substantiated reports; in this case, the reports resulted in the placement of one of the children.

3. The Current Child Protective Services System

1. In 1990, for example, the federal government provided 40 percent of the funding for child welfare (which is not synonymous with CPS but nevertheless overlaps a great deal), while state governments, with some help from local sources, provided the remaining 60 percent. U.S. House of Representatives, Committee on Ways and Means, *1994 Green Book: Background Material and Data on Programs within the Jurisdiction of the Committee on Ways and Means* (Washington, D.C.: U.S. Government Printing Office, 1994).

2. Although many of the staff doing child protective services work do not have social work degrees, I refer to CPS workers as social workers because they are expected by their agencies, and by the public, to perform a social work role.

3. The discussion here is limited to the role of private agencies in the formal CPS system. These agencies may undertake other activities related to child protection that are not funded or authorized by the government.

4. For an excellent overview of how cases move through the CPS system, see Peter Pecora, James Whittaker, and Anthony Maluccio, *The Child Welfare Challenge: Policy, Practice, and Research* (New York: Aldine de Gruyter, 1992), chap. 8.

5. In most jurisdictions, such cross-reporting between CPS and law enforcement on potentially criminal cases is now required by statute, and formal procedures have been established to facilitate it.

6. As we saw in Chapter 1, national statistics suggest that only about 40 percent of reported cases are substantiated, and of these only about 70 percent—or 28 percent of those originally reported—are kept open for services. This means that roughly 72 percent of reported cases receive no action or service from CPS beyond screening and investigation.

7. U.S. Department of Health and Human Services, National Center on Child Abuse and Neglect, *Child Maltreatment 1996: Reports from the States to the National Child Abuse and Neglect Data System* (Washington, D.C.: U.S. Government Printing Office, 1998), reports that 14 percent of substantiated cases were referred for court action in 1996, about the same share as in the five preceding years. This percentage is consistent with the estimate by Douglas Besharov that less than 5 percent of substantiated cases are brought to criminal court and 15 percent to civil court; "'Doing Something' about Child Abuse: The Need to Narrow the Grounds for State Intervention," *Harvard Journal of Law and Public Policy* 8 (1985), 549.

8. Only a small minority of children reported to CPS end up in foster care, and the increase in foster-care placements is not due entirely to CPS, as foster care is often used for other children (e.g., children who are status offenders or children with disabilities). Some of the recent increase reflects the reclassification of what is now known as "kinship care," as well as increases in this type of care. Until the mid to late 1980s, relatives such as grandmothers who took in abused or neglected children often received no payment from CPS and were not counted as part of the foster care system; instead, they typically received payments through the AFDC grantee relative program. Now, through the kinship care program, relatives can be formally approved and paid by CPS, and the children are therefore counted as part of the foster care caseload. For an overview of "kinship care," see Dana Burdnell Wilson and Sandra Stukes Chipungu, "Introduction to Special Issue: Kinship Care," *Child Welfare* 75 (1996), 387–395, and other articles in the same issue. For estimates of the size of the informal and formal kinship care population, see Allen Harden, Rebecca Clark, and Karen Maguire, *Informal and Formal Kinship Care*, 2 vols.

(Washington, D.C.: U.S. Department of Health and Human Services, Office of the Assistant Secretary for Planning and Evaluation, 1997).

9. On the rise in the value of children, see Viviana Zelizer, *Pricing the Priceless Child: The Changing Social Value of Children* (Princeton: Princeton University Press, 1994). On the role of women in advocating expanded services and programs for children and families, see Linda Gordon, *Pitied but Not Entitled: Single Mothers and the History of Welfare, 1890–1935* (Cambridge, Mass.: Harvard University Press, 1994).

10. Michael Katz, *In the Shadow of the Poorhouse: A Social History of Welfare in America* (New York: Basic Books, 1986), chap. 5. According to Katz, the proportion of children deemed to be in need of care and protection and placed in some form of out-of-home residential care doubled from 1900 to 1904 and fell sharply thereafter.

11. Linda Gordon, *Heroes of Their Own Lives: The Politics and History of Family Violence* (New York: Penguin, 1988), p. 28.

12. Henry Kempe, Frederic Silverman, Brandt Steele, William Droegemueller, and Henry Silver, "The Battered Child Syndrome," *Journal of the American Medical Association* 181 (1962), 17–24. See also Sheila Kamerman and Alfred Kahn, *Social Services in the United States* (Philadelphia: Temple University Press, 1976), chap. 3; and Barbara Nelson, *Making an Issue of Child Abuse: Political Agenda Setting for Social Problems* (Chicago: University of Chicago Press, 1984), chap. 6.

13. Kamerman and Kahn, *Social Services in the United States,* chap. 3.

14. Nelson, *Making an Issue of Child Abuse and Neglect,* chap. 7. Mandatory reporting, of course, turned out to be neither simple nor inexpensive. For two perspectives on mandatory reporting, see Douglas Besharov, "Gaining Control over Child Abuse Reports: Public Agencies Must Address Both Underreporting and Overreporting," *Public Welfare* 48, no. 2 (1990), 34–40; and David Finkelhor, "Is Child Abuse Overreported? The Data Rebuts Arguments for Less Intervention," *Public Welfare* 48, no. 1 (1990), 22–29, 46–47.

15. Child welfare is therefore a much broader area than child protection, and there is a wealth of scholarship on child welfare as distinct from child protection. See, e.g., the classic studies of children in foster care: Henry Maas and Richard Engler, *Children in Need of Parents* (New York: Columbia University Press, 1959); and David Fanshel and Eugene Shinn, *Children in Foster Care* (New York: Columbia University Press, 1978). For an excellent introduction to the recent child welfare literature, see Richard Barth, Jill Duerr Berrick, and Neil Gilbert, eds., *Child Welfare Research Review: Volume One* (New York: Columbia University Press, 1994).

16. The American Association for the Protection of Children, *Highlights of Official Child Abuse and Neglect Reporting—1986* (Denver: American Humane Association, 1987), table 4, found that 48.9 percent of families reported for child abuse or neglect in 1986 were receiving AFDC. See also

Gordon, *Heroes of Their Own Lives,* p. 308; Duncan Lindsey, *The Welfare of Children* (New York: Oxford University Press, 1994), p. 144; and Leroy Pelton, "The Role of Material Factors in Child Abuse and Neglect," in *Protecting Children from Abuse and Neglect,* ed. Gary Melton and Frank Barry (New York: Guilford Press, 1994), pp. 132–133 and 142–143.

17. In the discussion in the text I draw upon Katz, *In the Shadow of the Poorhouse;* and Theda Skocpol, *Protecting Soldiers and Mothers: The Political Origins of Social Policy in the United States* (Cambridge, Mass.: Harvard University Press, 1992).

18. Gordon, *Pitied but Not Entitled.*

19. Another important link between the public welfare and child protective systems is Medicaid, which in recent years has become increasingly important as a funding source for services provided for child protective cases. Thus Medicaid cutbacks will sharply curtail funding available for services to CPS clients and will boost CPS costs accordingly.

20. For national estimates, see Sheila Zedlewski, Sandra Clark, Eric Meier, and Keith Watson, "Potential Effects of Congressional Welfare Reform Legislation on Family Incomes" (Mimeograph, Urban Institute, Washington, D.C., 1996). For an example of a state-level estimate that takes state and local assistance into account, see Jane Waldfogel, Patrick Villeneuve, and Irwin Garfinkel, "The Impact of Welfare Reform for Families with Children in New York" (Paper presented at a meeting of the Association for Public Policy Analysis and Management, Washington, D.C., November 1997).

21. Mark Courtney, "Welfare Reform and Child Welfare Services," in *Child Welfare in the Context of Welfare "Reform,"* ed. Alfred Kahn and Sheila Kamerman (New York: Cross National Research Studies Program, Columbia University School of Social Work, 1997); and Douglas Besharov, "Child Protective Services Under Welfare Reform," Eighth Annual Nanette Dembitz Memorial Lecture, New York, April 1997.

22. There is a large literature on the long-term sequelae of childhood abuse and neglect. For an overview of the effects of maltreatment on children's development, see Dante Cicchetti and Vicki Carlson, eds., *Child Maltreatment: Theory and Research on the Causes and Consequences of Child Abuse and Neglect* (New York: Cambridge University Press, 1989); see also Lawrence Aber and Joseph Allen, "Effects of Child Maltreatment on Young Children's Socioemotional Development: An Attachment Theory Perspective," *Developmental Psychology* 23 (1987), 406–414; Raymond Starr, Darla MacLean, and Daniel Keating, "Life-Span Developmental Outcomes of Child Maltreatment," in *The Effects of Child Abuse and Neglect: Issues and Research,* ed. Raymond Starr and David Wolfe (New York: Guilford Press, 1991); and Penelope Trickett and Catherine McBride-Chang, "The Developmental Impact of Different Forms of Child Abuse and Neglect," *Developmental Review* 15 (1995), 311–337. For a review of evidence that childhood abuse or neglect may lead to poorer later outcomes such as delinquency, adult criminal behav-

ior, and violent criminal behavior, see Cathy Widom, "The Cycle of Violence," *Science* 244 (1989), 160–166. Although it is widely believed that childhood abuse leads to abusive behavior in adulthood, it appears that the links between childhood abuse and adult abuse have been overstated. See Joan Kaufman and Edward Zigler, "Do Abused Children Become Abused Parents?" *American Journal of Orthopsychiatry* 57 (1987), 186–192; and Cathy Widom, "Does Violence Beget Violence? A Critical Examination of the Literature," *Psychological Bulletin* 106 (1989), 3–28.

23. For a useful discussion of beliefs and assumptions about families and government intervention, see Joseph Goldstein, Albert Solnit, Sonja Goldstein, and Anna Freud, *The Best Interests of the Child* (New York: Free Press, 1996), chap. 9.

24. The Children's Bureau, for instance, tracks these three outcomes as it monitors states' child welfare programs. See Jane Waldfogel, "Conducting Research on the Child Welfare Population: Key Datasets and Outcome Measures" (Paper presented at a planning meeting of the National Research Council and Institute of Medicine Board on Children, Youth, and Families, Washington, D.C., May 1997). See also Lisa Merkel-Holguin and Nancy McDaniel, "National Overview of Child Welfare Outcome Measures Development Efforts" (Paper presented at the Third National Roundtable on Outcome Measures in Child Welfare Services, Aspen, Colo., 1995).

25. Comments from participants in a meeting of the Executive Session on Child Protective Services, Kennedy School of Government, March 17–18, 1994. The Executive Session group included a broad range of individuals who had experience with the child protective service system, including representatives from the federal government, state governments, judicial systems, community-based agencies, foundations, and other organizations involved with child protection, child welfare, and related issues such as substance abuse and domestic violence. All comments are unattributed in order to preserve the confidentiality of the discussions.

26. Quotes are from focus groups conducted in 1994 with CPS clients, workers, and supervisors. Vincent Breglio, *CPS: Conversations with Clients, Workers, and Supervisors* (Lanham, Md.: Research/Strategy Management, 1994).

27. See National Association of Public Child Welfare Administrators, *Guidelines for a Model System of Protective Services for Abused and Neglected Children and Their Families* (Washington, D.C., 1988). For a critical view, see Joan Rycraft, "Redefining Abuse and Neglect: A Narrower Focus Could Affect Children at Risk," *Public Welfare* 48, no. 1 (1990), 14–21, 46.

28. The guidelines are reproduced in Douglas Besharov, *Protecting Children from Abuse and Neglect: Policy and Practice* (Springfield, Ill.: Charles C. Thomas, 1988), chap. 13. Besharov, "Gaining Control over Child Abuse Reports," provides a brief overview.

29. Sheila Kamerman and Alfred Kahn, "Social Services for Children, Youth, and Families in the United States," *Children and Youth Services Review* 12

(1990), i–184; idem, "If CPS Is Driving Child Welfare—Where Do We Go from Here?" *Public Welfare* 48, no. 1 (1990), 9–13, 46; and Farrow, "Protecting Children While Supporting and Preserving Families."

30. American Public Welfare Association, *A Commitment to Change,* Report of the National Commission on Child Welfare and Family Preservation (Washington, D.C., 1991); U.S. Advisory Board on Child Abuse and Neglect, *Creating Caring Communities: Blueprint for an Effective Federal Policy on Child Abuse and Neglect* (Washington, D.C.: U.S. Government Printing Office, 1991); and idem, *Neighbors Helping Neighbors: A New National Strategy for the Protection of Children* (Washington, D.C.: U.S. Government Printing Office, 1993).

31. See Frank Farrow with the Executive Session on Child Protection, "Child Protection: Building Community Partnerships, Getting from Here to There" (Paper prepared for the Executive Session on Child Protective Services, Kennedy School of Government, 1997), and other papers produced for the Executive Session. See also Jane Waldfogel, "Rethinking Child Protection," *The Future of Children* 8, no. 1 (Spring 1998), 107–122.

32. Mary Jo Bane, "Integrating Family Services: The State Role" (Mimeograph, Malcolm Wiener Center for Social Policy, Kennedy School of Government, 1992); Alfred Kahn and Sheila Kamerman, *Integrating Services Integration: An Overview of Initiatives, Issues, and Possibilities* (New York: National Center for Children in Poverty, 1992); and Jane Waldfogel, "The New Wave of Service Integration," *Social Service Review* 71 (1997), 463–484.

33. For a review of the literature on family preservation, see Peter Pecora, "Family-Based and Intensive Family Preservation Services: A Select Literature Review," in *Families in Crisis: The Impact of Intensive Family Preservation Services,* ed. Mark Fraser, Peter Pecora, and David Haapala (New York: Aldine de Gruyter, 1991). Peter Rossi, in his comprehensive survey of existing research on family preservation, argued that the results to date were inconclusive and that placement prevention should not be the only criterion for success. Peter Rossi, "Assessing Family Preservation Programs," *Children and Youth Services Review* 14 (1992), 77–97. See also Peter Pecora, Mark Fraser, Kristine Nelson, Jacquelyn McCroskey, and William Meezan, *Evaluating Family-Based Services* (New York: Aldine de Gruyter, 1995), who agree that placement prevention should not be the only outcome that is measured in evaluations of family preservation programs. For an example of a controlled study, see John Schuerman, Tina Rzepnicki, Julia Littell, and Amy Chak, *Putting Families First: An Experiment in Family Preservation* (Hawthorne, N.Y.: Aldine de Gruyter, 1994), which found little difference in placement rates between families receiving regular services and those receiving family preservation, but did find differences on other outcome measures.

34. Michael Wald, for instance, criticized the rush to family preservation as being based on the untested assumption that children would be better off if they remained at home instead of being placed in out-of-home care. Michael Wald,

"Family Preservation: Are We Moving Too Fast?" *Public Welfare* 46, no. 3 (1988), 33–38, 46.

35. Conservative analysts such as Heather MacDonald fault family preservation for attempting to preserve "dysfunctional" families. Heather MacDonald, "The Ideology of 'Family Preservation,'" *Public Interest,* Spring 1994, p. 115. For a more extended critique of family preservation, see Richard Gelles, *The Book of David: How Preserving Families Can Cost Children's Lives* (New York: Basic Books, 1996).

36. Mary-Lou Weisman, "When Parents Are Not in the Best Interests of the Child," *Atlantic Monthly,* July 1994, pp. 43–63, argues that family preservation is inappropriate for a small percentage of children, particularly adolescents.

37. Lisbeth Schorr, *Within Our Reach: Breaking the Cycle of Disadvantage* (New York: Doubleday, 1988).

38. See Neil Guterman, "Early Prevention of Physical Child Abuse and Neglect: Existing Evidence and Future Directions," *Child Maltreatment* 2 (1997), 12–34, reviewing the evidence on home visiting.

39. Sidney Gardner and Nancy Young, "Alcohol and Drug Treatment: An Essential Ingredient in Community Partnerships for Child Protection" (Paper prepared for the Executive Session on Child Protective Services, Kennedy School of Government, 1997).

40. Sharon Lynn Kagan with Peter Neville, *Integrating Human Services: Understanding the Past to Shape the Future* (New Haven: Yale University Press, 1994); and Kahn and Kamerman, *Integrating Services Integration.*

41. Jane Waldfogel, "Integrating Child and Family Services: Lessons from Arkansas, Colorado, and Maryland" (Report to the Ford Foundation, Kennedy School of Government, 1994).

42. Mark Moore, *Creating Public Value* (Cambridge, Mass.: Harvard University Press, 1995).

4. Entry into the System

1. This chapter is based on a paper by Stacey Rosenkrantz and Jane Waldfogel, "Reporting, Screening, and Investigation of Child Maltreatment: Entry into the Child Protective Services System," prepared for the Executive Session on Child Protective Services, Kennedy School of Government, April 1996.

2. Henry Kempe, Frederic Silverman, Brandt Steele, William Droegemueller, and Henry Silver, "The Battered Child Syndrome," *Journal of the American Medical Association* 18 (1962), 17–24.

3. Barbara Nelson, *Making an Issue of Child Abuse: Political Agenda Setting for Social Problems* (Chicago: University of Chicago Press, 1984).

4. There has been a great deal of research on why reporters do not report. See, e.g., Robert Hampton and Eli Newberger, "Child Abuse Incidence and Reporting by Hospitals: Significance of Severity, Class, and Race," *American*

Journal of Public Health 75 (1985), 56–60; Rosonna Tite, "How Teachers Define and Respond to Child Abuse: The Distinction between Theoretical and Reportable Cases," *Child Abuse and Neglect* 17 (1993), 591–603; Jody Warner and David Hansen, "The Identification and Reporting of Physical Abuse by Physicians: A Review and Implications for Research," *Child Abuse and Neglect* 18 (1994), 11–25; Gail Zellman and Steven Antler, "Mandated Reporters and CPS: A Study in Frustration," *Public Welfare* 48 (Winter 1990), 30–47; Gail Zellman, "Report Decision-Making Patterns among Mandated Child Abuse Reporters," *Child Abuse and Neglect* 14 (1991), 325–345.

5. Elizabeth Hutchison, "Mandatory Reporting Laws: Child Protective Case Finding Gone Awry?" *Social Work* 38 (1993), 56–63.

6. U.S. Department of Health and Human Services, National Center on Child Abuse and Neglect (NCCAN), *Child Maltreatment 1995: Reports from the States to the National Child Abuse and Neglect Data System* (Washington, D.C.: U.S. Government Printing Office, 1997), pp. 3-7 and 3-8.

7. At the screening stage, the agency might try to reduce the volume of cases by changing the standards for screening in cases or by changing the procedures in such a way as to discourage or eliminate some reports. Similarly, at the investigation stage, the agency might raise the threshold for substantiation or raise the level of certainty required to establish that a case has met its threshold. Therefore, an increase in cases that are screened out or unsubstantiated does not necessarily reflect an increase in inappropriately reported cases.

8. The problem of false allegations is receiving an increasing amount of attention. However, few reports are found to be deliberately untrue. More often reports are unsubstantiated because there is insufficient evidence of abuse or neglect, or because the abuse or neglect does not seem to be serious enough to warrant coercive intervention. Brett Drake, "Unraveling 'Unsubstantiated,'" *Child Maltreatment* 1 (1996), 261, argues that "many or most unsubstantiated reports involve either some form of maltreatment or preventive service needs appropriate to CPS intervention." See also Jeffrey Leiter, Kristen Myers, and Matthew Zingraff, "Substantiated and Unsubstantiated Cases of Child Maltreatment: Do the Consequences Differ?" *Social Work Research* 18, no. 2 (1994), 67–82, who found that children who were the subject of unsubstantiated reports, like children with substantiated reports, had poorer outcomes (in the areas of schooling and delinquency) than nonreported children, suggesting that children who are reported but not substantiated have unmet needs that may be as serious as those of the children who are substantiated.

9. Douglas Besharov, "Unfounded Allegations—A New Child Abuse Problem," *Public Interest,* Spring 1986, pp. 18–33.

10. Ibid.

11. David Gil, *Violence against Children: Physical Child Abuse in the United States* (Cambridge, Mass.: Harvard University Press, 1970). These numbers

seem very low. Besharov cites a much higher figure (approximately 150,000) for 1963; see Douglas Besharov with Lisa Laumann, "Child Abuse Reporting: The Need to Shift Priorities from More Reports to Better Reports," in *Social Policies for Children,* ed. Irwin Garfinkel, Jennifer Hochschild, and Sara McLanahan (Washington, D.C.: Brookings Institution, 1996).

12. Linda Gordon, in her introduction to *Heroes of Their Own Lives: The Politics and History of Family Violence* (New York: Penguin, 1988), found that reports tended to increase in any period in which child maltreatment was the focus of national attention, even before the adoption of reporting laws.

13. In addition to the variation over time, there is also a great deal of variation in reporting rates across jurisdictions. In 1995 Pennsylvania had the lowest reporting rate in the nation (8.29 reports per 1,000 children), while the District of Columbia had the highest (107.64 per 1,000); NCCAN, *Child Maltreatment 1995,* p. 3-3. Examining these differences across states might be a useful way to identify the factors leading to higher reporting rates.

14. Vicky Albert and Richard Barth, "Predicting Growth in Child Abuse and Neglect Reports in Urban, Suburban, and Rural Counties," *Social Service Review* 70 (1996), 58–82.

15. This strong relationship between drugs and placement is consistent with the findings of other researchers. See, e.g., Susan Zuravin and Diane DiPanfilis, "Factors Affecting Foster Care Placement of Children Receiving Child Protective Services," *Social Work Research* 21, no. 4 (1997), 34–42, who found that "substance abuse problems had more influence on decision making than any other characteristic" (p. 40).

16. Jane Waldfogel and David Gilgoff, "Reports of Child Maltreatment in Pennsylvania, 1980–1990" (Manuscript in progress, Columbia University School of Social Work).

17. Another possible data source would be household surveys such as Murray Strauss, Richard Gelles, and Suzanne Steinmetz, *Behind Closed Doors: Violence in the American Family* (Garden City, N.Y.: Anchor Press/Doubleday, 1980); and Richard Gelles and Murray Strauss, *Intimate Violence* (New York: Simon and Schuster, 1988); but these studies focused on only one type of child maltreatment, physical abuse.

18. The first national incidence study was conducted in 1979 and 1980; the second was conducted in 1986 and 1987. For a description of those two studies and their results, see Andrea Sedlak, *National Incidence and Prevalence of Child Abuse and Neglect: 1988, Revised* (Rockville, Md.: Westat, 1991); see also idem, *Supplementary Analysis of Data on the National Incidence of Child Abuse and Neglect* (Rockville, Md.: Westat, 1991). The third national incidence study was conducted from 1993 to 1995. Its results are reported in Andrea Sedlak and Diane Broadhurst, *Third National Incidence Study of Child Abuse and Neglect* (Washington, D.C.: NCCAN, 1996). Each national incidence study used a similar methodology, collecting data from a repre-

sentative sample of U.S. counties and surveying staff in both CPS and non-CPS agencies, such as schools, child-care centers, hospitals, and police departments. The researchers asked staff in the non-CPS agencies to tell them about all the cases of suspected maltreatment they had seen. The researchers unduplicated the data so that each child was counted only once. Then these cases were matched with those that CPS was aware of to estimate how many cases of abuse and neglect seen by outside agencies made it into the CPS system. Taken together, the three studies provide estimates of the incidence of abuse and neglect at three points in time from 1980 to 1995. Unfortunately, no similar study was conducted before the passage of the reporting laws in the 1970s.

19. A confounding factor here is the fact that the *Third National Incidence Study,* though designed to be comparable to the first two, identified many more cases of abuse or neglect than the previous studies had. While it is possible that the true incidence of abuse and neglect rose substantially from 1986 to 1993, it is also possible that the 1993 survey for some reason identified too many cases of abuse and neglect. Such overidentification would at least in part explain the lower rate of identified cases known to CPS in that year.

20. There is no time series of data before 1990. After 1993 the National Committee to Prevent Child Abuse continued to track this issue, but fewer than half the states reported.

21. American Humane Association (AHA), *Twenty Years after CAPTA: A Portrait of the Child Protective Services System* (Denver, 1994); Ching-Tung Wang and Deborah Daro, *Current Trends in Child Abuse Reporting and Fatalities: The Results of the 1996 Annual Fifty-State Survey* (Chicago: National Committee to Prevent Child Abuse, 1997), and earlier reports; and NCCAN, *Child Maltreatment 1996,* and earlier reports. Some estimates (e.g., Douglas Besharov, "Gaining Control over Child Abuse Reports: Public Agencies Must Address Both Underreporting and Overreporting," *Public Welfare* 48, no. 2 [1990], 34–40) are even lower. The disparity seems to be due mainly to differences in the definition of substantiation. Several states (12 as of 1996, according to NCCAN, *Child Maltreatment 1996*) have an "indicated" disposition (reflecting a determination that it is more likely than not that a child has been maltreated or is at risk of abuse or neglect, but with a level of certainty below that required for substantiation) in addition to the substantiated and unsubstantiated dispositions. In NCCAN, *Child Maltreatment 1993,* for instance, the proportion of cases that are substantiated would be only 33 percent if one counted the "indicated" cases as unsubstantiated, but the substantiation rate rises to nearly 40 percent when cases that are "indicated" are included in the numerator. Other sources of variation across studies include the treatment of duplicate reports and the definition of the denominator (i.e., whether all reports are included or just those that were investigated).

22. Besharov, "Gaining Control over Child Abuse Reports"; and David Finkelhor, "Is Child Abuse Overreported? The Data Rebuts Arguments for Less Intervention," *Public Welfare* 48, no. 1 (1990), 22–29, 46–47.

23. Figures from the National Committee to Prevent Child Abuse show a similar trend over the 1990s. See Wang and Daro, *Trends in Reporting, 1996,* and earlier reports.

24. AHA, *Twenty Years after CAPTA;* Victor Flango, "Can Central Registries Improve Substantiation Rates in Child Abuse and Neglect Cases?" *Child Abuse and Neglect* 15 (1991), 403–413.

25. Author's calculations based on data in NCCAN, *Child Maltreatment 1993,* p. 3-5. The National Committee to Prevent Child Abuse (NCPCA) found a similar range (a low of 11 percent and a high of 83 percent) in their 1994 data; see David Wiese and Deborah Daro, *Current Trends in Child Abuse Reporting and Fatalities: The Results of the Annual 1994 Fifty-State Survey* (Chicago: National Committee to Prevent Child Abuse, 1995).

26. Author's calculations based on NCCAN, *Child Maltreatment 1993,* p. 3-5. State-level data from the 1994 NCPCA survey look similar: of the 23 states in the survey, only 2 (9 percent) have a rate above 50 percent, 4 (17 percent) have substantiation rates between 40 and 50 percent, 9 (39 percent) have rates between 30 and 40 percent, and 8 (35 percent) have rates below 30 percent. I am grateful to NCPCA for providing me with unpublished state-level substantiation rate data (without state identifiers).

27. John Eckenrode, Jane Powers, John Doris, Joyce Munsch, and Niall Bolger, "Substantiation of Child Abuse and Neglect Reports," *Journal of Consulting and Clinical Psychology* 56 (1988), 9–16, found that in New York State reports from professionals were more likely to receive court action; they also resulted in more case-worker contacts with the subjects of the reports and the reporters. See also John Eckenrode, Joyce Munsch, Jane Powers, and John Doris, "The Nature and Substantiation of Official Sexual Abuse Reports," *Child Abuse and Neglect* 12 (1988), 311–319.

28. Almost all the data compare professionals with nonprofessionals (rather than mandated with nonmandated reporters), but in most jurisdictions the category of professionals is nearly synonymous with mandated reporters.

29. AHA, *Twenty Years after CAPTA,* p. 20.

30. Eckenrode et al., "Substantiation of Reports." Even when their reports are unsubstantiated, mandated reporters seem to be more "successful," in that their reports are more likely to receive preventive services. See Brett Drake, "Predictors of Preventive Services Provision among Unsubstantiated Cases," *Child Maltreatment* 1 (1996), 168–175.

31. Massachusetts Department of Social Services (DSS), *Massachusetts Child Maltreatment Statistics, January 1–December 31, 1992* (Boston, 1993), table A2.

32. Ibid.

33. Hampton and Newberger, "Child Abuse Incidence and Reporting by Hospi-

tals"; and Janine Jason, Nathan Andereck, J. Marks, and C. W. Tyler Jr., "Child Abuse in Georgia: A Method to Evaluate Risk Factors and Reporting," *American Journal of Public Health* 72 (1982), 1353–58.

34. See, e.g., Hutchison, "Mandatory Reporting Laws."

35. This is not to say that eliminating mandated reporting could not result in a decrease in inappropriate reports, but rather that we have no evidence to suggest that this would occur. One scenario under which eliminating the mandate to report could lead to a reduction in inappropriate reports is if mandated reporters currently report inappropriate cases because the mandate causes them to err on the side of overreporting. To the extent that this is a reason for inappropriate reporting, eliminating the mandate might reduce it. If, however, overreporting is due to reporters' differential perceptions about what constitutes abuse or about what warrants CPS intervention, then changing the mandate to report would not affect the number of inappropriate reports. For this reason, I conclude that other reforms (such as changing or clarifying the definitions) are more likely to lead to a reduction in the number of inappropriate reports.

36. Brett Drake, "Associations between Reporter Type and Assessment Outcomes in Child Protective Services Referrals," *Children and Youth Services Review* 17 (1995), 503–522, makes the point that even anonymous reporters sometimes refer cases of very serious abuse or neglect.

37. One outcome of discretionary reporting might be improved relationships between reporters and CPS. See David Finkelhor and Gail Zellman, "Flexible Reporting Options for Skilled Child Abuse Professionals," *Child Abuse and Neglect* 15 (1991), 335–341.

38. Screening and investigation are also stages at which CPS agencies may adjust the size of their caseloads by raising thresholds when caseloads threaten to get too high. This type of triage is distinct from screening (which entails determining whether a case meets the definitions of abuse and neglect and whether it constitutes an emergency).

39. Others have suggested improvements in screening tools such as risk-assessment matrices. See, e.g., Howard Doueck, Diana English, and Diane DiPanfilis, "Decision-Making in Child Protective Services: A Comparison of Selected Risk-Assessment Systems," *Child Welfare* 72 (1993), 441–452; Jane Downing, Susan Wells, and John Fluke, "Gatekeeping in Child Protective Services: A Survey of Screening Practices," *Child Welfare* 69 (1990), 357–368; and Susan Wells, Jane Downing, and John Fluke, "Responding to Reports of Child Abuse and Neglect," *Children and Youth Services Review* 15, no. 2 (1991), 63–72.

40. Wiese and Daro, *Current Trends in Reporting, 1994*, p. 2.

41. Douglas Besharov, *Protecting Children from Abuse and Neglect: Policy and Practice* (Springfield, Ill.: Charles C. Thomas, 1988), p. 347.

42. This is particularly important given the current unevenness of screening activity, but it is important even when screening is well done, because contacting

the reporter provides the investigator with firsthand and up-to-date information.

5. Narrowing as a Strategy to Improve Child Protection

1. We saw in Chapter 1 that only about 40 percent of reports are substantiated and that only about 70 percent of substantiated cases remain open for services after the investigation.
2. Comments by members of the Executive Session on Child Protective Services, Kennedy School of Government, 1994. All comments are unattributed in order to preserve the confidentiality of the session proceedings.
3. Linda Gordon, *Heroes of Their Own Lives: The Politics and History of Family Violence* (New York: Penguin, 1988); Leroy Pelton, "Child Abuse and Neglect: The Myth of Classlessness," *American Journal of Orthopsychiatry* 48 (1978), 608–617; idem, *For Reasons of Poverty* (New York: Praeger, 1989); Duncan Lindsey, *The Welfare of Children* (New York: Oxford University Press, 1994), p. 155.
4. Comments at the Executive Session on Child Protective Services, Kennedy School of Government, 1994.
5. Douglas Besharov, "Gaining Control over Child Abuse Reports: Public Agencies Must Address Both Underreporting and Overreporting," *Public Welfare* 48 (1990), 34–40, provides a brief overview. See also idem, "'Doing Something' about Child Abuse: The Need to Narrow the Grounds for State Intervention," *Harvard Journal of Law and Public Policy* 8 (1985), 539–588.
6. National Association of Public Child Welfare Administrators, *Guidelines for a Model System of Protective Services for Abused and Neglected Children and Their Families* (Washington, D.C., 1988).
7. Sheila Kamerman and Alfred Kahn, *Social Services for Children, Youth, and Families in the United States* (Greenwich, Conn.: Annie E. Casey Foundation, 1989); Sheila Kamerman and Alfred Kahn, "If CPS Is Driving Child Welfare—Where Do We Go from Here?" *Public Welfare* 48 (1990), 9–13, 46.
8. Elizabeth Hutchison, "Mandatory Reporting Laws: Child Protective Case Finding Gone Awry?" *Social Work* 38 (1993), 56–63.
9. Child Welfare League of America (CWLA), *Child Protection: It's Everybody's Business* (Washington, D.C., 1996).
10. See, e.g., Leroy Pelton, "A Functional Approach to Reorganizing Family and Child Welfare Interventions," *Children and Youth Services Review* 14 (1992), 289–303.
11. Lindsey, *The Welfare of Children*.
12. Lela Costin, Howard Karger, and David Stoesz, *The Politics of Child Abuse and Neglect in America* (New York: Oxford University Press, 1996).
13. Leroy Pelton, "Beyond Permanency Planning: Restructuring the Public Child Welfare System," *Social Work* 36 (1991), 337–343.
14. Mark Moore refers to these three dimensions as the "strategic triangle"

in *Creating Public Value* (Cambridge, Mass.: Harvard University Press, 1995).

15. Some CPS agencies and their communities also include in their mission the provision of nonprotective services. For example, although it is becoming less common, some CPS agencies provide some services to nonprotective children and families (whether referred by the community or applying voluntarily), acting as a catchall for children and families not served by other agencies. This role may be spelled out in statutes (as in the case of status offenders) or may simply reflect informal practice (as in the case of voluntary applicants for service).

16. This percentage and those that follow are intended to be illustrative. For a thoughtful discussion of the questions of how many cases of maltreatment there are, their level of severity, and what share need authoritative intervention, see Julie Boatright Wilson, "Cases of Child Abuse and Neglect: How Many Are There? How Serious Is the Maltreatment? What Share Could Only Be Reached through Coercive Intervention?" (Paper prepared for the Executive Session on Child Protective Services, Kennedy School of Government, 1996). Clearly, the answers to these questions will also vary a great deal by jurisdiction, as different areas will have different standards for situations serious enough to warrant intervention against the wishes of the parents.

17. Patricia Schene, "Chronic Neglect in St. Louis City," Report prepared for the Missouri Department of Social Services, Division of Family Services, St. Louis, 1996.

18. Using the criteria of severity and the need for coercive intervention seems to be the approach most commonly envisioned by those who advocate narrowing. Other approaches, of course, are possible (for example, using parental willingness and ability to protect the children as the criterion).

19. *The American Heritage Dictionary, Revised College Edition* (Boston: Houghton Mifflin, 1991), defines the terms as follows. Neglect: "1. The act or an instance of neglecting something. 2. The state of being neglected. 3. Habitual lack of care." Negligence: "*Law.* The omission or neglect of reasonable precaution, care, or action."

20. The alternative system would not pick up all the cases excluded from the narrowed CPS. For example, cases of nonparental abuse or negligence presumably would be picked up by another agency, either criminal justice or the state agency with supervisory responsibility for the institution involved.

21. Sheila Zedlewski, Sandra Clark, Eric Meier, and Keith Watson, *Potential Effects of Congressional Welfare Reform Legislation on Family Incomes* (Washington, D.C.: Urban Institute, 1996), p. 1.

22. On the likely effects of block-granting funds for CPS and child welfare, see William Meezan and Jeanne Giovannoni, "The Current Threat to Protective Services and the Child Welfare System," *Children and Youth Services Review* 17 (1995), 567–574.

23. The terms *closed referral* and *open referral* are commonly used in social ser-

vices to denote whether a program is closed to the public unless referred by the funding agency (in this case CPS) or whether a program is open to the public without case-by-case authorization by the funding agency. With day care, for example, CPS funds the programs and controls some but not all intake, while with family support, CPS funds the program but all intake is open referral. This distinction would be important if funding for the alternative service delivery system was to come from CPS.

24. States are already making such distinctions at the conclusion of investigation. Many are using risk-assessment tools to identify lower-risk cases that though substantiated for abuse or neglect are nevertheless a lower priority for CPS intervention than other, more serious cases.

6. Differential Response

1. Throughout this chapter I use the term *CPS* to refer to the public agencies that have traditionally had responsibility for child protection, as distinct from the community agencies that under the approach described here would form part of the response to child maltreatment. Note also that although it is typically assumed that the community agencies who will now be partners in child protection will all be private agencies, this is not necessarily the case. A community might elect to use some public providers, such as public health nurses or school attendance officers, as partners in child protection. A community might also choose to redeploy some CPS employees to carry out some of the community partner functions.

2. For an excellent review of the dominant paradigms in child protection, see Lela Costin, Howard Karger, and David Stoesz, *The Politics of Child Abuse and Neglect in America* (New York: Oxford University Press, 1996).

3. The latest swing of the pendulum, toward more of a child-rescue orientation, can be seen in the passage of child welfare legislation in November 1997 that shortens the time frames for permanency planning established by federal legislation (P.L. 96-272) in 1980. See Katharine Seelye, "Clinton to Approve Sweeping Shift in Adoption," *New York Times,* November 17, 1997, p. A20.

4. Edward Zigler, "Controlling Child Abuse: Do We Have the Knowledge and/or the Will?" in *Child Abuse: An Agenda for Social Action,* ed. George Gerbner, Catherine Ross, and Edward Zigler (New York: Oxford University Press, 1980), p. 14.

5. For a comprehensive review of the research on the correlates of child maltreatment, see National Research Council, *Understanding Child Abuse and Neglect* (Washington, D.C.: National Academy Press, 1993). For research on how various types of cases respond to particular treatment modalities, see Deborah Daro, *Confronting Child Abuse* (New York: Free Press, 1988); and idem, "Child Maltreatment Research: Implications for Program Design," in *Child Abuse, Child Development, and Social Policy,* ed. Dante Cicchetti and Sheree Toth (Norwood, N.J.: Ablex, 1993).

6. See Linda Gordon, *Heroes of Their Own Lives: The Politics and History of Family Violence* (New York: Penguin, 1988).

7. See Leroy Pelton, "The Role of Material Factors in Child Abuse and Neglect," in *Protecting Children from Abuse or Neglect: Foundations for a New National Strategy on Child Abuse and Neglect*, ed. Gary Melton and Frank Barry (New York: Guildford, 1994). We also know that more cases of neglect and other forms of maltreatment are reported from neighborhoods in which a higher proportion of residents are poor or low-income, and that more children from such areas are also placed in foster care. Data from the Administration for Children's Services (ACS) for New York City in 1994 indicate that reporting rates are much higher in poor neighborhoods than in other parts of the city. Citywide, 29 children per 1,000 are reported to child protective services. In the 10 community districts with the highest rate of AFDC recipiency, the average reporting rate is 48 per 1,000 children. With regard to foster care, Fred Wulczyn's data from New York City indicate that poverty areas have higher placement rates than nonpoverty areas. Areas where more than 40 percent of the population are in poverty (areas that meet the technical definition for ghetto poverty) have a placement rate of 14.5 per 1,000 children; areas with poverty rates from 30–39 percent have about 9.6 children per 1,000 in placement; areas with poverty rates from 20–29 percent have 6.5 children per 1,000 in placement; and areas with poverty rates below 20 percent have under 3 children per 1,000 in placement. ACS data for 1994 confirm this pattern. Citywide, on average 7 per 1,000 children are in placement; however, the placement rate in the 10 districts with the highest AFDC recipiency rate was twice as high (15 per 1,000). See ACS, "Child Protection Intervention Rates in Ten Highest Child AFDC Recipiency Communities, 1994" (Mimeograph, ACS, New York City, 1996); and Fred Wulczyn, "Child Welfare Reform, Managed Care, and Community Reinvestment," in *Children and Their Families in Big Cities: Strategies for Service Reform*, ed. Alfred Kahn and Sheila Kamerman (New York: Cross-National Studies Research Program, Columbia University School of Social Work, 1996). For a comprehensive review of the research on child protective services and poverty, see Duncan Lindsey, *The Welfare of Children* (New York: Oxford University Press, 1994).

8. See Sidney Gardner and Nancy Young, "Alcohol and Drug Treatment: An Essential Ingredient in Community Partnerships for Child Protection" (Paper prepared for the Executive Session on Child Protective Services, Kennedy School of Government, 1997), and the references therein.

9. However, most adults who were abused as children are not themselves abusive. See, e.g., Edward Zigler and Nancy Hall, "Physical Child Abuse in America: Past, Present, and Future," in *Child Maltreatment: Theory and Research on the Causes and Consequences of Child Abuse and Neglect*, ed. Dante Cicchetti and Vicki Carlson (Cambridge: Cambridge University Press, 1989).

10. For a more detailed discussion of the barriers to collaboration, see Jane Waldfogel, "The New Wave of Service Integration," *Social Service Review* 71 (1997), 463–484.

11. For a very helpful discussion of the issues of substance abuse in child protective services, see Gardner and Young, "Alcohol and Drug Treatment."

12. The discussion of "bootstrapping" reform, "learning by doing," and "learning by monitoring" draws on Charles Sabel, "Learning by Monitoring: The Institutions of Economic Development," in *The Handbook of Economic Sociology,* ed. Neil Smelser and Richard Swedberg (New York: Russell Sage and Princeton University Press, 1994); and Waldfogel, "The New Wave of Service Integration."

13. See Ross Thompson, *Preventing Child Maltreatment through Social Support: A Critical Analysis* (Thousand Oaks, Calif.: Sage, 1995), for an excellent discussion of the limitations of family support as a resource for the prevention of child maltreatment. See also Diane DiPanfilis, "Social Isolation of Neglectful Families: A Review of Social Support Assessment and Intervention Models," *Child Maltreatment* 1 (1996), 37–52.

14. See Suzanne Salzinger, Sandra Kaplan, and Connie Artemyeff, "Mothers' Personal Social Networks and Child Maltreatment," *Journal of Abnormal Psychology* 92 (1983), 68–76; Raymond Starr, "A Research-Based Approach to the Prediction of Child Abuse," in *Child Abuse Prediction,* ed. Starr (Cambridge, Mass.: Ballinger, 1982); and Isabel Wolock and Bernard Horowitz, "Child Maltreatment and Material Deprivation among AFDC-Recipient Families," *Social Service Review* 53 (1979), 175–194.

15. Jill Korbin, "Social Networks and Family Violence in Cross-Cultural Perspective," in *The Individual, the Family, and Social Good: Personal Fulfillment in Times of Change,* ed. Gary Melton (Lincoln: University of Nebraska Press, 1998); idem, "'Good Mothers,' 'Babykillers,' and Fatal Child Abuse" (Paper presented at the annual meeting of the American Anthropological Association, Chicago, 1991); idem, "Fatal Maltreatment by Mothers: A Proposed Framework," *Child Abuse and Neglect* 13 (1989), 481–489.

16. Deborah Belle, ed., *Lives in Stress* (Beverly Hills: Sage, 1984).

17. Elizabeth Seagull, "Social Support and Child Maltreatment: A Review of the Evidence," *Child Abuse and Neglect* 11 (1987), 41–52; and Marybeth Shinn, Stanley Lehmann, and Nora Wong, "Social Interaction and Social Support," *Journal of Social Issues* 40 (1984), 55–76.

18. Teresa Eckrich Sommer, "Low-Income Families as Customers of the Social Service Delivery System: Implications for Practice and System Reform" (Ph.D. diss., Kennedy School of Government, Harvard University, 1995).

19. James Garbarino was one of the first researchers to document the relationship between child maltreatment and neighborhood social indicators. See James Garbarino, "A Preliminary Study of Some Ecological Correlates of Child Abuse: The Impact of Socioeconomic Stress on Mothers," *Child Development* 47 (1976), 178–185; and James Garbarino and Ann Crouter, "Defin-

ing the Community Context of Parent-Child Relations: The Correlates of Child Maltreatment," *Child Development* 49 (1978), 604–616. Other research, reviewed in Susan Zuravin, "The Ecology of Child Abuse and Neglect: Review of the Literature and Presentation of Data," *Violence and Victims* 4 (1989), 101–120, provides further documentation of this relationship. For more recent studies at the neighborhood level, see Claudia Coulton, Jill Korbin, Marilyn Su, and Julian Chow, "Community Level Factors and Child Maltreatment Rates," *Child Development* 66 (1995), 1262–76; and Frank Furstenburg, "How Families Manage Risk and Opportunity in Dangerous Neighborhoods," in *Sociology and the Public Agenda,* ed. William Julius Wilson (Newbury Park, Calif.: Sage, 1993).

20. Belle, *Lives in Stress.*
21. Korbin found this tension in several child-fatality cases. See Korbin, "Social Networks and Family Violence in Cross-Cultural Perspective"; "'Good Mothers,' 'Babykillers,' and Fatal Child Abuse"; and "Fatal Maltreatment by Mothers."
22. Thompson, *Preventing Child Maltreatment through Social Support,* provides several examples of successful programs that combine formal and informal supports.
23. The discussion of the Missouri case draws on a case study by Kari Burrell, "Missouri's Child Protective Services System and Current Differential Response Demonstration Project" (Paper prepared for the Executive Session on Child Protective Services, Kennedy School of Government, 1995).
24. Ibid., p. 14.
25. Currently, a reporter in Missouri may ask to be informed of the outcome of the CPS investigation, but in practice this does not always occur. With reports being made locally, this may change.
26. It is also consistent with what clients have said they wanted in focus groups convened as part of the reform project.
27. This section draws upon a case study and update by Stewart Wakeling, "Child Protective Services Reform in Florida" (Paper prepared for the Executive Session on Child Protective Services, Kennedy School of Government, 1995) and "Child Protective Services Reform in Florida: A Brief Update" (Paper prepared for the Executive Session on Child Protective Services, Kennedy School of Government, 1996).
28. Although Florida's published statistics indicate that 66 percent of all reports were substantiated, the base used in calculating this percentage is the number of screened-in reports, not the total number of calls made to the hotline. Since the substantiation rate is usually defined as the number of cases substantiated divided by the total number reported, I recalculated Florida's rate as a percentage of all reports and obtained the 40 percent figure used in the text.
29. These are understandable reactions in CPS, given its rollercoaster experience with reforms and its record of sometimes scapegoating social workers when children die.

30. Wakeling, "Child Protective Services Reform in Florida: Update," p. 9.

31. Mario Hernandez and Beth Barrett, *Executive Summary of the Evaluation of Florida's Family Services Response System* (Tampa: University of South Florida, Florida Mental Health Institute, Department of Child and Family Studies, 1996).

32. For a detailed report on the Patch Project, see Paul Adams, Catherine Alter, Karin Krauth, Mark St. André, and Martin Tracy, "Strengthening Families and Neighborhoods: A Community-Centered Approach. Final Report on the Iowa Patch Project" (Mimeograph, University of Iowa, Des Moines, 1995).

33. For more on decategorization in Iowa, see Charles Bruner and Dick Flintrop, "Developing Comprehensive, Family-Centered Child Welfare Systems— Emerging State Strategies" (Mimeograph, National Maternal and Child Health Resource Center, University of Iowa, Iowa City, 1991). For more on service integration more generally, see Sharon Lynn Kagan with Peter Neville, *Integrating Human Services: Understanding the Past to Shape the Future* (New Haven: Yale University Press, 1994); Alfred Kahn and Sheila Kamerman, *Integrating Services Integration: An Overview of Initiatives, Issues, and Possibilities* (New York: National Center for Children in Poverty, 1992); and Waldfogel, "The New Wave of Service Integration."

34. Adams et al., "Strengthening Families and Neighborhoods: The Iowa Patch Project," p. 118.

35. Lisa Merkel-Holguin, *Innovations for Children's Services for the 21st Century: Family Group Decision Making and Patch* (Denver: American Humane Association, 1996).

36. The Edna McConnell Clark Foundation is funding community partnerships for protecting children in four sites—St. Louis, Missouri; Jacksonville, Florida; Louisville, Kentucky; and Cedar Rapids, Iowa—and is chronicling the progress of the sites in a newsletter published by the Center for the Study of Social Policy in Washington, D.C. See, e.g., "Four Sites Launch Community Partnerships," *Safekeeping* 1 (1996), 1; "From Investigation to Assessment in Iowa," ibid., p. 2; and "Moving into Action: How Four Communities Are Keeping Their Children Safer," *Safekeeping* 2 (1997), 1.

7. Working Together

1. For a chronology of legislation and other initiatives related to child protection, see Peter Reder, Sylvia Duncan, and Moira Gray, *Beyond Blame: Child Abuse Tragedies Revisited* (London: Routledge, 1993).

2. Matthew Colton, Charlotte Drury, and Margaret Williams, *Children in Need: Family Support under the Children Act 1989* (Aldershot: Avebury, 1995), p. 16. For a history of the development of the British welfare state since World War II, see Howard Glennerster, *British Social Policy since 1945* (Oxford: Basil Blackwell, 1995).

3. Seebohm Committee, *The Report of the Committee on Local Authority*

and Allied Personal Social Services (London: Her Majesty's Stationery Office, 1968).

4. As late as 1974, an inquiry recommended that medical professionals take the lead in the local interagency teams; Staffordshire Area Health Authority, *Report of the Committee of Enquiry Set Up to Enquire into the Circumstances Surrounding the Admission, Treatment, and Discharge of Baby David Lee Naseby, Deceased, at Burton-on-Trent General Hospital from February to May 1973* (London: Her Majesty's Stationery Office, 1974). However, later that year the Maria Colwell report recommended that social services departments take the lead; Department of Health and Social Security, *Report of the Committee of Inquiry into the Care and Supervision Provided in Relation to Maria Colwell* (London: Her Majesty's Stationery Office, 1974).

5. An important exception is health services authorities, which may have different boundaries.

6. Why Britain never instituted mandatory reporting is an interesting question from the U.S. perspective, but one that has not attracted a great deal of attention in Britain. It may be that there was a stronger tradition in Britain of professionals referring families to the local social services departments; there also appears to have been a stronger sense that local professionals had a role to play in child protection. Thus, there apparently was less perceived need than in the United States for laws requiring professionals to report. Seen in the European context, Britain's lack of mandatory reporting laws is not unusual. Many other European countries do not require reporting by professionals who come in contact with children. See James Christopherson, "European Child-Abuse Management Systems," in *Child Abuse: Public Policy and Professional Practice,* ed. Olive Stevenson (Hemel Hempstead: Harvester, 1989); and Neil Gilbert, "Conclusion: A Comparative Perspective," in *Combatting Child Abuse: International Perspectives and Trends,* ed. Gilbert (New York: Oxford University Press, 1997).

7. Department of Health, *Child Protection: Messages from Research* (London: Her Majesty's Stationery Office, 1995), pp. 29, 31.

8. Department of Health, *Children and Young People on Child Protection Registers* (London: Department of Health, 1996), table 1.21, p. 34.

9. Jane Gibbons, Sue Conroy, and Caroline Bell, *Operating the Child Protection System: A Study of Child Protection Practices in English Local Authorities* (London: Her Majesty's Stationery Office, 1995), chap. 2. For a study of four Welsh local authorities' decisionmaking regarding registration, see Henri Giller, Caroline Gormley, and Peter Williams, *The Effectiveness of Child Protection Procedures: An Evaluation of Child Protection Procedures in Four A.C.P.C. Areas* (Cheshire: Social Information Systems, 1992).

10. See Michael Little and Jane Gibbons, "Predicting the Rate of Children on the Child Protection Register," *Research, Policy and Planning* 10 (1993), 15–18, for further details.

11. The 1973–1989 inquiries are reviewed in two reports: Department of Health

and Social Security, *Child Abuse: A Study of Inquiry Reports, 1973–1981* (London: Her Majesty's Stationery Office, 1982); and Department of Health, *Child Abuse: A Study of Inquiry Reports, 1980–1989* (London: Her Majesty's Stationery Office, 1991). For more recent reviews see Eileen Munro, "Avoidable and Unavoidable Mistakes in Child Protection Work," *British Journal of Social Work* 26 (1996), 793–808; idem, "Common Errors of Reasoning in Child Protection Work" (Mimeograph, London School of Economics, 1996); and Reder, Duncan, and Gray, *Beyond Blame.*

12. Stuart Bell, *When Salem Came to the Boro: The True Story of the Cleveland Child Abuse Crisis* (London: Pan Books, 1988).

13. Frances Hill, *A Delusion of Satan: The Full Story of the Witch Trials* (London: Hamish Hamilton, 1996).

14. Lord Justice E. Butler-Sloss, *Report of the Inquiry into Child Abuse in Cleveland 1987* (London: Her Majesty's Stationery Office, 1988), quoted in Mary Greenwood and Jan Van Wagtendonk, "After Cleveland: A Crisis of Confidence," in *Responses to Cleveland: Improving Services for Child Sexual Abuse,* ed. Peter Riches (London: National Children's Bureau, 1989), p. 51.

15. The story of the "dawn raids" on the children's homes is chronicled in Robert Black, *Orkney: A Place of Safety?* (Edinburgh: Canongate Press, 1992).

16. Lord Justice J. Clyde, *The Report of the Inquiry into the Removal of Children from Orkney in February 1991* (London: Her Majesty's Stationery Office, 1992), quoted in Robert Black, *Orkney: A Place of Safety?* (Edinburgh: Canongate Press, 1992), p. 184.

17. Department of Health and Social Security, *Social Work Decision-Making in Child Care* (London: Her Majesty's Stationery Office, 1985).

18. See Cressy Cannan, *Changing Families, Changing Welfare: Family Centres and the Welfare State* (New York: Harvester/Wheatsheaf, 1992).

19. Department of Health, *An Introduction to the Children Act* (London: Her Majesty's Stationery Office, 1989), sec. 1.31.

20. Ibid., sec. 1.33.

21. Evidence from registers maintained by the National Society for the Prevention of Cruelty to Children (NSPCC) (covering about 10 percent of the child population in Britain) suggests that rates were fairly constant until the mid-1980s and then doubled between 1984 and 1987; the NSPCC data also confirm the rise from 1988 to 1990. See S. J. Creighton and P. Noyes, *Child Abuse Trends in England and Wales, 1983–1987* (London: NSPCC, 1989); and S. J. Creighton, *Child Abuse Trends in England and Wales 1988–1990, and an Overview from 1973–1990* (London: NSPCC, 1992). See also Elizabeth Birchall, "The Frequency of Child Abuse," in *Child Abuse: Professional Practice and Public Policy,* ed. Olive Stevenson (London: Harvester Wheatsheaf, 1989). According to Birchall, if one extrapolates from Department of Health and Social Services data from 1974, there were 8,360 registered cases that year. The NSPCC data (for 10 percent of the child population) then show 997 cases in 1977; 1,066 in 1978; 1,081 in 1979; 1,123 in 1980; 1,176 in

1981; 1,071 in 1982; 1,109 in 1983; 1,115 in 1984; 1,586 in 1985; and 2,138 in 1986.

22. The narrowing of the criteria seemed to reduce the listing of girls more than that of boys. Before the change, girls were more likely to be listed than boys; after the change, their numbers and rates equalized. This probably reflects the fact that the change affected listings for grave concern related to sexual abuse, which was more commonly a reason for listing girls than for listing boys.

23. Department of Health, *Introduction to the Children Act,* sec. 4.2.

24. Ibid., sec. 4.4.

25. Ibid., sec. 4.11.

26. Ibid., secs. 4.16 and 4.21.

27. Department of Health, *Child Protection: Messages from Research,* p. 19.

28. Ibid.

29. Ibid., p. 30.

30. Christine Hallett, *Interagency Coordination in Child Protection* (London: Her Majesty's Stationery Office, 1995).

31. Ibid.; see also Audit Commission, *Seen but Not Heard: Coordinating Community Child Health and Social Services for Children in Need. Detailed Evidence and Guidelines for Managers and Practitioners* (London: Her Majesty's Stationery Office, 1996).

32. Colton, Drury, and Williams, *Children in Need,* p. 21.

33. Audit Commission, *Seen but Not Heard.*

34. Elaine Farmer and Morag Owen, *Child Protection Practice: Private Risks and Public Remedies. A Study of Decision-Making, Intervention, and Outcome in Child Protection Work* (London: Her Majesty's Stationery Office, 1995), p. 112.

35. Audit Commission, *Seen but Not Heard.*

36. See Department of Health, *Children in Need: Report of a Social Services Inspectorate National Inspection of Social Services Departments Family Support Services, 1993/1995* (London: Her Majesty's Stationery Office, 1996). See also a recent study of Welsh local authorities, Colton, Drury, and Williams, *Children in Need.*

37. This is not a complete list of the concerns raised about the reforms in Britain. For instance, one school of thought challenges the emphasis that is placed on the notion of risk. See Nigel Parton and Olive Otway, "The Contemporary State of Child Protection Policy and Practice in England and Wales," *Children and Youth Services Review* 17 (1995), 599–617; and Nigel Parton, David Thorpe, and Corinne Wattam, *Child Protection: Risk and the Moral Order* (London: Macmillan, 1997).

38. Department of Health, *Child Protection: Messages from Research.*

39. Audit Commission, *Seen but Not Heard.*

40. Gerry Mulcahy, Westminster Social Services Department, personal communication, August 1997.

41. See C. Pelham, "A Lighter Touch" (M.Sc. diss., London School of Economics,

1996), p. 48. This dissertation reported the results of a series of interviews with social workers in one inner London local authority that had changed its procedures in response to the release of the Department of Health's 1995 report.

42. Ibid., p. 49.

43. Gerry Mulcahy, Westminster Social Services Department, personal communication, August 1997.

44. Ibid.

45. Farmer and Owen, *Child Protection Practice,* chap. 3.

46. Pelham, "A Lighter Touch," p. 37.

47. The British model is described by Kate Morris and Jo Tunnard, *Family Group Conferences: Messages from UK Practice and Research* (London: Family Rights Group, 1996). For a discussion of family group conferences in other countries, see Burt Galaway, Joe Hudson, and Allison Morris, eds., *Family Group Conferences: Perspectives on Policy and Practice* (Monsey: Willow Tree Press, 1996).

8. Changing Frontline Practice

1. Vincent Breglio, *CPS: Conversations with Clients, Workers, and Supervisors* (Lanham, Md.: Research/Strategy/Management, 1994), p. 21. See also Marc Parent, *Turning Stones: My Days and Nights with Children at Risk* (New York: Harcourt Brace, 1996); Patrick Murphy, *Wasted: The Plight of America's Unwanted Children* (Chicago: Ivan R. Dee, 1997).

2. Alex Gitterman, "Testing Professional Authority and Boundaries," *Social Casework* 70 (1989), 165–171.

3. Edward Mullen and James Dumpson, *Evaluation of Social Intervention* (San Francisco: Jossey-Bass, 1972).

4. Breglio, *CPS: Conversations,* p. 27.

5. Neil Guterman and Srinika Jayaratne, "'Responsibility at-Risk': Perceptions of Stress, Control, and Professional Effectiveness in Child Welfare Direct Practitioners," *Journal of Social Service Research* 20 (1994), 99–120.

6. See Lela Costin, Howard Karger, and David Stoesz, *The Politics of Child Abuse and Neglect in America* (New York: Oxford University Press, 1996), for an excellent discussion of this issue.

7. Paul Anderson, "The Origin, Emergence, and Professional Recognition of Child Protection," *Social Service Review,* June 1989, pp. 222–244. See, e.g., Dorothy Hutchinson, "Some Thoughts on Being Non-Judgmental," *CWLA Bulletin* 21 (1942), 3–4.

8. Henrietta Gordon, "Protective Services for Children," *CWLA Bulletin* 25 (1946), 2.

9. For this reason, some theorists have used the term *mandated* to describe the authoritative character of CPS intervention. See, e.g., Elizabeth Hutchison, "Use of Authority in Direct Social Work Practice with Mandated Clients," *Social Service Review,* December 1987, pp. 581–598.

10. Elliot Studt, "An Outline for Study of Social Authority Factors in Casework," *Social Casework* 35 (1954), 231–238; Judith Cingolani, "Social Conflict Perspective on Work with Involuntary Clients," *Social Work* 29 (1984), 442–446; and Hutchison, "Use of Authority."

11. See, for example, Porter Lee, "Changes in Social Thought and Standards Which Affect the Family," *Proceedings of the NCSW* 50 (1923), 286–294; Studt, "An Outline for Study"; Elliot Studt, "Worker-Client Authority Relationships in Social Work," *Social Work*, January 1959, pp. 18–28; and Lela Costin, *Child Welfare: Policies and Practices* (New York: McGraw-Hill, 1972).

12. Studt, "An Outline for Study"; Hutchison, "Use of Authority."

13. This discussion draws on two case studies of the Massachusetts program: Pamela Varley, "Partners in Child Protective Services: The Department of Social Services and La Alianza Hispana" (Kennedy School of Government Case Program, 1996); and idem, "High Stakes and Frightening Lapses: DSS, La Alianza Hispana, the Public-Private Question in Child Protection Work" (Kennedy School of Government Case Program, 1994).

14. For a social network program that was effective in improving the parenting of neglectful families, see James Gaudin, John Wodarski, Mary Kelly Arkinson, and Luciclair Avery, "Remedying Child Neglect: Effectiveness of Social Network Interventions," *Journal of Applied Social Sciences* 15 (1991), 97–123. See also Diane DiPanfilis, "Social Isolation of Neglectful Families: A Review of Social Support Assessment and Intervention Models," *Child Maltreatment* 1, no. 1 (1996), 37–52, who concludes that "modest improvements in the parenting behavior of neglectful parents can be achieved through the following: (a) differential assessment; (b) a multi-service approach; (c) intensive social contacts with a volunteer, lay therapist, or parent aide; (d) use of modeling, coaching, reframing, or feedback to improve social interaction skills; (e) development of personal networks; and (f) structured parenting and support groups for socialization, support, and social and parenting skill building" (p. 37). See also Sharon Lynn Kagan and Bernice Weissbourd, *Putting Families First: America's Family Support Movement and the Challenge of Change* (San Francisco: Jossey-Bass, 1994), who provide many examples of successful family support programs.

15. Comment by a member of the Executive Session on Child Protective Services, Kennedy School of Government, March 1994.

16. For a recent review, see Howard Doueck, Diana English, and Diane DiPanfilis, "Decision-Making in Child Protective Services: A Comparison of Selected Risk-Assessment Systems," *Child Welfare* 72 (1993), 441–452.

17. Jacquelyn McCroskey and Alexandra Sladen, "The Family Assessment Form: A Practice-Based Approach to Assessing Family Functioning" (Mimeograph prepared for Frontline Practice Workshop, Community Partnerships for Protecting Children, St. Louis, Mo., June 1996); and Child Welfare League of America, *A Multi-Level Assessment Tool* (Washington, D.C., 1997).

18. Daniel Kahneman, Paul Slovic, and Amos Tversky, *Judgement under Uncer-*

tainty: Heuristics and Biases (Cambridge: Cambridge University Press, 1990); Eileen Munro, "Common Errors of Reasoning in Child Protection Work" (Mimeograph, London School of Economics, 1996); idem, "Avoidable and Unavoidable Mistakes in Child Protection Work," *British Journal of Social Work* 26 (1996), 793–808.

19. Eileen Munro, "The Power of First Impressions," *Practice* 7, no. 3 (1995), 59–65.

20. Robert Dingwall has written extensively on the rule of optimism in CPS casework practice. See, e.g., Robert Dingwall, John Eekelaar, and Topsy Murray, *The Protection of Children: State Intervention and Family Life* (Oxford: Blackwell, 1983).

21. Munro, "Common Errors of Reasoning"; and Donald Schon, "Reflective Inquiry in Social Work Practice" (Paper presented at the Center for Social Work Practice, Columbia University School of Social Work, 1993).

22. Donald Schon, "Reflective Inquiry in Social Work Practice." See also idem, *The Reflective Practitioner* (New York: Basic Books, 1983).

23. See Jill Kinney, Kathy Strand, Marge Hagerup, and Charles Bruner, "Beyond the Buzzwords: Key Principles in Effective Frontline Practice" (Falls Church, Va.: National Center for Service Integration, 1994); Lisbeth Schorr, *Within Our Reach: Breaking the Cycle of Disadvantage* (New York: Anchor Press, 1988); idem, "Attributes of Effective Services for Young Children," in *Effective Services for Young Children,* ed. Lisbeth Schorr, Deborah Both, and Carol Copple (Washington, D.C.: National Academy Press, 1991); and Thompson, *Preventing Child Maltreatment through Social Support,* for the United States. See the Department of Health, *Child Protection: Messages from Research* (London: Her Majesty's Stationery Office, 1995), for Britain.

24. The slowdown in placements was not long-lasting, but the upturn in the mid and late 1980s is probably due less to the reduced effectiveness of permanency planning than to changes in the caseload, in particular, a surge in reports of drug-involved families. Many of the provisions of the 1980 law were superseded by new legislation passed in November 1997.

25. Charles Bruner and Dick Flintrop, "Developing Comprehensive Family-Centered Child Welfare Systems—Emerging State Strategies" (Mimeograph, National Maternal and Child Health Resource Center, University of Iowa, 1991).

26. Ibid.

27. Jane Waldfogel, "Integrating Child and Family Services: Lessons from Arkansas, Colorado, and Maryland," Report to the Ford Foundation, Kennedy School of Government, 1994.

28. Bruner and Flintrop, "Developing Comprehensive Family-Centered Child Welfare Systems."

29. Waldfogel, "Integrating Child and Family Services."

30. Costin, Karger, and Stoesz, *The Politics of Child Abuse and Neglect,* pp. 96–97.

31. The city's reform plan is described in Nicholas Scoppetta, *Protecting the Children of New York: A Plan of Action for the Administration for Children's Services* (New York: Administration for Children's Services, 1996).

32. Ibid., p. 81.

33. By October 1997 the average caseload was 14. The agency, however, was continuing to experience problems. Rachel Swarns, "Experts Denounce Children's Agency," *New York Times,* October 22, 1997, p. 1.

34. Ibid.

35. For cross-training materials on domestic violence and child protection, see Anne Ganley and Susan Schecter, *Domestic Violence: A National Curriculum for Child Protective Services* (San Francisco: Family Violence Prevention Fund, 1996); and Susan Schecter and Anne Ganley, *Domestic Violence: A National Curriculum for Family Preservation Practitioners* (San Francisco: Family Violence Prevention Fund, 1995). Sacramento County has developed a complete curriculum for cross-training on substance abuse and child protection. See Legal Action Center, *Making Welfare Reform Work: Tools for Confronting Alcohol and Drug Problems Among Welfare Recipients* (New York, 1997), for a description of the Sacramento initiative. See Nancy Young and Sidney Gardner, "Chemical Dependency Training—Level II Findings and Interim Report on the Initiative Evaluation" (Sacramento County Department of Health and Human Services, July 1996) for a preliminary evaluation. Although we might think that CPS social workers are already familiar with issues of domestic violence and substance abuse, this is not the case. Domestic violence specialists argue that CPS workers are not always aware of the domestic violence that is present in their caseloads, and recent efforts have focused on heightening that awareness. See, e.g., N. Cummings and A. Mooney, "Child Protective Workers and Battered Women's Advocates: A Strategy for Family Violence Intervention," *Response to the Victimization of Women and Children* 11, no. 2 (1988), 4–9; Susan Schecter and Jeffrey Edleson, "In the Best Interest of Women and Children: A Call for Collaboration between Child Welfare and Domestic Violence Constituencies" (Paper presented at the Conference on Domestic Violence and Child Welfare: Integrating Policy and Practice for Families, Racine, Wis., June 1994); Mary McKay, "The Link between Domestic Violence and Child Abuse: Assessment and Treatment Considerations," *Child Welfare* 73 (1994), 29–39; and Randy Magen, Kathryn Conroy, Mary Margaret Hess, Ann Panciera, and Barbara Levy Simon, "Evaluation of a Protocol to Identify Battered Women during Investigations of Child Abuse and Neglect" (Paper presented at the Fourth International Family Violence Research Conference, University of New Hampshire, July 1995). In the area of substance abuse, prior research has found that CPS workers often have little knowledge about substance abuse and that they can gain a great deal from training. See Martha Morrison Dore, Joan Doris, and Pearl Wright, "Identifying Substance Abuse in Maltreating Families: A Child Welfare Challenge," *Child Abuse and Neglect* 19 (1995),

531–543; Thomas Gregoire, "Assessing the Benefits and Increasing the Utility of Addiction Training for Public Child Welfare Workers," *Child Welfare* 73 (1994), 69–81; and Elizabeth Tracy and Kathleen Farkas, "Preparing Practitioners for Child Welfare Practice with Substance-Abusing Families," ibid., pp. 57–68.

36. Richard Weissbourd, *The Vulnerable Child: What Really Hurts America's Children and What We Can Do about It* (Reading, Mass.: Addison-Wesley, 1996).
37. Connie Roberts, San Diego Partners for Success, personal communication, February 18, 1997.
38. Child Protection Enforcement Group, *A Joint Project on Child Abuse and Neglect Investigations: Final Report* (Chicago, 1996), p. 13.
39. See Kagan and Weissbourd, *Putting Families First: America's Family Support Movement and the Challenge of Change,* on family support programs; and Deanna Gomby, Carol Larson, Eugene Lewit, and Richard Behrman, "Home Visiting: Analysis and Recommendations," *The Future of Children* 3, no. 3 (1993), 6–22, on home visiting programs.
40. Waldfogel, "Integrating Child and Family Services."
41. Paul Vincent, Child Welfare Policy and Practice Group, Montgomery, Ala., personal communication, March 1997.
42. Susan Kelly, Michigan CPS, personal communication, March 1997.
43. In some instances, changing casework practice will also mean changing who is hired to do the work. Illinois, for example, will no longer accept a degree in criminal justice, in order to support its move toward a more assessment-oriented as opposed to investigative approach to cases that are not high-risk. See Illinois Department of Children and Family Services, "Front End Redesign: Workplan for Implementing Pilot Projects" (Chicago, 1996).
44. Paul Vincent, Child Welfare Policy and Practice Group, Montgomery, Ala., personal communication, March 1997.
45. Bruner and Flintrop, "Developing Comprehensive Family-Centered Child Welfare Systems—Emerging State Strategies"; and Jane Waldfogel, "The New Wave of Service Integration," *Social Service Review* 71 (1997), 463–484.
46. John Goad, Cook County Child Protective Services, Chicago, personal communication, March 1997.
47. See, e.g., McCroskey and Sladen, "The Family Assessment Form."
48. Child Welfare League of America, *A Multi-Level Assessment Tool;* idem, *A Planning Guide to Assessment in Child Protective Services* (Washington, D.C., 1997).
49. See, e.g., Kinney, Strand, Hagerup, and Bruner, "Beyond the Buzzwords"; Schorr, *Within Our Reach;* idem, "Attributes of Effective Services for Young Children."
50. This was a problem in the Nadine Lockwood case in New York City, where investigators accepted at face value the mother's introduction of a neighbor's

child as Nadine and failed on another occasion to verify the mother's story that Nadine was visiting an aunt out of town.

51. Child Protection Enforcement Group, *Joint Project on Child Abuse and Neglect Investigations,* p. 12.

52. The mandate for the New Zealand family conference comes from the New Zealand Children, Young Persons, and Families Act of 1989. For more information on the family group conference model, see Mark Hardin, "Family Group Conferences in New Zealand," *ABA Juvenile and Child Welfare Law Reporter,* May 1994, pp. 4–8; and Joan Pennell and Gale Burford, "Widening the Circle: Family Group Decision Making," *Journal of Child and Youth Care* 9 (1994), 1–11. See also Chapter 7 above.

9. Reforming Child Protection

1. U.S. Advisory Board on Child Abuse and Neglect, *Child Abuse and Neglect: Critical First Steps in Response to a National Emergency* (Washington, D.C.: U.S. Government Printing Office, 1990), p. 2. See also idem, *Creating Caring Communities: Blueprint for an Effective Federal Policy on Child Abuse and Neglect* (Washington, D.C., 1991); idem, *Neighbors Helping Neighbors: A New National Strategy for the Protection of Children* (Washington, D.C.: U.S. Government Printing Office, 1993).

2. See National Association of Public Child Welfare Administrators, *Guidelines for a Model System of Protective Services for Abused and Neglected Children and Their Families* (Washington, D.C., 1988); and Douglas Besharov, *Protecting Children from Abuse and Neglect: Policy and Practice* (Springfield, Ill.: Charles C. Thomas, 1988).

3. Frank Farrow with the Executive Session on Child Protective Services, "Child Protection: Building Community Partnerships. Getting from Here to There" (Paper prepared for the Executive Session on Child Protective Services, Kennedy School of Government, 1997).

4. See, e.g., Leroy Pelton, "Child Abuse and Neglect: The Myth of Classlessness," *American Journal of Orthopsychiatry* 48 (1978), 608–617; Douglas Besharov, "'Doing Something' about Child Abuse: The Need to Narrow the Grounds for State Intervention," *Harvard Journal of Law and Public Policy* 8 (1985), 539–588; and Duncan Lindsey, *The Welfare of Children* (New York: Oxford University Press, 1994).

5. Sheila Kamerman and Alfred Kahn, *Social Services for Children, Youth, and Families in the United States* (Greenwich, Conn.: Annie E. Casey Foundation, 1989).

6. See case number 15 in Chapter 1.

7. For early results from Missouri, see Kari Burrell, "Missouri's Child Protective Services System and Current Differential Response Demonstration Project" (Paper prepared for the Executive Session on Child Protective Services, Kennedy School of Government, 1995). Mario Hernandez and Beth Barrett, *Ex-*

ecutive Summary of the Evaluation of Florida's Family Services Response System (Tampa: University of South Florida, Florida Mental Health Institute, Department of Child and Family Studies, 1996), report the results of a preliminary evaluation of the Florida reforms. Paul Adams, Catherine Alter, Karin Krauth, Mark St. Andre, and Martin Tracy, "Strengthening Families and Neighborhoods: A Community Centered Approach. Final Report on the Iowa Patch Project" (Mimeograph, University of Iowa, 1995), evaluate the Iowa Patch Project. See also Stephen Christian, *New Directions for Child Protective Services* (Washington, D.C.: National Conference of State Legislatures, 1997).

8. Hernandez and Barrett, *Executive Summary of the Evaluation of Florida's Family Services Response System,* p. 3.

9. See case number 5 in Chapter 1.

10. Farrow, "Child Protection: Building Community Partnerships," provides a detailed discussion of the pathways to reform. The discussion in the text draws on this paper and the comments of participants in the Harvard Executive Session.

11. For a discussion of "bootstrapping reform," see Jane Waldfogel, "The New Wave of Service Integration," *Social Service Review* 71 (1997), 463–484.

12. For further discussion of learning by doing and learning by monitoring, see Charles Sabel, "Learning by Monitoring: The Institutions of Economic Development," in *The Handbook of Economic Sociology,* ed. Neil Smelser and Richard Swedberg (New York: Russell Sage and Princeton University Press, 1994); and Waldfogel, "The New Wave of Service Integration."

13. Stewart Wakeling, "Child Protective Services Reform in Florida: A Brief Update" (Paper prepared for the Executive Session on Child Protective Services, Kennedy School of Government, 1996).

14. Illinois Department of Children and Family Services, "Substance Exposed Infants and Their Families: A Protocol of Clinical Practice and Collaborative Intervention" (Mimeograph, Illinois Department of Children and Family Services, Chicago, 1996).

15. See "Moving into Action: How Four Communities Are Keeping Their Children Safer," *Safekeeping* 2 (1997), 1.

16. Richard Krugman, "Universal Home Visiting: A Recommendation from the U.S. Advisory Board on Child Abuse and Neglect," *The Future of Children* 3, no. 3 (1993), 184–191.

17. France's preventive home-visiting program provides an interesting example of a more targeted program. France tracks all pregnant women and refers all cases that might be at risk of abuse or neglect for home visiting as a means of detecting and preventing abuse and neglect. In the Rhone region, for example, half of all infants receive such visits, and about one in five or six children is followed until age three or four. Originally, these visits to high-risk cases were made by child protective social workers, but because families found the social workers intimidating, the French public health service gradually shifted to using public health staff such as nurses and midwives. The results have been

very impressive, with a positive response to the program from high-risk families and a sharp reduction in referrals to formal child protective services. See Barbara Bergmann, *Saving Our Children from Poverty: What the United States Can Learn from France* (New York: Russell Sage, 1996), chap. 5; see also Colette de Saint Sauveur, *Protection de la maternité et de l'enfance* (Paris: Masson, 1985).

18. For a recent review of home-visiting programs as a means to prevent child abuse and neglect, see Neil Guterman, "Early Prevention of Physical Abuse and Neglect: Existing Evidence and Future Directions," *Child Maltreatment* 2 (1997), 12–34. See also Deanna Gomby, Carol Larson, Eugene Lewit, and Richard Behrman, "Home Visiting: Analysis and Recommendations," *The Future of Children* 3, no. 3 (1993), 6–22; David Olds and Harriet Kitzman, "Review of Research on Home Visiting for Pregnant Women and Parents of Young Children," ibid., pp. 53–92; Sheila Kamerman and Alfred Kahn, *Starting Right: How America Neglects Its Youngest Children and What We Can Do about It* (New York: Oxford University Press, 1995); and Lisbeth Schorr, *Common Purpose: Strengthening Families and Neighborhoods to Rebuild America* (New York: Anchor Books, 1997).

19. Connie Roberts, San Diego Partners for Success, personal communication, 1997.

20. Peter Digre, County of Los Angeles Department of Children and Family Services, personal communication, May 1997.

21. See Mary Margaret Hess and Brenda McGowan, "Final Report of a Study of the Center for Family Life in Sunset Park," Report to the Annie E. Casey Foundation (Columbia University School of Social Work, November 1997). See also Schorr, *Common Purpose,* chap. 2.

22. Kathryn Conroy, Columbia University School of Social Work, personal communication, 1997.

23. Illinois Department of Children and Family Services, "Front End Redesign: Workplan for Implementing Pilot Projects" (Mimeograph, Illinois Department of Children and Family Services, Chicago, 1996).

24. Susan Kelly, Michigan CPS, personal communication, 1997.

25. See, e.g., Alfred Kahn and Sheila Kamerman, *Integrating Services Integration: An Overview of Initiatives, Issues, and Possibilities* (New York: National Center for Children in Poverty, 1992); Sharon Lynn Kagan with Peter Neville, *Integrating Human Services: Understanding the Past to Shape the Future* (New Haven: Yale University Press, 1994); and Jane Waldfogel, "The New Wave of Service Integration."

26. For more on the patch model, see Lisa Merkel-Holguin, *Innovations for Children's Services for the 21st Century: Family Group Decision Making and Patch* (Denver: American Humane Association, 1996).

27. John Goad, Cook County Child Protective Services, Chicago, personal communication, March 1997.

28. Wakeling, "Child Protective Services Reform in Florida: A Brief Update."

29. Jane Waldfogel, "Conducting Research on the Child Welfare Population: Key

Datasets and Outcome Measures" (Paper prepared for a planning meeting of the National Research Council and Institute of Medicine Board on Children, Youth, and Families, Washington, D.C., May 1997).

30. See, e.g., Lela Costin, Howard Karger, and David Stoesz, *The Politics of Child Abuse in America* (New York: Oxford University Press, 1996), who propose a children's authority.

31. Farrow, *Child Protection: Building Community Partnerships.*

Index